MYTH, OIL, AND POLITICS

MYTH, OIL, AND POLITICS

Introduction to the Political Economy of Petroleum

Charles F. Doran

THE FREE PRESS
A Division of Macmillan Publishing Co., Inc.
NEW YORK
Collier Macmillan Publishers
LONDON

Copyright © 1977 by The Free Press
A Division of Macmillan Publishing Co., Inc.

The Free Press
A Division of Macmillan Publishing Co., Inc.
866 Third Avenue, New York, N.Y. 10022

Collier Macmillan Canada, Ltd.

Library of Congress Catalog Card Number: 77–4571

Printed in the United States of America

printing number

1   2   3   4   5   6   7   8   9   10

Library of Congress Cataloging in Publication Data
Doran, Charles F
  Myth, oil, and politics.

  Includes bibliographical references and index.
    1. Petroleum industry and trade. 2. Energy
policy. I. Title.
HD9560.6.D64   338.2'7'282   77-4571
ISBN 0-02-907580-7

To Mother

Contents

Preface

How MYTH OBSCURES oil politics, the theme of this book, is perhaps effectively conveyed by a personal anecdote on an otherwise unrelated topic. During happier days in the beautiful city of Beirut, a taxi driver and I were engaged in conversation. At one point, the driver—a large, jovial man— asked with a chuckle, "How many wives do you have?" A bit startled by the question, I answered, "Why, one, of course," whereupon he responded, "Aha! A poor man huh?"

Myth obscures understanding in somewhat the same way that my companion evoked humor namely, by supplying erroneous explanation. Since 1973 Americans have been startled by a series of complex questions about energy matters and must now work through the maze of explanations to formulate a coherent petroleum policy. In this study I examine a number of major "explanations" that have engendered false understanding. Some may be right but for the wrong reasons, others wrong though based on essentially correct information; some may be neither right nor wrong but strongly supported, for instance, by arguments of justice or power politics. In short, this book represents a search for valid explanation in oil politics.

A number of individuals from a variety of backgrounds, perspectives, and institutions have contributed directly or indirectly to the evolution and completion of this work. These individuals often disagreed broadly among themselves or with me regarding energy policy or matters of approach or interpretation. But in one way or other I have benefited from the many discussions, comments, and criticisms. Any shortcomings of fact or judgment are nonetheless solely my own responsibility.

I would first like to thank the representatives of government, industry, and academia who participated in the plenary session, "U.S. Energy Policy: Towards Dependence, Self-sufficiency, or Interdependence?", which I was fortunate to chair at the Southwest Social Sciences Association meeting in April 1976. The presentations of Kenneth Boulding, Department of Economics, University of Colorado; John Hill, deputy director of the Federal Energy Administration; Robert North, Department of Political Science, Stanford University; and John Roorda, vice-president, planning and economics, Shell Oil Company, as well as their informal discussions, lent perspective to my understanding of the energy crisis.

A group representing the fields of economics, mathematics, political science, and chemistry met at Rice University in August 1975 for a symposium on game-theoretic applications to energy policy sponsored by the National Science Foundation. Among the many participants who ought to be acknowledged for their helpful discussions are Robert Thrall, chairman of the Mathematical Sciences Department, Rice University, and Thomas Sparrow, then director of the Advanced Productivity, Research, and Technology Division of the National Science Foundation and professor of economics, Johns Hopkins University.

Separate trips in the spring and summer of 1974 to several European capitals and to leading producer nations in the Middle East provided important information through interviews and discussions. A further trip in the spring of 1977 reinforced earlier findings. Additional feedback was received at various talks and lectures I delivered over the past three years. Two lectures given about a year apart are of special note because they each tested main themes of this book before knowledgeable audiences. One lecture prepared for the biannual President's Executive Luncheon Series at Rice University in early September 1975 challenged the myth of OPEC cohesion; the other explored U.S. energy strategy with members of the Forty-sixth Advanced Management Program of the Harvard School of Business at their annual Continuing Education Seminar. Unfortunately, I cannot mention all of the many individuals at these gatherings whose analyses of the energy problem and related matters were helpful to this study, but for their insights in personal discussions I would in particular like to thank Robert Mabro, St. Anthony's College, Oxford University; Dan Pattir, chairman of the National Federation of Israeli Journalists; Ragaei El Mallakh, editor of the *Journal of Energy and Development*; Fuad Itayim, publisher of the *Middle East Economic Survey* (Beirut); and I. William Zartman, Department of Political Science, New York University. A grant from the Institute for World Order and the University of Texas to establish a course on the political economy of cartels and world energy supply created a further opportunity to test a number of the ideas expressed herein this time before a group of sharp-witted students. Mary Ann Tetreault, a graduate student in political science, collected and coded data on the International Energy Agency; Terrance Ward and Duane Roberts provided computer assistance.

An anonymous reviewer made useful suggestions with respect to strengthening and extending the manuscript. Appreciation also goes to Stanley Besen and Richard Butler of the Department of Economics, Rice University, who provided excellent criticism on various sections of the manuscript, and to Tita Gillespie, who gave important advice while editing the text with care. I also thank Jaquie Ehlers for typing interminable drafts, my wife for her encouragement and good humor, and our two sons for all of those extra weekends spent at home.

C.F.D.
Houston

MYTH, OIL, AND POLITICS

Introduction: Myths and Mythmakers in the Great Oil Polemic

> And that distill'd by magic sleights
> Shall raise such artificial sprites
> As by the strength of their illusion
> Shall draw him on to his confusion.
> Hecate, act 3, scene 5
> *Macbeth*

THE POLITICAL ECONOMY OF OIL: CRUCIBLE FOR MYTHMAKING

Since the second world war no event has seemingly so transformed the norms of international politics and commerce as the 1973 takeover of the world oil market by the Organization of Petroleum Exporting Countries (OPEC). Some analysts have gone so far as to interpret the OPEC takeover and the subsequent oil price increases as symbolic of the final deterioration of superpower, bipolar dominance. What is unmistakably clear, however, is that the takeover foretells a new era of resource scarcity and global resource consciousness, an era in which petroleum has become the new bargaining instrument in international affairs.

Accompanying the sudden rise in importance of oil matters is a series of myths regarding the origins and impact of oil politics. Some elements of myth are expedient, perhaps even valid; others are unproven, distorted, and perhaps deleterious to good policy. One task of this book is to examine these myths and to separate fantasy from fact, distortion from reality, placing the political economy of oil in a context meaningful to actor and observer alike. We begin by assessing the meaning of myth and its relevance to the petroleum setting.

Recipes for Myth

Like the Trobriand Islanders studied by Bronislaw Malinowski, for whom myth was a "living legend," members of global society today have created a series of oil myths that incorporate glimpses of a larger weltanschauung, personal and cultural.[1] On the one hand, myth is not as sweeping and integrated as *ideology*, whose relatively systematic body of notions and aims constitutes a sociopolitical program.[2] On the other hand, myth is not as definite, authoritative, or established as *dogma*, which often consists of a code of ethics or a doctrine concerning faith and morals. Myth is at

1

once narrower and more flexible, more subtle and more voluntarily compelling than these kindred concepts.

Myth for our purposes will be defined as *a complex of beliefs and assertions professed by large groups of people that purports to explain reality and fulfills important functions of a psychological and political nature but that is false in significant, although often not very evident, respects.* Oil myths are thus not simple statements of detail but edifices of complicated argumentation sometimes concealed within rather simplistic phraseology. Oil myths also contain a history of experience with petroleum questions that explains or is used to justify them. Myths can be either propagated or believed, or both, by the same or separate sources. Myth may also be conscious or unconscious in origin. Two aspects of myth above all, however, are critical to analysis.

First, myth seems to meet the needs of the individual, institution, or society that believes and articulates it. These needs may be genuine and purposeful. For example, a government may rely upon myth to rally mass support for its foreign policy or to strengthen a regime. The wider the circle of believers, the more successful the myth from the viewpoint of the propagators. Those who propagate myth, insofar as its origins can be traced, may also believe in it, although this condition is not essential to the myth's success and in politics is often missing, a situation described as hypocrisy or duplicity by critics.

Psychological needs of the believer are usually met in part by myth, giving myth its extraordinary appeal. Fear, hatred, and guilt can often receive embodiment in myth when reality is too painful or too filled with uncertainty to bear.[3] Manipulated by political authority, myth can exort sacrifice and other behavior that from the believer's own perspective may be rational or nonrational. Myth is by no means merely a religious vestige of primitive society: it is as much a secular product of modern society, the more compelling when tinged with the aura of scientific truth.

Second, myth contains elements of falsehood that normally are not apparent to the myth-taker or are discounted. Other things being equal, the degree to which myth fails to account accurately for reality yet retains its appeal is the measure of the *power* of the myth. By incorporating elements of truth, myth reinforces faith because the believer translates partial validation into confidence in total authenticity. Insofar as opponents accept myth in lieu of a more accurate statement of their own interests and thus substitute myth for reality, political myth has achieved perhaps its ultimate purpose, a situation not so unusual where conditions of empirical test are difficult or impossible. Since governments tend to create their own reality, myth can confuse them or obstruct the realization of plausible objectives. But myths that appear convincing to one society or interest group are likely to appear less so to individuals accustomed to a differing cultural and political perspective on events. Differences in interest perception and political background constitute a safeguard against the overwhelming dominance of false ideas.

Turning to an application of this more general discussion of myth to oil politics, why, we ask, is the political economy of oil prone to mythmaking?

Witchcraft and Oil

A partial answer is that most of the components of myth generation are present in the brew of international oil matters: uncertainty, shock, lack of technical information, contrived secrecy, power, exaggeration, politicization, heavy media involvement, and the immediacy, intensity, and scope of the energy question. Torn between the fear and shock associated with the energy shortage and the absence of clear solutions advocated by decisive political leadership, the American public has relied on myth to explain the consumer dilemma. Reluctant to admit its lack of technical information and facing contradictory, often strongly partisan, political crosscurrents within Congress, the executive branch of the U.S. government has politicized energy as a major issue without supplying the rational groundwork for the passage of effective legislation. Presidents have failed to convince constituents of the validity of the energy problem. Uncertain of America's motivation and direction in the energy field because of the existence of comparatively sizable U.S. petroleum reserves (which lessen the immediate pressure for action) and indexed by the virtual absence of a U.S. conservation effort (the U.S. ranks fourteenth out of fourteen in a recent International Energy Agency survey of member conservation programs), the other consumer countries are prone to accept comfortable energy myths in lieu of policy coordination. Bitter because of what it discerns as unjustified criticism of its methods, achievements, and purposes, the oil industry remains inward and highly suspicious of other actors and potential rivals. Newly experiencing the rush of political success and enormous financial revenue, the petroleum exporting countries need myth to contribute a sense of legitimacy and permanence to their achievements. Throughout, in part because of the complexity of oil matters, the press and other media often tend to popularize the simple and spectacular in a news atmosphere that already is permeated with some exaggeration. No dearth of myth-takers awaits the shaping and dissemination of convenient oil parables.

Each of the major sets of actors in turn becomes a *mythmaker* of sorts, sometimes through a rather conscious formulation of beliefs, more often through a less explicit process of welding together fears, biases, aspirations, and defense mechanisms. When the atmosphere is conducive to myth projection, a variety of actors is likely to arise in pursuit of this craft.

The United States, for example, must resolve contradictions in its purpose through myth. It must reconcile maintenance of one of the highest standards of living in the world, accompanied by one of the highest levels of per capita energy consumption, with an OPEC policy that would slow down this growth in wealth while lifting a number of OPEC countries out of comparative poverty. It must explain why artificial props under the price of crude after 1973 are any less morally acceptable than artificial constraints on price before 1973. Second, the United States must contend with the assertion that it is willing to provide small amounts of economic aid, totaling less than three-quarters of a percent of the nation's GNP as conscience money, while exploiting the resources of the recipients at unusually favorable prices. On the other hand, the United States must deprecate forcible transfers of wealth via small-state collusion while extolling voluntary transfers of wealth as political charity, supporting this argument with data showing that OPEC aid to the poor Fourth World countries does not equal the increase in oil revenue extracted from them. Third, the United States and the consumer countries in general find immobilism a seductive, if dangerous and self-defeating, strategy. Leadership crises in the United States, Japan, and West Germany combined with economic problems and parliamentary challenges in Britain, Italy, and France have encouraged governmental inaction within the International Energy Agency (IEA). Inefficacy necessitates a rationale to divert criticism and to preserve a modicum of legislative respectability. A propensity for inaction leaves the consumer countries vulnerable to myth that will ease and justify the lack of a vigorous energy program.

In contrast, the oil exporting countries expound myth with the dual task of externally defending the tactics and gains of OPEC and of internally espousing the merits of collective enterprise. OPEC seeks to divide the consumers through implied threat, promises of special treatment, and the pious hope of conditional price reduction. But the principal task of myth creation for OPEC is to legitimize governmental collusion as a means of extracting revenue from hesitant clients among both the rich and poor. Without ritualized acknowledgment as a respected member of the international system, OPEC will find self-perpetuation much more difficult and precarious. Mythmaking is difficult for OPEC because the cartel must justify today the existence of dependency relations of precisely the type that the founding of OPEC in 1960 was designed to counter. Having berated the multinational corporation for ruthlessness, arrogance, and avarice in the past, the OPEC countries find themselves attempting to transform an image increasingly identified with these same characteristics. OPEC's "natural" enemy, the multinational oil company, moreover, becomes the chief ally in a setting of mutual dependence in which the hierarchy of roles has been inverted and changed.

Mythmaking for the oil industry, the other major actor in the triumvirate of oil politics, focuses on a single theme, credibility. (Myth-taking by the industry is far more heterogeneous.) But credibility is different for different people, influenced to a great degree by their needs or desires. Consumer societies want delivery of large amounts of oil and gas at modest prices. Oil exporting governments want sale of crude oil at high prices and on terms that suit producer needs. Not being able to satisfy both of these sets of demands, and recognizing that the "credibility" of the industry must not be allowed to suffer, the multinational corporation stresses efficiency, reliability, and service to both groups of countries. But neither group of countries is interested primarily in efficiency, nor is efficiency the kind of principle one can market and sell except in its absence, and by that time the mode of production responsible for that efficiency may have changed radically.

Mythmaking for the industry must overcome the companies' divisive responsibility of working for two masters. Consumer governments must be shown that exploration activity is convincingly ahead of what normal economic models of incentive would predict for reasons of competition, the lottery mentality of discovery, and the national interest. Producer governments must learn that only the industrial leadership can provide the discipline, skills, and distribution network that can optimize long-run production and benefits to OPEC's advantage. Consumer governments must be made confident that continuity of supply is possible regardless of political contingency; producer governments must be assured that reliable implementation of supply interruption is feasible if the call should go out. Again and again the image of the industry embodied in myth is what might kindly be labeled multifaceted. In practice, to survive the assaults from producer and consumer, the industry must project a record and an image of credibility, counting upon myth to balance or conceal contradictions.

In oil matters myths have tended to predominate because the milieu is conducive to them. There have been an ample number of myth-takers—individuals, institutions, nations—that need myth, internalize it, and find it useful. There have also been numerous mythmakers who consciously or implicitly spin the fabric of myth. Myths of oil politics thus meet the apparent needs of both the myth-takers and the mythmakers, for without this concurrence no myth could be truly compelling.

GHOSTS, GOBLINS, AND OTHER MYSTERIOUS CREATURES

Since a government to some extent ordains its own destiny, the myths that it borrows or decrees for itself have an impact on the policies that it adopts. Like O'Neill's protagonist the Emperor Jones, who allowed mysterious little fears to become gigantic nocturnal figures, so a society embodies its fears, guilts, and unfulfilled aspirations in myth, which in turn can imprison it. The variety of political ghosts and goblins that nations and other global actors fabricate is quite endless and not usually interesting unless a particular myth grows in size and plausibility to the extent that it begins to create mischief within the decision process.

Chosen for study in this book are six oil myths of substantial proportions that affect different societies differently. They are interesting for their complexity and scope of political impact. But they are also fascinating because they entail a rich synthesis of fact and fiction, a transposition of time elements, reciprocal contributions of mythmaker and myth-taker in the perpetuation of myth, and a potential for shaping global oil matters throughout the last quarter of the twentieth century. A stupendous myth, especially one that also is arcane, is inherently more intriguing than a trivial one.

Chapter I addresses the question of whether the current price of petroleum is fair or unfairly high. It sifts argumentation on behalf of the view that the price increases have created hardships for the advanced industrial nations and further impoverishment of the world's poor. It explores alternative defenses for the price behavior of the OPEC states as well. Having reached a conclusion concerning the nature of myth and oil prices, the chapter ends with an examination of likely OPEC price strategies.

Chapter II probes the often asserted association between Israel and the oil price increases and, conversely, the political impact of oil and the future of Israel. By exploring the historical antecedents of the 1973 oil crisis and the basis of OPEC price motivation, one can reach conclusions regarding the nature of the association between Israel and oil. But the impact of oil on Israel is a different and more speculative problem. It involves not only an estimate of the trend of revenues in the Arab world and the uses to which these revenues will be put but also an analysis of the foreign policies of the major powers relative to Israel, especially the United States, in the new era of petroleum dependence.

Chapter III focuses upon the myth of excessive oil industry profits. This myth is important not just because of the number of its advocates but also because the industry is experiencing something of an identity crisis. The way in which corporate profit is viewed is likely to affect the role the multinational company will play in oil matters, particularly its capacity to act as a buffer between consumer and producer nations. Whether oil profits are indeed excessive is examined in terms of a number of standards across time and across industries. Conclusions are then drawn regarding how profits and the perception of profits are likely to impinge on the structure of industry relationships.

Chapter IV examines the myth of divestiture as a means of solving the energy problem. It considers two traditional doctrines of antitrust—the structural market approach and the behavioral approach—and rejects both on the ground that they do not apply to the oil industry's situation in the current period. Upon what basis, then, is the divestiture legislation founded? The answer is that divestiture has a political foundation, not a legal foundation, and that its political purpose is to subvert OPEC cohesion by attacking the corporations that process, transport, and sell OPEC oil. The hopelessness of affecting OPEC by this indirect and cumbersome method constitutes the myth of divestiture.

Chapter V explores the structure and aims of the International Energy Agency (IEA). Consumer solidarity is an image that the IEA seeks to project. But the actual achievements of the IEA fall within a single limited area; whereas the myth of consumer solidarity is that it can become, through this broadly composed organization, an effective counterweight to OPEC. An examination of the similarity of energy characteristics across all the member states makes rather evident the flaw in this vision of solidarity.

Chapter VI treats the final, and possibly the most central, myth of the current petroleum debate, the myth of OPEC durability and cohesion. An exploration of the criteria for cartel unity and an application of these criteria to the present OPEC setting reveals the degree to which commercial and political tensions exist inside the cartel. The compelling nature of the OPEC myth is that the cartel will be able to do what most other cartels have not been able to do; namely, survive despite increasing external competition, internal crises and challenges, and the absence of a production share agreement that both the major producer, Saudi Arabia, and the other, marginal producers find efficient and equitable. Among contemporary oil myths, the myth of OPEC's perpetual unity is perhaps most significant for the direction and pace of world oil politics.

In Chapter VII we seek to disentangle U.S. energy policy from the body of myth that presently contains it. We distinguish idealistic and realistic energy strategies and detail a set of four recommended strategies that emerge out of the prior analysis and that meet needs in critical problem areas.

In the final chapter we sum up the conclusions of the preceding chapters and place these ideas in the context of a theory of co-dependence between consumer and producer nations. The implications of myth in petroleum matters become clear in assessing the capacity of the three actors —the consumer nations, OPEC, and the oil industry—to forge a new linkage.

Throughout the study we attempt to get beneath the rhetoric of positioning and maneuver employed by the respective actors.[4] In so doing, the complexity of the oil problem in human terms is revealed, a complexity going far beyond the mere citation of statistical fact, barrel counts, or tax levies. International oil involves a blend of politics and economics. Pure economic models lose the meaning of the struggle over petroleum among governments and corporations because control rather than Pareto optimality is at the core of oil relations. The longer the interval one discusses, the more relevant are equilibrium notions of the market; however, the more closely one examines actor motivation and behavior, the more relevant become power-oriented conceptions of the oil market.

Myth serves to mask the outlines of the oil struggle. But myth can also be used to strengthen a bargaining position or to weaken that of an opponent. Knowing the content and origins of myth thus becomes critical to a full examination of oil matters. Since the components of petroleum myth are often obscure, a few analytic guidelines may help.

OIL MYTHS: ORIGINS AND IMPACT

A battery of four questions eases the job of disrobing the myths of oil politics: who creates myth; how is myth conjoined; for whom is myth meant; who actually *believes* myth. Not all of these questions in practice will be answerable, but together they put the analyst on guard against illusion. Illusion, of course, is the stuff of which myth is made.

In assessing who is responsible for the six myths examined in this book, we offer some partial insights. Consumer governments, the press, and many scholars in the advanced industrial world are responsible for the myths concerning price inequity. The members of OPEC have created the myth of the association between Israel and oil, while a number of Israel's deepest sympathizers (perhaps for fear of alarmism) must assume the burden of concealing the political impact of oil on Israel. Largely to avoid framing genuine solutions to the energy problem, critics of the industry located in the consumer countries are responsible for the "obscene profits" arguments. Similarly, drawing upon an undercurrent of populism that still exists in modern, urban America, advocates of divestiture have attempted to rationalize their dissatisfaction with the "anti-American" oil industry as a means to destroy the foreign oil cartel. Consumer solidarity becomes a comfortable crutch for those analysts located primarily in the Atlantic community who prefer the image of successful, if untested, confrontation to the perils of effective action. OPEC cohesion is a myth generated by the members of the producer cartel for purposes of soliciting cooperation and compromise from the membership and for purposes of dismantling opposition to the cartel. Undoubtedly, others within and outside these constellations of interests are influential in promulgating various of these myths as well. Homogeneity of viewpoint is by no means expected, particularly in pluralistic communities. Yet these allocations of responsibility for myth creation do not miss the mark by far.

Regarding the mode of creation, large subconscious motivation underlies the generation of the second and third myths, namely, the myths placing responsibility for the oil crisis on Israel and the oil industry respectively. In each case the subject of the myth is as much a diversion from the central struggle over energy distribution as it is a genuine commercial issue. Psychological needs of the mythmakers and myth-takers explain these myths at least as well as do political needs. In contrast, myths one and four —price inequity and OPEC cohesion—are more strictly political in design and more overt. That they operate in opposite directions through the advocacy of opposed groupings of states is scarcely accidental. Nor, is their elaborate intellectual (as opposed to unconscious or prejudicial) foundation without note.

For whom are the oil myths meant? Insofar as one can attribute conscious manipulation to myth projection, and surely this is at least in part feasible, the targets of each myth seem rather clear. What is more curious, however, is the effort by the propagators of myth to convince others, especially their opponents, by convincing themselves. Hence, the argument that the fourfold price increase for crude is fair is not likely to be well received in the consumer countries. Likewise, the assertion that the Israeli question has nothing to do with oil prices or that OPEC is subject to fragmentation is hardly a popular point of view among the decision elites of the oil exporting countries. Most of the members of the IEA want to believe that consumer solidarity is working, just as the advocates of divestiture prefer to think that the existence of OPEC justifies a position that under other circumstances they could also find legitimate. Ironically, the truth of a perspective in such instances is demonstrated not by the preferences of the majority but by the courage of the iconoclast.

Hardest of all questions perhaps is that which asks who actually believes these myths. So much myth propagation is instrumental. For this reason it may be impossible to discern by objective measures whether a sample of respondents genuinely believes in a particular oil myth or merely finds convenient the pretense. One suspects, for example, that the censuring of Israel by the Security Council in the winter of 1976 was for a number of states of instrumental value. Similarly, the U.S. congressional campaign against the oil companies and price decontrol legislation (notwithstanding the feasibility of subsidies or other protection for low-income groups) was based more on the popularity of the stance in home districts than on the rational attractiveness of the orientation as long-term energy policy.

A remarkable characteristic of oil myth is that it emerges in a period of political uncertainty when data and theory regarding the oil situation are either unavailable or still broadly contested by experts. Myth fills the interstices of fact. In the absence of facts on the nature of the new relations between the oil producing nations and the oil industry, the myth of divestiture supplies an explanation. Lacking sufficient analysis regarding the diversity of consumer interests and capabilities, the IEA leadership has concealed heterogeneity under the banner of consumer solidarity. Failure to form a smaller, more homogeneous entity hinders the effort to create an effective counterweight to OPEC. Because of the simplicity and convenience of mythical statement, however, myth also soon may *replace* fact for many observers of petroleum politics. More disturbingly, myth in such situations often begins to provide the basis for policy as well.

By convincing themselves that price strategies of oil exporting countries are fundamentally unjust, the consumer nations, for example, could respond with the use of military force in an atmosphere of war fever heightened by the emotionalism of ethical absolutes. Conversely, by accepting the thesis of the producers that OPEC cohesion is permanent and irremediable, the consumer governments could convince themselves that any effort to reduce their foreign oil dependency is essentially futile. Sacrifice involved in conservation programs seems less than worthwhile if it has little potential effect on the reduction of oil imports. Faith in the myth of the OPEC monolith could discourage investment in new non-OPEC exploration and in the development of alternative energy sources. It could postpone large-scale energy investment insurance programs to reduce risk and to speed up the development of innovative processing of coal, shale, and geothermal and solar energy. Excessive respect for the power of OPEC also is likely to discourage vigorous policy coordination within the International Energy Agency to achieve concerted reduction in foreign petroleum dependence.

Part and parcel of the mythology of oil politics is a self-fulfilling prophecy. By accepting the tenets of myth, government can inadvertently transform myth into reality. Statesmen, like most people, seemingly want to believe in a closed reality. In the absence of clear evidence they, too, are likely to cling to secular myth. Since myth regarding oil matters abounds, it is imperative that analysts provide society with a delineation of myth and its consequences, both positive and negative, for choice in the long-term evolution of energy policy.[5]

I

Unfair Oil Prices: The Myth of Inequity

A REVOLUTION IN OIL MATTERS upset the system of international politics in the late fall of 1973, changing abruptly the relation of the consumer to the producer nations. Ending decades of relative price stability, the oil price increase shattered economic planning and some of the commonplaces of modern diplomacy. Governments in Italy and Britain struggled to maintain flagging standards of living. A few oil producing countries that had previously been thought of as weak, sparsely populated, agricultural states now dictated the terms of economic exchange to some of the most militarily powerful states in the system. Oil price changes accelerated the decline of certain Western and non-Western democracies in both material and ideational terms. Some of the rich became poorer and some of the poor became richer as the very structure of post-1945 politics trembled.

Revolutions precipitate, if they have not already subsumed, notions of justice and injustice, the province of law and politics. Not surprisingly, the rapid climb in the price of crude oil triggered sharp criticism in the United States, Western Europe, and Japan, as well as more muted comment in some of the non-oil developing nations. What is a fair price for a barrel of crude oil? How high can the price of oil go before damage to the world economy and to fragile political institutions outweigh any possible gains to the producer countries? These are the questions that are still being asked in the wake of price hikes by OPEC.

Revolutions often are characterized by the magnitude of the disturbances they cause. The oil price revolution of the mid-1970s adds gravity to the issue of fairness because of the scope and magnitude of its effects. If price shifts could be dismissed as minor perturbations of the market having

11

a direct impact on only a few countries or a small segment of a nation's economy, the question of fairness would not arise or at least would not be so interesting. But the oil price increases transcend many recent politico-commercial developments and rank with such events as the Marshall Plan of the post–World War II period and the Rome treaties founding the European Common Market. Whether the medium-term significance of cartel politics is as great as was the significance of the Kennedy tariff talks, for example, is still uncertain. But the short-term political ramifications of OPEC policy can scarcely be denied, nor can we ignore the emotion surrounding the question of the injustice or inequity of large-scale nonvoluntary commercial transfers of wealth from nation to nation.

THE CASE FOR THE UNFAIRNESS OF OIL PRICES

First among the grievances against the OPEC price escalation is the naked fact of its size. Between November 1973 and April 1974 the price for a barrel of oil rose four times. A barrel of Arabian crude that cost $2.50 in November 1973 cost more than $10 the following spring. Nor is this increase the last that the consumers have absorbed.

The size of the price increases makes them less socially acceptable and therefore less justifiable than incremental increases. In fact, most of the objections to price increases for crude oil can be linked to the size of the original demands. When combined with suddenness and lack of predictability, the oil price increases add a devastating quality of uncertainty that upsets trade relations and dampens entrepreneurial initiative in the same way that devaluations have been disruptive of commercial ties between nations and orderly business relations within countries. Regardless of these other characteristics, however, if the increases had been (and would continue to be) smaller, the issue of the fairness of price would be less loudly debated.

A further criticism of OPEC price policy is that it has been inflationary on a world scale. Studies differ on the degree to which inflation in 1974 was attributable to oil price increases. Figures of anywhere from 2 percent to 9 percent have been confidently quoted for the United States. Whatever the true rate, the inflationary consequences have been both real and substantial.

Moreover, inflation linked to oil price increases affects countries differently depending upon the amount of energy they use and the source of their supply. Countries long accustomed to comparatively low rates of inflation, the advanced industrial countries, suddenly become the greatest targets for inflationary pressure since they import the largest amounts of foreign oil. But since they also supply the bulk of industrial goods to the developing nations, including the oil producing countries themselves, these latter nations in turn import the oil-linked inflation. Iran, for example, the second largest oil exporter, sustained a rate of inflation in excess of 20 percent in 1975. Therefore, policies that encourage inflation, so these arguments run, return to trouble the original perpetrators. Escape from commercial responsibility is brief.

Perhaps a more serious challenge to large oil price increases falls in the realm of domestic political instability. No one who is a serious student of conflict analysis will assert that the upheaval in Portugal, the student political unrest in Italy, the belligerence of labor unions in Britain, and the disrespect of constitutional liberties in India (which either necessitated Gandhi's mass arrests or embodied them) were in any direct way collectively linked to tensions between the oil producers and consumers. Yet coming in a period in which inflationary pressures were already high, the add-on inflation of the oil price increase surely aggravated political problems in each of these nations. It should not surprise the reader accustomed to capitalist theory that when economic and political tensions combine to shake the foundations of the international political system, the governments "on the margin" in terms of stability are the first to suffer.

Democracy was marginal in Portugal because following years of dictatorship the government was weak and inexperienced. Italy is a society marked by ideological cleavage and precariously stabilized only by the calculated prudence of the communist left. Britain was experiencing difficulty adjusting its standard of living to its real income and level of productivity. Democracy was vulnerable in India because that nation, with all of its population problems, has long been ungovernable—indeed, India's longevity amazes political scientists. In all of these instances the unintentioned but inevitable blows applied by the oil cartel to democracy cost the West dearly in a period of collateral recession and post-Vietnam adjustment.

The thesis of price unfairness is reinforced for some critics by "terms of trade" arguments. A concept from international trade theory, the terms of trade expresses as a ratio the value of a nation's exports to its imports. If the nation is an importer of industrial goods and an exporter of primary commodities, the ratio obtains ideological significance from the Third World perspective of dependence. Examining South American economies, Raul Prebisch and other development economists have asserted that the terms of trade have been steadily shifting unfavorably against commodity producing countries, a view that may be extended in defense of the oil price increase. This view has not been widely accepted among more traditional economists and policymakers in the advanced industrial countries, however, and critics of the OPEC price rise offer evidence to the contrary.

Despite high import costs for many OPEC countries, there seems to be evidence that in the period 1950–1970 the increase in oil prices kept up pretty well with the average cost of imported foodstuffs and industrial goods.[1] In any case, the fourfold price increase of 1973 substantially exceeded any unfavorable shift in the terms of trade to the oil producers. Technological advances and other qualitative improvements in industrial goods during this time of rapid innovation, moreover, would further have discounted any negative shifts in OPEC's terms of trade. Hence, if the terms of trade are taken as a measure of fairness in oil pricing, the fourfold price hike wiped out the basis of commercial reciprocity and fairness. Less esoteric and difficult to calculate indexes of fairness might lead to similar conclusions.

It could be argued, for instance, that a number of members of OPEC, like Venezuela and Kuwait, are actually members of the world's middle class. They belong among neither the full participants in the advanced industrial elite nor the poor nations. As the bourgeoisie of the international system, the argument goes, these nouveaux riches states not only have taken from the rich but also have stolen from the poor, thus creating a disparity in wealth between themselves and the bulk of the non-oil developing countries.

This rapid divergence in status between the bourgeois oil producers and the systemic proletariat has to some extent been paid for at the *direct expense* of the latter group. A gallon of gasoline in Bolivia may have increased in cost by the same percentage as in West Germany, but the peasants of La Paz have far less ability to pay than the Bavarians of south Germany. Unless covered by an equivalent increase in the value of exports or by aid or an inflow of capital, both the balance of payments and the welfare of the poor countries will suffer significantly.

Not unmindful of these problems of exploitation, individual members of OPEC have established a number of foreign assistance programs. On paper at least, Saudi Arabia has contributed 10 percent of its revenue in 1975 to various kinds of foreign assistance, a feat matched nowhere among the industrial nations in a single year. Concealed within this figure are dollars for arms purchased from the United States, France, and Britain and contributions to Syria and Egypt in the struggle with Israel. Whether all of these pledges of external assistance are actually honored, the relative magnitude of the proposed effort is impressive. Indeed, collectively the oil producers have pledged a volume of foreign assistance almost equaling that of the advanced industrial nations combined.

One characteristic of the aid program devised by the oil producers is that it is naturally weighted in the direction of those who possess the largest financial reserves. These countries happen to be the ones that have large reservoirs of petroleum but little capacity to put capital in large amounts into productive investments. This confluence of large petroleum reserves and small capital absorbency is marked for three countries, Saudi Arabia, Kuwait, and the United Arab Emirates, all of them Arab. Furthermore, in distributing economic assistance, the Arab countries have established the priorities that in effect exclude certain developing countries from aid while channeling it toward others. The three concentric circles of diminishing priority are the poor Arab countries, including Israel's principal rivals—Egypt, Syria, and Jordan; non-Arab Moslem countries such as Pakistan and Bangladesh; and black Africa. Other poor countries in Latin America and Asia may receive loans through OPEC contributions to the World Bank or through regional grants, for example from Venezuela or Iran, although internal demands within each of these polities circumscribe the magnitude of the latter assistance.

Almost unavoidably, a net surplus in favor of the oil producing countries will drain capital and foreign exchange away from a number of poor countries. In many instances OPEC assistance either will fail to erase the deficit or will leave it untouched. This deficit may be pointed to as the measure to which the achievements of the new middle class of nations have grown at the expense of those nations at the bottom of the socioeconomic hierarchy.

A final argument heard on behalf of the unfairness of the current oil prices is based on grounds of egalitarianism, an argument that has curiously been used to defend the increases more often than to oppose them. The egalitarian critique stems not just from the fact that a small fraction of the nations in the world have benefited from oil exportation or that the populations of the bulk of these (excluding Indonesia, Nigeria, and Iran) are quite small, thus creating per capita incomes that are enormous—exceeding in the cases of Saudi Arabia, Kuwait, and the United Arab Emirates the per capital wealth of the richest advanced industrial nations. (Indeed it is true that even Iran, with a population of some 30 million, will shortly exceed the per capita wealth of the poorer European states such as Italy.) The real heart of the egalitarian attack lies in how the new oil wealth is distributed among *people*, that is, among families and individuals.

Without significant exception, the per capita distribution of wealth within each member of the OPEC group is highly unequal. It is well known, for example, that some twenty families control the bulk of Kuwait's income and that an even smaller number of extended families connected with the throne in Saudi Arabia enjoy preeminent economic status there. Names such as Aalam, Sadri, Bakhtiyari, and Eqbal are familiar among the Iranian elite of some forty powerful families linked through complex political and kin ties to the ruling Pahlavis. Nor are the military governments in Nigeria, Iraq, and Indonesia immune to favoritism and the concentration of wealth despite lip service to socialist values. Advancement within the army is as much a route to personal wealth as it is to power or social prestige, and the military is careful to preserve its ties with concentrated wealth in the private sector.

Corruption, moreover, is often such a conventional method of reinforcing privilege that at least one of the larger OPEC states, Venezuela, has for reasons of social discipline consciously adopted the somewhat antieconomic policy of reducing oil production substantially below the historical level. This policy is antieconomic because alternative investments with high rates of return theoretically exist both inside and outside the country. But as former petroleum minister Juan Pablo Pérez Alfonso (one of the founders of OPEC) lamented, the new oil income is being squandered by the government, diverted into political corruption, siphoned out of the country into the personal bank accounts of certain members of the governing elite, and otherwise prevented from finding its way into investments that would benefit the society as a whole. Hence, more than $8 billion is being held in a special fund for future Venezuelan investment under more carefully controlled and planned development programs.

The upshot of the egalitarian critique is that on an individual basis vast inequities are emerging within the OPEC countries in terms of the acquisition of personal wealth. Insofar as one accepts the thesis that increasing economic inequality is bad, the enabling force behind such inequality may likewise be construed as undesirable, namely, the sudden fourfold increase in the price of crude oil and the additional increases thereafter. The egalitarian argument would not hold if it could be shown that the oil price increases and the huge concomitant bulge of revenues had occurred without causally exaggerating the disparity of wealth within OPEC nations. Similarly, the argument would not hold if it could be shown that through effective taxation schemes or other reforms the trend toward social inequality were likely to be reversed in such a way that the overall economic development of a society would be enhanced not harmed. In the absence of either of these qualifications, the indictment of the price increases as a poor vehicle for the transference of wealth within the international system seems from this perspective rather well sustained.

In general, the unfairness-of-oil-price doctrine rests on the extraordinary size of the initial price increases, the negative impact on world inflation, the resulting political disturbances that in part have been associated with OPEC's actions, the widespread feeling that the terms of trade have not shifted against the oil producers, the damage done to the economies of some of the poorest nations, and the great accruals of wealth to a handful of individuals within a few countries.[2] Whether these arguments attacking the current high price for oil justify, from the viewpoint of equity, a concerted effort to change the global policy of the oil producing nations through any of several strategies depends further, however, upon the appropriate determination of what is meant by a fair price for oil, taking into account the preferences of consumers, producers, and the system as a whole. It is to this task that we now turn.

WHAT IS A FAIR PRICE FOR OIL?

Since the negative consequences of the new higher oil prices appear legion, the adoption of a reasonable price for oil necessitates weighing a number of price alternatives. Several approaches to price determination have been suggested, each displaying a different level of public attention and appeal.

Free Competition Price

Some of the first econometric models in the recent wave projecting the world price of crude oil more than a decade into the future adopt the conceptually rather simplifying assumption of free, or perfect, competition.[3] While the free competition price is quite useful to an economist as a benchmark against which to measure the actual price of oil, it is likewise a very misleading notion for policymakers and noneconomists if it is taken to mean even a hypothetically feasible price let alone a more equitable one. Notwithstanding such restraints on trade as the OPEC cartel (which in the absence of dissolution will continue to set the price for oil), the fact that there is a relatively small number of fairly concentrated firms in the oil industry and that there are only about 150 consumer nations is sufficient to make it unlikely that the market will ever approach perfect, or free, competition. For the same reason, it does very little good to compute estimated or proven world reserves of petroleum and then calculate the long-term availability of this resource by reference to historical increases in the growth rate of consumption. Both consumption and exploration (and thus the size of reserves) are as much a function of price as price in turn is a function of them. The "free" competition price for crude or its products is an artifact of the methodology we employ to analyze economic relations and in no way corresponds either to the politico-economic reality of the market or to a possible basis for judging what is fair for consumers to pay or for producers to charge.

Cost plus Profit

Suppose instead that one adopts, somewhat in the tradition of utility regulation, the practice of ascertaining the cost of producing a barrel of oil and then adding on a reasonable profit calculated against some historical standard or industrial average. We might, for example, conclude from the experience of America's 500 largest corporations that a 15 percent return on investment (based on a ratio of revenue to total assets) above cost is an ample profit level. Apart from the accounting difficulty of agreeing upon how costs should be defined (e.g., are commissions to facilitators within a foreign bureaucracy appropriate costs?), this standard might be readily accepted by most consumers. But I suspect that the oil producers would reject the scheme as totally unfair.

First, costs of drilling, transporting, and ultimately of refining and marketing oil vary widely from region to region. In Saudia Arabia the cost of producing a barrel of crude is still significantly under $.50, while in the

North Sea the cost is higher by a factor of more than ten. An irony of the proposed pricing system is that the higher one's costs, the greater one's absolute profits. Hence, there is no incentive for efficiency. Nor is there any rational reason why low-cost producers should be remunerated so poorly. But more seriously from the producer's perspective, the net rates of return in oil production by historical standards have been far higher than the 15 percent return the consumers might think valid according to the cost plus profit criterion.

This problem leads to the second major difficulty regarding producer acceptance. Why should norms for industrial pricing be applied to market contexts in which societies are the actors? If instead one used markets between governments or other proxies for the society as a whole, the average net rate of return in such trading might be far larger. But even here history is used as a guide to price "reasonableness." There is no reason to believe that justice guided the determination of prices in the past any more than there is reason to believe on the basis of this criterion that current prices are unjust. Why should history reflect anything more than the equilibrium of political and economic power among countries and firms, an equilibrium that may or may not have reflected social equity?

Third, assert the producers, the analogy between industrial production and the exploitation of a natural resource is totally fallacious. Consumers who have this conception of value, they argue, are bound to be confused about price fairness. Most industrial production has a very long, perhaps infinite, time horizon assuming the capacity for a modicum of technological innovation on the part of the entrepreneur. But oil is an exhaustible resource and as such must be treated differently. Once oil is used up it cannot be replaced. Hence, the normal profit earned by the entrepreneur in industrial production is a very poor standard for determining the economic rent associated with the exhaustible resource. Accordingly, oil prices determined by cost plus rent calculations are likely to be far higher than those conceived in terms of some sort of cost plus profit criterion.

Societal Needs

Perhaps a shortcut to the selection of a fair price for oil can be discovered via the route of social need. A clear-cut disparity in the needs of consumers and producers would indicate in which direction price ought to tilt. While scarcely precise, this rationale for setting price levels has the advantage of intuitive plausibility and indeed is the essential guideline for establishing foreign assistance programs.

Since the largest buyers of OPEC oil are the advanced industrial countries, whose wealth is substantial, producers tend to believe that these countries can afford even higher prices for oil than they currently pay—especially because energy, while an important component of an economy, is only a single component and because the consumer governments actually increase the cost to users by attaching heavy taxes to the price of delivered crude. According to the producers, their own preeminent social needs are self-evident and fairness dictates global acknowledgment of these needs. Immediately, however, two difficulties arise in accepting this rationale for higher prices.

First, despite the poverty of a country like Indonesia, with an estimated per capita annual income of $90, the per capita wealth of a number of the most influential OPEC states exceeds that of most of the consumer countries. Moreover, even if the majority of the poorest nations of the world were compensated by OPEC for their net trade deficits created by the increased oil import bill, a number of so-called advanced industrial societies —Spain, Greece, Austria, Italy, and the East European bloc of nations— would find their incomes trailing those of many of the OPEC states by 1980. By no means is the disparity between rich consumers and poor producers self-evident, largely because each group is so heterogeneous in income terms.

Second, following the arguments familiar in an earlier section, income inequality within the producer countries is particularly marked and is further aggravated by the recent bulge of oil revenues only poorly digested. Yet the existence of income inequality in such countries as the United States makes cross-national comparisons even more problematic. It is difficult to argue that the Turkoman of northeastern Iran, although he is a farmer and nomad, is worse off in social terms than the poor black in the American ghetto or the poor white farmer in Appalachia. Indeed, insofar as quality of life and health indexes are used as measures of social well-being, the Turkoman nomad has a life-style, cultural outlook, and personal longevity that many Americans would envy.

Not only does the problem of personal income inequality cloud the price fairness issue, but the philosophic problem becomes relevant of whether one has the right analytically to question the distribution of wealth within another society. If a government represents its people, maintains order, yet still tolerates vast and increasing personal economic inequality, on what grounds is this inequality to be disputed? Such a conclusion would simplify the fairness question because one would then treat nations as aggregates and make judgments on the basis of cross-national differences in aggregate personal income. But even if this rather challengeable approach to social needs is adopted, this discussion should have made quite apparent that one will never approximate price fairness unless some better technique for assessing and comparing social needs is developed employing a concept like utility.

A Global Welfare Function and the Theory of Welfare Maximization

Since the disparity in social needs between consumers and producers has been seen by no means to be uniform, we are forced to consider some type of global welfare function for determining valid compromises among preferences across broadly heterogeneous wealth classifications.[4]

Hence, discussion of the "just price" notion raises an important political question: fairness, or equity of distribution. According to W. S. Vickrey,

> the notion that each article had a "just price" which truly represented its intrinsic value had as a corollary the notion that in trading articles at the just price neither party gained or lost, while any departure from this price involved a gain to one party at the expense of the other. As long as circumstances changed slowly, this idea did much to prevent exploitation in potentially monopolistic situations.[5]

OPEC control of oil prices certainly constitutes a "monopolistic situation." Therefore, is use of the just price notion theoretically justified in the context of the petroleum debate? In order to explore this idea in terms of the history of welfare thought, we are going to attempt to condense more than fifty years of extended argumentation into a few paragraphs. Our purpose is to illustrate some of the theoretical difficulties as well as the theoretical promise underlying the determination of a *global welfare function*, a concept that if derived would lend considerable weight to the use of the just price notion in the current oil polemic.

While Samuelson's grand synthesis in *Foundation's of Economic Analysis*, written at mid-century, and Pareto's ideas of welfare maximization, written at the beginning of the century, perhaps stand out most clearly in the evolution of welfare theory, dozens of analysts helped establish the foundations of welfare thought, including Lerner, Bergson, Kaldor, Hicks, and Scitovsky.[6] Kenneth Arrow slammed the door on one pathway to welfare calculation, namely that via *interpersonal ordinal utilities*, in his famous "impossibility theorem"; other economists like J. E. Meade have extended welfare economics into such areas as the gains from international trade.[7] For our purposes in questioning the use of the concept of just price in the current oil debate, it is sufficient to sketch the static determination of inputs and outputs and of equity, but we shall secondly consider the problem of dynamic extension and analysis of intertemporal production efficiency. A now classic article by Francis Bator is helpful in each of these tasks.[8]

Static treatment of welfare maximization assumes a set of production functions, ordinal preference functions, and a social welfare function that permits only an intrapersonal preference ordering for individuals in their own preference fields. First, the model connects "factor endowments" such as land and labor related through production functions to a "production possibility curve" showing what can be produced from the endowments. Second, the static model relates the production possibility curve to a utility-possibility frontier, or set of indifference curves, showing what production is possible given an individual's value preferences. Third, each utility-possibility frontier is evaluated to determine a single best configuration of such frontiers, or a social welfare function. Finally, once the social welfare function is established, we can retrace our steps to determine the "best" choice of inputs and outputs associated with the original production function.

But while the static model can be constructed with seemingly little difficulty, the dynamic model is more complex. For example, dynamic treatment must include leads and lags with respect to temporal processes such as the delay involved in moving from exploration to drilling and from drilling to production of oil and gas. Also, stocks and inventories are of critical significance in an industry such as petroleum although the static model neglects them. Spacial and transport problems become important as well. Finally, intertemporal judgments have to be made regarding preference and regarding allocations and distributions of stocks. Calculation of intertemporal flows is complicated by the instability of intrapersonal preferences over time and by necessary judgments concerning the availability of inputs today and tomorrow and the relative desirability of certain outputs on each of these occasions. Knowledge of tomorrow's preferences is critical to today's production, but to some degree today's production is responsible for tomorrow's preferences. Problems of this kind, as well as many more involving the actual distribution of income, diminishing returns to scale, curves with ambiguous maxima and minima, and various kinds of "externalities" that are not directly reflected in price but affect social output, tend to broaden and blur definitive welfare conclusions.

But the blow struck by Arrow to the use of ordinal utilities in the comparison of *interpersonal* preferences in a community of more than two individuals was perhaps the most devastating attack on the theory of welfare maximization. It should be intuitively apparent that even at the theoretical level, our analytic capacity at this time to conceive of the kind of underlying models that would permit satisfactory calculations of a just price for oil is seriously flawed. We have not demonstrated that the determination of a just price for oil is impossible; far less have we shown that the question is politically unimportant. We merely despair in the contemporary development of a reliable theoretical calculus for proper welfare maximization. Moreover, the data on the preference of samples of the population within each nation-state, as well as on production, flows, inventories, and income, present formidable tasks of coding, collection, and analysis.

Having described the process and assumptions involved in the determination of a global welfare function we can appreciate more fully how far short we fall in the actual calculation of such a function. And without the information that such a function could yield, we see how hopeless the task is of concluding whether $7, $11, or $20 a barrel of oil is a just price. These analytic problems do not deny either that in principle there must be a just price for oil or that knowledge of such a price would be an invaluable guide to policy. This discussion only demonstrates the impossibility of precise welfare judgments given our current ability to treat complex questions of value in the social sciences.

If we cannot presently determine an equitable price for the sale and purchase of crude oil, perhaps we can at least identify whether there are any upper bounds on price. Perhaps we can also say something regarding alternative price paths and regarding the various price strategies that producers or consumers might adopt.

WHAT IS A PLAUSIBLE UPPER BOUND TO PRICE?

In theory there is no magic involved in the answer to this question. The *substitution threshold,* namely, that price at which substitution takes away a significancet share of the OPEC market, creates the upper limit on price advances. The exploitation of alternative energy sources such as shale oil, coal liquification or gasification, nuclear breeder reactors, and solar energy and the discovery of major new (although perhaps high-cost) petroleum deposits all set limits to price as these sources or discoveries come on line and begin to compete with OPEC oil. But in practice the difficulty in identifying the locations of the substitution threshold (or thresholds) in advance and the problem of assessing how the various players in the market game are likely to perceive the threshold complicate the answer by introjection of political factors.

The Substitution Threat
OPEC decisionmakers set prices by considering not only current conditions but also future investment behavior of the consumers. As prices rise, a panoply of new energy options are opened to the consumer nations. Perceptions concerning these options become critical to understanding how the OPEC cartel may act.

Currently, OPEC tends to minimize the importance of new energy sources and tends perhaps to exaggerate the height of the substitution threshold. One Arab source, for example, concludes that meaningful substitution from shale oil could not occur at less than $17 a barrel (1973 prices).[9] The reason for deemphasizing the seriousness of the substitution threat is severalfold.

First, the producers are aware (more aware than were some members of the Nixon administration at the time that Project Independence was unfolded) of the enormous front-end costs of meaningful substitution from so-called exotic sources. The magnitude of the capital costs alone ranges from a low estimate of $150 billion to a high of $1 trillion spread over ten years. Given other priorities and overall constraints on capital, particularly in the period of recent recession, the producers have expressed doubts that the consumers will embark on any broad-scale energy development programs.

The second deterrent to substitution that the producers count on is the combination of current rigidities and uncertainties. They recognize that insofar as the oil industry itself is called upon to develop oil shale or to exploit coal liquification in order to drive down OPEC prices by eroding OPEC's market share, this task is really not in the industry's commercial interest. Why should it embark on a massive project to destroy the stability of its own market? This in no way implies that OPEC and the oil industry have colluded in price increases, even if such collusion were possible. Rather, it suggests merely that the oil industry has few real commercial incentives to undermine its own price structure.

Coupled with downward price rigidity is price uncertainty, uncertainty created by the possibility that OPEC could drag the price of oil below the substitution threshold once massive investments had been begun, thus wiping out any possible profits from the enterprise. Unless consumer governments are willing to subsidize the production of crude oil on a massive scale (or alternatively guarantee to purchase a given amount of synthetic crude oil if the world price for crude falls below a minimum), no private investor is likely to absorb the risks of innovation in the face of so much market uncertainty.

Finally, the producers perceive that they will have considerable leverage over market price during the next decade because of lags and delays in the substitution effort. Environmental delays involved in laying the Alaskan pipeline are the sort of obstacle that the consumers must overcome in launching a crash energy program. Even without unanticipated delays, a lag of approximately seven years exists between the time exploration is begun and the time the first gallon of gasoline is pumped into the tank of an automobile. In addition, much of the technology that will be needed for drilling on the outer shelf, and much of the chemical research needed to make synthetic crude processing economically feasible is unavailable or incomplete. In a sector of the scientific and engineering communities where employment is rather full, the prospects are not very high for sudden increases in the rate of innovation.

Given these three kinds of leverage—the cost deterrent, market rigidities and uncertainties, and development lags and delays—the producers remain confident that very little pressure from substitution will occur through 1985. They are far more concerned however about the prospect of large new discoveries of petroleum, perhaps in the South China Sea. They may be more sensitive to petroleum discovery because of the ease with which large new deposits have been found and developed in the Middle East. They are also aware of the probabilistic character of discoveries and the "lumpiness" involved in the discovery process. A single major new oil field of the size of one of the fields in the Ras Tanura area (Saudi Arabia) could rapidly shift the supply picture. On the other hand, offshore drilling in the

Gulf of Mexico and along the Atlantic coast does not concern the producers very much because they know that this is high-cost production, much like that in the North Sea, the effect of which is to build a floor under the price rather than significantly to undercut it.

In response to the diffidence of the producers concerning the substitution threat, the consumers have several advantages that are either discounted or ignored by the producers and that thus give the United States and its allies potential leverage. First, while few economies of scale seem to be associated with offshore drilling, economies of scale are very pronounced in the production of synthetic crude and perhaps as well in the production of coal by conventional methods. One estimate suggests that the cost of some now novel production processes could be reduced by one-third over some years.[10] The practical implication here is that oil shale plants substantially bigger than 100,000 barrels per day may enjoy cost savings that tend to bring down the price of oil. If the economies of scale are great enough, countries like the United States, with important shale deposits and a huge domestic energy market, can afford to invest heavily in such technology because the payoffs will be large and increasing.

Second, in the area of alternative sources, the learning curve effect may speed up technological innovation and further reduce costs of production. Estimates suggest that by exploiting possible technological breakthroughs in synthetic crude production one could reduce production costs by a factor of three. Together the learning curve effect and economies of scale could transform what appear to be noneconomic processes at today's prices into very competitive future sources of energy.

Whether the leverage that the producers perceive they have is greater than the leverage obtainable by the consumers is difficult to estimate. Regardless of the medium-term outcome, the reality is clear of an upper bound on price created by the substitution threshold. Since from the consumer point of view meaningful substitution is years away at best, it may be instructive to explore types of price strategies that the producers could employ prior to the time when a significant share of the OPEC market will be lost to energy substitution or to large new petroleum discoveries.

Alternative Price Strategies (1975–1985)

1. Counterinflationary strategy. A much debated policy within OPEC is whether to continue to seek ad hoc price increases or to attempt to tie the price of crude to the rate of inflation embodied in industrial imports. If the latter course is chosen, a subsidiary problem is how to select a bundle of industrial goods that cumulatively reflects "inflation" for each of the varied producer economies with their varied import needs. What the hypothetical strategy under discussion reveals, however, is that regardless of whether the consumers agree to a program tying the price of consumer goods to the price of crude oil (a program that under any but the most

dire commercial pressure the advanced industrial states would be unlikely to accept in part because of its awkwardness), the producers can achieve the same objective unilaterally as long as they remain price makers rather than price takers on the world oil market. Annual or semiannual increases in crude prices could be improvised so as just to offset the impact of inflation, thereby freezing-in the initial gains from the fourfold price increase of 1973–1974.

One advantage of this strategy is that it would have less of a negative impact on the OPEC production share over the next decade than other strategies yielding somewhat higher revenues (recalling that depending upon price elasticity, price and quantity produced are somewhat inversely proportional since it would tend neither to reduce the overall rate of oil consumption so greatly nor to increase the purchase of oil from new non-OPEC sources. The trouble with this strategy from the OPEC viewpoint is that it may not produce revenue fast enough to please the most capital-hungry of the cartel partners.

2. Long-term stabilization strategy: This hypothetical strategy is likely to appeal to those members of the cartel with large petroleum reserves and thus a long time horizon over which to stretch returns. The objective of the strategy is to increase price slowly, thus minimally accelerating the innovation of new energy sources and the process of new discoveries while at the same time increasing net returns from the sale of OPEC oil.[11] Insofar as the OPEC production share is not significantly diminished during the period required to bring new sources on line, and insofar as the period required to develop new sources is not severely abbreviated through crash consumer programs triggered by the fear of rapid increases in OPEC prices, the price stabilization strategy aimed at a point just below the cost of producing significant amounts of synthetic crude ought to receive considerable support from a number of cartel members. Uncertainty as to whether price increases will in fact have much to do with shrinking the potential lag time involved in the consumer substitution effort could, however, make this strategy less popular.

3. Short-term revenue maximization. At the opposite extreme, a strategy designed to exploit what seems to be perceived as an inevitable lag time in consumer efforts of seven to ten years might attempt to maximize revenue in the short run by raising price well above the substitution threshold and then lowering it precipitously as synthetic crude, massive coal production, or major new discoveries of moderate-cost oil came on stream. Theoretically, the price of crude could go very high indeed, perhaps above $30 a barrel. For those actors with good alternative investments inside or outside their own countries, this strategy makes much more sense than the prior one since oil left in the ground is not likely to provide returns equal to those from education, heavy industry, infrastructure, or safe foreign investments. The only extra economic cost this strategy entails is a rapid de-

cline in the OPEC market share caused by the overall decline in the world demand for oil, particularly oil used for heating and, to a lesser extent, transportation purposes. Insofar as the interval required to bring in new oil cannot be further contracted for reasons of market rigidities, personnel shortages, and technical encumbrances, the impact on OPEC would not be great from the supply side even for so aggressive a strategy as this one.

4. Substitution-delay strategy. By far the most imaginative strategy from the producer country perspective is one that would both maximize the economic return to the cartel in the short run and postpone the negative price effects of energy substitution. But how could OPEC achieve such a combination of opposed objectives? A rather obvious trade-off seems possible in a static model in which the producer country is not able to alter its strategy.

When one considers the strategic possibilities in a dynamic setting, however, the conclusion regarding the trade-off is far from ineluctable. The way OPEC could obtain both maximum revenues and substitution delays is through price juggling. OPEC could raise prices as rapidly as is feasible based on the internal preferences of the cartel membership. It should be pointed out that not all members, particularly countries with the characteristics of Saudi Arabia, are likely to prefer very rapid or very major price increases (see Chapter VI). At the first sign of major *production* activity regarding oil shale, coal liquification, or breeder reactors, OPEC could drop the price of crude oil precipitously. The potential effect of this action on private investment in major synthetic crude activities would be devastating. The impact on government-sponsored programs in democracies in which continuity of leadership is often lacking and fickleness of public resolve is an obstacle would be one of program slowdowns if not outright cancellations. Having upset ongoing development programs and added uncertainty to investment calculations, the producers would also have tempted the consumer societies to exploit the cheaper supplies of crude oil and to forget about new, more ambitious energy projects for a time. (Lower cost crude would also quickly drive high-cost marginal drilling operations out of business.)

Having eliminated some of the pressure from competing sources and postponed, in some cases indefinitely, high-cost research and production efforts not easily revived, OPEC could then raise prices again to prior levels. This process of raising and lowering prices could be repeated at intervals dictated by the imminence and magnitude of the substitution danger. Prices according to this strategy could be raised well above the substitution threshold because the awareness of price uncertainty would tend to outweigh the positive inducement to high-cost exploration or substitution of high crude prices. Given the apparent plausibility of this schema for maximizing revenue and delaying price competition, how realistic is the strategy from a political viewpoint?

A number of considerations seem to discount the attractiveness of substitution-delay strategies for the producers. First, although the producer countries cannot afford to be too concerned about the impact of their policies on the economies and societies of the consumer nations, the oscillation of prices involved in substitution-delay strategies would send waves of uncertainty and disequilibrium throughout the entire trade network. Insofar as this resulting disequilibrium would threaten the flow of industrial goods into the OPEC countries, particularly in the current rapid phase of their economic development, when a steady flow of goods at reasonable prices is critical to balanced growth, substitution-delay could have undesirable secondary effects. Admittedly, a reduction in prices would hardly be criticized in terms of disruptiveness, but for the strategy to be fully successful and for OPEC members to capture a maximum amount of revenue, the price of crude would again have to be raised sending a shock through the economies of the industrialized nations.

Second, the prospect of a price decline, no matter how abbreviated, would be hard for members of the political elites within OPEC countries, and hence for the governments themselves, to accept. Temporary losses of revenue are not likely to be palatable to regimes precariously balanced among powerful families, communal groupings, and the military. Weak governments cannot easily convince the planners of development programs to sacrifice current projects for the possibility of substantial increases in future revenue when the risk associated with such a strategy is large or unknown. Inertia built into the development process demands a continuity of policy.

For a few governments—Saudi Arabia, Kuwait, the United Arab Emirates—implementation of price declines would be easier because of vast financial reserves earning only poor rates of return. These revenues could find an immediate employment in tiding the development program over the period required to delay the substitution effort in the consumer countries. But these three OPEC states are the very states that are the most financially cautious and reluctant to upset producer-consumer relations with overly bold policies. For the other OPEC members the strategy would be less feasible because after 1977 excess financial reserves for the majority of the membership will be virtually nonexistent.

The consequence is that the price decline side of the substitution-delay strategy is not going to be easy for the membership to achieve. The awkwardness, uncertainty, and complexity of the strategy makes it a difficult one to sell to risk-averse decisionmakers.

Third, when facing the possible repetition of price rises and declines, the consumer countries would not likely remain passive. Awareness that price declines approximated a Trojan horse and were calculated only to foil the substitution effort might stimulate reprisals. Government-sponsored "insurance programs" for the private investor involved in generating new energy sources also would be a likely consequence of substitution-delay strategies. While the establishment of such programs in the consumer countries is problematic for reasons of capital shortages, interference with the philosophy of free enterprise, and investor skepticism, continued use of the substitution-delay strategy would surely drive the consumer governments to protect themselves.

The combination of negative secondary trade effects, opposition from the elites in the producer countries to price declines, and protectionist policies on the part of the consumers all tend to undercut the prospects of success for the substitution-delay approach. Of the four proposed price strategies for OPEC adoption, which is the most feasible and why?

If the substitution-delay strategy is too complex and radical for some of the most powerful members of OPEC to embrace, the long-term stabilization strategy is too pusilanimous and unremunerative for the majority of the cartel membership to adopt. The substitution-delay approach is unlikely ever to receive a serious hearing within the upper OPEC decision echelons, just as the long-term revenue stabilization strategy will never persuade the rank and file that it is sufficiently aggressive.

This leaves the first and third strategies, counterinflation and short-term revenue maximization, as more broadly attractive. Indeed, these two price paths can be thought of as the probable dynamic lower and upper bounds, respectively, of crude oil prices through 1980. The rate of U.S. inflation is the rate upon which the counterinflation strategy would focus. Short-term revenue maximization as reflected in models incorporating lags in the adjustment of supply and demand suggests that the price could theoretically go as high as $30 or 40 a barrel in 1975 prices. Practical limits on the advancement of price, as well as intense opposition to massive price increases from certain members of the cartel such as Saudi Arabi, reduce the probability of this level of revenue accentuation. Barring a very efficient and perceptibly equitable distribution of revenue within the cartel, moreover, short-term profit maximization for the cartel as a whole would not necessarily benefit each member equivalently. But neither would the counterinflationary strategy. Indeed, many of the OPEC governments may settle for retaining the fourfold price increase in the face of U.S. inflation (i.e., the counterinflationary strategy) regardless of whether it wrings the last dollar of possible revenue out of the consumers, especially since a collapse of cartel policies could leave all of the members somewhat worse off.

POSTSCRIPT ON PRICE

Reduced to its essence, the problem with the increase in crude oil prices is that it occurred over too short a time period to be readily absorbed by the world economy. If the fourfold price increase had been averaged over the fifteen-year interval since the birth of OPEC, the consumer nations would not have experienced stressful financial and commercial adjustment. The price increases would still have outpaced the inflation the industrial world would have transmitted to the producing countries.

But there is a legitimate question from the OPEC perspective of whether for political reasons the increases could have come in any other way. The producer countries could not take command of prices until a shift of power occurred in their favor. Two forces—unprecedented increases in world demand for crude oil, which outstripped non-OPEC production capacity, and erosion of the strength of the multinationals regarding production decisions—combined to facilitate this shift of power. OPEC had to take advantage of the "existential moment" at which commercial and political forces created an opportunity for a revolution in the price structure. Prior to 1973 an attack on the price structure would have been premature; much subsequent to this point in time demand and supply conditions might have changed, making unilateral price increases less feasible. Thus, a gradual increase in prices over the entire history of OPEC's existence was probably impossible, attractive though this hypothetical price pattern might be to economic theorists.

But if most of the world's commercial problems have stemmed from the rapidity of the price increases for crude oil, the question of a just, ultimate price remains. Not able to determine a just price, however, the analyst is in a poor position to argue that any price is unjust. Inability to calculate an equitable price suggests that much of the debate over fair market prices for oil is based less on the foundations of political economy than on ideological preference.

Lacking convincing evidence from either side, one can anticipate that the fairness argument is a myth that will be used by both the consumers and the producers for instrumental purposes. In such circumstances, where gross imperfections in the market also exist, the outcome is determined in the larger politico-economic setting in which the amount of information available to the producers, the ability of the producers to surmount political differences among themselves, the concerns regarding national security and access to industrial goods, and the energy strategies of the consumer governments together will significantly affect price decisions. Perceptions rather than market realities in the short run become the guide to policy.

Regardless of the hardships caused by the changes in the petroleum price structure, the global system of states will recognize that a positive benefit enjoyed by everyone is the more efficient and more prudent use of the world's energy resources.[12] Waste presumably benefits no one. Elimination of waste thus benefits producers and consumers of energy alike. A 25 percent reduction in the long-term growth of energy demand in the United States, for example, may include some involuntary shifts in preference. Americans may buy fewer Cadillacs and Mercedes and more Gremlins and

Toyotas. But by an insightful examination of industrial and residential practices, Americans and others may instead be able to conserve energy without changing their preferences. Innovation in energy conservation is as feasible as development of new ways to employ energy. Price increases may to some degree hinder the productive growth in energy use, but this effect must be qualified by the incentives created to use energy better.

Petroleum is a natural resource with a large variety of possible applications in drugs, plastics, chemicals, and food. Substitutes for petroleum in several of these areas may be far from satisfactory even fifty years from now. There is no guarantee that mankind necessarily exploits the cheapest resource first because this practice would assume technological omniscience and perfect foresight. If much of the world's oil is used for heating and transportation today because it is cheap, then far more important future uses may be precluded. OPEC may have done the world a favor by forcing a modicum of conservation and a bit more attention concerning mankind's plight once petroleum reserves have been depleted.

From the world perspective the assertion of OPEC countries that oil is their "ticket into the twentieth century" bears respectful examination.[13] Current disparities in the level of per capita income have little significance here. What OPEC is arguing is that it seeks for its future citizens an industrial base not just a good living today off temporary rents. Since in most cases the time required to industrialize is limited to the life of an OPEC country's petroleum reserves, the per capita income of the country may have to be very high indeed during this relatively short period in order to overcome the *encumbrances of haste* in the development process.

The global consequence of OPEC development is an enlarged industrial world (qualified by the damage done to the industrial hopes of the poorest countries) one likely to provide more goods and services for mankind not less. Global welfare will have been increased by the emergence of a new middle class of nations capable of exchanging something more than the naked resources of their lands for the increasingly sophisticated and productive manufactures from ours. While there is no guarantee that the distribution will be equitable, some power is likely to shift toward the new middle class of nations. But given an effective dynamic response from the advanced industrial economies, OPEC should not garner an unreasonably large share of the increased benefits of world trade. With the passing of the old commercial order, we should not so much lament the loss of a producer of cheap commodities as we should hail the arrival of a new trading partner capable of expanding the variety and abundance of the world's created surplus.

II

Israel and Oil:
The Myth of Association

SOURCES OF THE MYTH

An argument commonly heard in some circles is that the Israeli question and oil price increases are causally related. Israeli actions are held to be responsible in part for the plight of the oil consuming nations. The argument that the two forces are one, namely, that the oil price hikes and Israeli hesitance to return occupied territory prior to negotiation are synonymous, is based on a variety of contentions and evidence: assertions by Arab petroleum ministers in the summer and fall of 1973 that price increases would follow an Israeli refusal to withdraw from the occupied territories; the actual concurrence of price increases and the October war; and the expectation that Israeli concessions will bring about a future reduction in the price of oil. Each of these factors is complex and requires detailed, careful explication and treatment. Insofar as we are dealing with the perceptions of statesmen and petroleum officials, publicly expressed opinion must be sifted and measured against the realities of politics and the oil market.

With increasing vehemence, oil officials in the Arab exporting countries warned the United States in 1972 and early 1973 that oil could be used as a weapon against Israel. In April 1973 the Washington Post reported that Saudi petroleum minister Yamani felt his country could not significantly increase production (and thus maintain price levels) unless Washington changed its pro-Israeli stance. In August, Prince Abd Allah ibn'Abd al-Aziz, commander of the Saudi Arabian National Guard, noted in an interview with the Beruit weekly *al-Hawadith* that the new Saudi Petroleum Council

31

possessed a brief "not limited to purely economic matters." Rather, its purpose was to "maximize the use of oil in the service of the Arab cause." Similarly, Prince Saud al-Faisal, deputy minister of oil and mineral resources, observed in an interview with *al-Hawadith* on August 31 and in an earlier radio interview that both Arab oil and reserve funds could be used as a political lever in the Arab-Israeli confrontation. Finally, King Faisal himself in a *Newsweek* interview (as well as on a rare television appearance spoke of extreme difficulty in increasing exports to the United States because of American support of Zionism against Arabs.[1]

This barrage of comments linking Israel with oil production and price came largely but not solely from Saudi Arabia, the largest oil exporter, and hence the country most capable of putting its program into action. Some Saudi government officials like Prince Saud al-Faisal recognized the cumbersomeness of the oil weapon.[2] It was designed to affect the United States but, whether broadly or selectively applied, it would end up affecting everybody, particularly those countries more dependent upon OPEC oil than is the United States.

Iraq chose to dissociate itself from collective Arab policy partly on the ground that the production cut approach was too diffuse. According to Sadoon Hammadi, Iraq's minister of oil and minerals, the Arab governments must "fight this enemy" by "confront[ing] him directly and seriously."[3] This meant nationalization of U.S. economic interests in Iraq, rupture of diplomatic relations, and withdrawal of Arab financial reserves from U.S. banks, Iraqi policy toward the United States also reflected the government's desire to increase its oil production for economic reasons in a period in which the rest of OPEC was cutting back production (a move justified largely by awareness that the Iraqi rate of increase of oil production in the 1960s had been the lowest in OPEC). One suspects that Iraq's own commercial ambitions actually overshadowed its disenchantment with the commonly accepted Arab strategy for dealing with the Israeli issue. Although Iraq's stubborn autonomy probably did not undermine the joint strategic effort of the Arab governments, it served to call the effectiveness of the strategy into question.

Regardless of the actual prospects for success, the political warnings and threats announced by the major Arab oil exporters left little doubt that they wanted the United States and its allies to modify relations with Israel. The implied quid pro quo of continued large increases in the production of crude oil in exchange for pressure on Israel had to be taken on faith, just as the power of the oil weapon to force an alteration of foreign policies remained for the time being conjectural.

Second among the arguments supporting the causal link between Israel and oil is the pattern of events associated with the October 1973 war. OPEC demands had already begun to shatter long-standing price structures in the summer of 1973 as the Teheran pricing agreement, signed in 1971 and supposedly valid for a seven-year period, came up early for revision. The war itself, however, added a dimension that affected profoundly both the timing and the magnitude of the changes in commercial policy.

One must bear in mind that prior to October 1973, no concerted or calculated effort by OPEC to cut back production massively *in order to boost price* had occurred. The information required to coordinate joint commercial policies was thought to be monumental. The level of cooperation and trust among the members necessary to make collusion work and to prevent cheating was uncertain and feared to be unattainable. The possibility of some sort of retaliation by the consumers was sufficient to cause several OPEC members to hold back. Only a cataclysm of some sort could overcome simultaneously all of these obstacles to a vigorous OPEC policy.

What the October war provided was this cataclysm, independent of commercial issues yet impinging upon them in an invaluable way. The principal Arab oil producers, with the notable exception of Iraq and the curious partial exception of Gaddafi's Libya, cut back oil production across the board when the United States airlifted arms to Israel late in the war. Although the purpose of the embargo was to isolate the United States, Saudi Arabia and the other major producers recognized that implementation of their policies was only partially in their hands and that selective embargoes would "leak" badly. Hence it was necessary to reduce total production to affect the United States appreciably. The purpose of this embargo strategy was political—to obtain a reorientation of policy toward Israel. Insofar as Japan and Western Europe also suffered from the production cutbacks, they, too, would be induced to treat Arab interests more evenhandedly. Because of their vulnerability to interruptions of crude supply, the West European governments (with the exception of Holland) and Japan could be counted on to put pressure on the United States to come to more favorable terms regarding Israeli territorial exchanges and, as it turned out later, relations with OPEC. Despite the manifest political character of the production cutbacks, their most important long-term impact was economic and commercial.

In the brief interval from October to December 1973 OPEC discovered with euphoria that there seemed to be virtually no upper limit to the price the exporters could charge for their crude. In the panic that typified the reaction of the consumers, wild bids were submitted by certain consumer governments, bids that soared as high as $20 a barrel for light, low-sulfur Libyan crude. The enabling force behind the incredible fourfold price increase that ultimately prevailed was the existence of broad-scale production cutbacks. It mattered not that the embargo had been instigated for political reasons. The economic impact was just as real and just as supportive of price hikes that months earlier no one inside or outside the cartel had thought possible.

Since the price increases could be sustained only by corresponding production cutbacks, and since the major Arab producers led the way, difficult negotiations within the cartel over who should be responsible for what level of production were avoided. Basking in the financial glow of enormous revenue increases, the OPEC governments devoted all of their quite limited administrative and financial manpower to determining how the new surpluses should be spent rather than on the quarrelsome issue of an efficient and just distribution of market shares. The cataclysm of the October war thus made easier what under other circumstances would have involved extended and difficult intra-OPEC negotiations, that is, a shift in power toward the producers in such a fashion that they could obtain control over price.

The October war did for OPEC what Hiroshima did for Russian scientific efforts on the nuclear bomb. In each case a monumental event proved that a process was technically feasible. Once demonstrated to be workable, the process could be manipulated properly by the administrators of the resource in order to achieve the desired consequence, in the case of OPEC high prices for crude at controlled levels of production.

A third basis for the view that the Israeli question and oil prices are linked is the asserted hope that Israeli territorial concessions perhaps back to the 1967 borders, or acceptance of U.N. Resolution 242 (founded on the same territorial principle), would bring about a price decline. In some cases this view is encouraged by statements of Kuwaiti or Saudi officials. In other cases the view rests on the confidence of some Western diplomats that a bargain could be established with the Arab oil producers along these lines, given the nascent improvement in the relations between Egypt and the United States following the interim peace agreement.

According to some of its proponents, a more balanced U.S. position in the Middle East would strengthen the hand of the moderates in OPEC, thus stemming price increases or possibly even achieving a price reduction. Inasmuch as Saudi Arabia was (1975–1976 period) producing at about only half the rate of its potential output, Saudi Arabia appears to have a degree of control over the export oil market. If the Saudi government chose to double its output, the impact on the price would be appreciable, particularly in the short run.

Each of these three sets of arguments—the warnings of price increases by Arab statesmen in 1973, the scenario of the October war, which triggered the commercial shifts, and the pious hope of future price reductions based upon political criteria—creates the same analytic task. To what degree are they accurate estimates of both the intentions and capabilities of governments to bring about price declines, and to what degree are they mere rationalizations for action or misperceptions of the underlying structure of diplomatic and commercial reality surrounding world oil?

COUNTERARGUMENTS AND CRITIQUE

A number of interconnected aspects of OPEC relations dispute the thesis that Israeli policy stands are a source of much upward pressure on the price of crude oil. Part of the confusion regarding the issue stems from the failure to distinguish the quite separate consumer problems of the continuity of oil supply (absence of embargoes), on the one hand, and price, on the other.

The former problem is directly traceable to the Arab-Israeli conflict, while the latter problem, which tends to prevail in the near term, is not. Economic criteria provide persuasive and sufficient grounds for price escalation. Reinforcing this fact is the behavior of the non-Arab members of OPEC, which despite essentially warm relations with Israel, have gone along with the price increases wholeheartedly. Indeed, at least one of these basically non-Arab countries, Iran, has been described as the true "burr under the saddle" on the rise of prices. Finally, we note the sagacity of the Arab commercial bargaining position and the wisdom of including political as well as economic considerations within it. Let us treat each of these counterarguments in turn.

Price versus the Certainty of Oil Supply

Price hikes and oil embargoes are generally quite dissimilar aspects of OPEC policy despite the concurrence of both phenomena during the October war. The explanation for the concurrence is that oil embargoes, especially if they lead to widespread and rather permanent cutbacks in production, will induce an increase in the price of crude oil in accordance with the laws of economic supply and demand. Indeed, the elasticities of supply and demand (i.e., the percentage of change in output associated with a given change in price) together explain the magnitude of the embargo's effect on price.

What distinguishes price strategies and termination of supply, however, is that the former normally operate in the absence of the latter. In other words, a vigorous embargo, well supported and disciplined, inevitably will yield price increases for crude oil; but the converse, namely, that all price increases involve embargo, is not the case. Price increases for crude oil may and probably will in a period of slack demand require extensive production constraints, but these constraints are not and should not be construed for analytic purposes to be the equivalent of a market embargo or interruption of supply. In most cases a cartel will gradually constrain production in order to drive prices for its product higher or will announce a price increase and then reduce production accordingly, sometimes claiming that shortages or labor difficulties necessitated this move. However, the difference in motivation and implementation should be clear in each case. Embargoes are announced for political reasons. They are abrupt and are defined independently of price. Their purpose is not to increase revenue to the cartel membership but rather to use the cost and hardship induced by the embargo for political ends. When these ends are achieved or when the embargo has outlived its political utility, perhaps because of the resistance and counterembargo activity that it has stimulated or because of defections by cartel members that attempt to cheat, the embargo is lifted and the market returns to normal. When price and revenue are the producers' chief objectives, however, the cartel leadership seeks to sustain production cutbacks over a long time period, thus enabling the proponents of collusion to enjoy the economic benefits of market power.

Sufficiency of Economic Arguments

Once price strategies and supply interruptions have been clarified as to motivations, a further reason for believing that Israel as an issue area has little to do with the prices charged by OPEC is that economic arguments *alone* are sufficient to justify these prices. Regardless of what certain members of the cartel may have asserted as their rationale for raising prices at certain times (or conversely for applying brakes on increases at other times), very little noneconomic market behavior has occurred on the part of any OPEC member since 1973.

The only way OPEC could increase its total revenue was to raise prices and reduce production, a strategy that was markedly effective in a period of runaway demand and with a commodity such as oil, which was essential to all industrial economies and which had few short-term substitutes. Saudi Arabia's complaints in the summer of 1973 that it had to rein in production beneath the projected needs of U.S. consumption for 1980 reflected its basic concern that despite the enormous size of Saudi petroleum reserves, crude oil is an exhaustible resource. The most plausible strategy was to combine the conservation ethic with a plan to increase financial revenues. Production constraints would achieve both economic aims simultaneously. The only reason the strategy had not been implemented earlier was that the proper confluence of market forces, information, and political power to affect the changes had not previously existed.

Arab and Non-Arab Price Behavior

If the motivations regarding an issue like Israeli policy are primarily political, as is certainly the case, then one would think that those OPEC countries for which only economic objectives dictate manipulating the price of crude would dissociate themselves from OPEC policies impelled by political considerations. In other words, if oil is to be used as a political weapon by Arab producers, as it was with varying success in the 1956, 1967, and 1973 crises, then one would expect the non-Arab producers, with basically no grievances against Israel, to refuse to participate or to participate in joint policies only if the economic benefits were sufficiently great. In 1956 and 1967 this very situation occurred. The reason the boycott efforts in each of these crises failed was because the non-Arab oil exporters increased their production by the same margin that certain Arab oil exporters attempted to cut back. By 1973 the difference in technique was that instead of increasing their production to capture a larger share of the market as the Arab producers implemented the embargo, the non-Arab members of OPEC, largely Iran and Venezuela, also cut back production—thus forcing prices upward. Regardless of approach, however, either increasing production to garner a larger share of the market or reducing production to sustain cartel prices, the non-Arab members acted in their own economic self-interest. What is so fascinating analytically is that both Arab and non-Arab producers after 1973 found that a policy of production constraints was in their common economic interest. Far from differentiating their behavior along political lines, the Arab producers did what was economically very rational for them to do. They acted to increase their financial revenue just as non-Arab OPEC and even non-OPEC producers like Canada have done. Thus, in the absence of a clear delineation of behavior between sets of producers over a period of several years, one is led to conclude that common economic logic rather than diverse political orientation is at the heart of contemporary OPEC price policy.

Arab Commercial Bargaining Position

One should not treat the policies of the OPEC countries as naive or impetuous, as was the tendency of the industrialized countries prior to 1973, nor as omniscient and perfectly coordinated, as has been the tendency since that time. Rather, the commercial policies of the cartel have followed closely the lines of the short- and medium-term economic self-interest of the members. They have compromised when they have come to realize that hanging together can be postponed by not hanging separately. In this regard, the policies of Saudi Arabia, the largest producer, warrant a bit more attention.

Aside from the very strong religious feeling that Faisal held with respect to his role as protector of the Holy Places, and from the pan-Arab sentiment that encouraged the Saudi government to oppose Israel, several very solid commercial reasons existed for combining both political and economic arguments in a single rationale for commercial pressure on the West and the United States. For one thing, the combination of political and economic justifications tends to divide the consumer opposition. Governments like Holland and the United States, which have strongly defended pro-

Israeli policies, are separated from France and Japan, which have not. Disagreement of consumer nations over foreign policy tends to spill over into commercial policy, hindering the collective effort to generate a satisfactory response to the OPEC challenge. By touching the right keys, the OPEC leadership can play discordant notes at a time when the United States is attempting to direct the consumer symphony.

Alternatively emphasizing both the economic rationale for price increases, including conservation, and the political rationale based on Israeli pressure, the Arab leadership is able to shift the grounds of the debate over price at crucial times. When the United States asserts that the price increases are not justified by a negative shift in the terms of trade, the Saudis respond that the real issue is Israel and territorial withdrawal, in which area progress has been minimal. When the interim peace agreement was signed between Sadat and Rabin in 1975, however, Yamani remarked in Vienna at the September OPEC price conference that price is an *economic* issue that has to be resolved on that plane. Either way, the consumers are likely to lag behind the rapidly shifting sands of Middle East commercial discourse.

Having divided the consumers on political issues and confused them regarding Arab price motivations, OPEC inherits a further advantage, that of delay and postponement of consumer commercial decisions. The longer the consumers waffle on energy policy, the longer OPEC can garner, unimpeded, revenue from extraordinary price increases. Every year of delay adds uncertainty to the consumer effort to escape the bonds of petroleum dependence. The sagacity of the Arab commercial bargaining position from the OPEC perspective can scarcely be faulted. A better mix of rationales and justifications to keep the consumers off balance could hardly have been devised.

In short, the set of arguments holding that Israel is responsible for the dilemma in which the consumers find themselves is grossly overstated and wrong in major details. Assertions of Arab petroleum ministers and others in the spring and summer of 1973 that price increases would follow lack of a serious attempt to reverse Israeli policy were more a recognition that a embargo was being planned and that production would have to be cut back for reasons of conservation and economic incentive than indication of a decision to employ price for strategic purposes. Price increases were significantly associated with the interplay of political and commercial forces during the October war, but the increases were by no means a calculated product of that war. Some margin may exist in the future for Saudi Arabia either to hold the line on prices or to increase them, depending in part on progress in the peace negotiations, but such a policy must also conform to economic logic and is not likely to lead to actual price reductions.

Indeed, the counterarguments regarding the connection between oil politics and Israel are more compelling: interruptions of oil supply and price strategies have unfortunately been confused; the economic grounds for price escalation are themselves a *sufficient* explanation for the price policies; and the behavior of the non-Arab producers with no Israeli grievances coincides with the behavior of the Arab producers, tending to confirm the essentially commercial character of OPEC price preferences since 1973. Despite the conclusion that there is no causal relationship between the oil price increase and Israeli policy, the myth of this relationship is undeniably useful for strategic purposes and the Arab capacity to exploit this instrument has probably strengthened the short-term OPEC bargaining position. But if we cannot convincingly link Israeli policy stands to oil price behavior, we nonetheless ought to ask the converse question, namely, what has been the significance of the price hikes for Middle East politics?

REAL IMPORTANCE OF OIL FOR ISRAEL

While Israeli policy did not cause the oil price increases, the oil price increases will have an observable impact on the political future of Israel.[4] This thesis is likely to become increasingly arguable over the next decade. The reason is not so much that the perceptions of the mass public and even the governing elite may fail to distinguish correctly aspects of petroleum strategy and Middle East politics. Nor is the reason supply interruptions, which will continue to hold potential for coercion and pressure despite increased oil storage capacity approaching a one-year's supply for some of the consumer nations. Rather, the reason the oil price increases will so affect Israel's future is that they have elicited a shift in the balance of Middle East power.[5]

Increasingly, the moderate position of Saudi Arabia and Egypt during the fall of 1975 will become the norm for the Middle East and the measure for Israeli accommodation. Accommodation will become more essential and perhaps feasible for Israel in the wake of the 1973 price increases for at least three reasons.

First, the increase in the price of oil enabled a number of Arab regimes, including Egypt and Iraq, to become more inward looking and development oriented. In order to do this the governments needed improved relations with the West, which would provide the skilled services and manufactured goods required for industrialization. Concentrating on economic development, less attention has been devoted to Israeli policy, with the result that the apparent level of tensions has somewhat diminished (although guerrilla activity continues). This reduction of hostility at the governmental level has taken some of the immediate political pressure off Israel from the Arab side, allowing the United States to work out terms that would be acceptable to the middle echelons of Israeli opinion.

Second, the interim peace agreement between Sadat and Rabin led to a de facto split in the ranks of Israel's opponents with Saudi Arabia and Kuwait lining up behind Egypt and on the other side Libya and Iraq supporting Syria. A debit was the closer military coordination of Hussein's and Assad's military forces, but Jordan remained sufficiently dependent upon Saudi Arabia not to act without tacit Saudi approval. The temporary split in Arab ranks further reduced short-term political pressure on Israel while the Kissinger effort to get step-by-step diplomacy back on track on the Golan heights issue contributed to further easing of tensions. Israel obtained time to consolidate and respond to initiatives and to reflect on the longer view of changes in Middle East relations.

Third, and most important however, the price increases have spawned a fundamental shift of military power.[6] In four years (1970 to 1974) the military budgets of Saudi Arabia increased seven times; Kuwait, four times; and Iraq, more than twice. Together these three Arab countries spent almost $3 billion on arms for themselves in 1974, while providing billions of dollars of economic and military aid to Syria, Egypt, and Jordan. Despite the more than $2.5 billion of American military aid to Israel accompanying the interim peace agreement, the *rate of increase* did not match that of Arab military spending.

But increases in the size and quality of Arab military forces is only part of the overall shift of power in the Middle East. The OPEC producers have gained in importance as trading partners both in Europe and Japan. Leverage is obtained not only on the oil export side, where consumer dependence has increased since 1973, but also on the import side as industrial countries jockey for a larger share of the Arab import market. Alterations in policies of diplomatic recognition and exchange regarding Israel in the aftermath of the October war reveal only partially the new attention given Arab interests. U.N. resolutions censoring Israel reflect not so much an alteration in the structural pattern of U.N. voting as a new climate of world opinion under the weight of Arab oil money. While not entirely effective, the Arab boycott of corporations doing business in Israel is symptomatic of the problems Israel faces on the economic front. Whether or not the flag does indeed *follow* trade, as the adage suggests, both the flag and trade do seem to move in the same direction, in this case against Israel's long-term advantage.

Assessing the Arab Trade Boycott

A twofold objective underlies the Arab trade boycott of Israel from the perspective of OAPEC (Organization of Arab Petroleum Exporting Countries). First, by interdicting a portion of the foreign trade and investment that would otherwise go to Israel, the Arab governments seek to reduce the growth rate of the Israeli economy and thereby to erode Israel's political power base. An associated aim is to create discomfort and frustration for the average Israeli citizen, which in turn might be translated into dissatisfaction with the government; in other words, the immediate hardships caused by the boycott may provoke loss of confidence in government policies that fail to alter the boycott situation. Hence, an initial boycott aim is to impact Israel directly.

A second objective of the boycott—and by no means a subordinate one —is to try to force the American electorate into making a deliberate choice. The choice is between strong emotional and sentimental ties to Israel, on the one hand, and issues of national interest and economic benefit, on the other. By polarizing the nature of this choice, OAPEC hopes to lay bare the trade-off facing U.S. foreign policy in terms of emotion versus self-interest, moral commitment versus brutal power politics. Most Arab governments assume that when the nature of this trade-off is clarified for the American electorate through boycott pressures, a number of Americans will opt for economic self-interest, especially if antiboycott policies increase the danger of war involving the United States.

Even if the first objective of the boycott fails, its proponents count on this second objective regarding American public opinion to justify use of the boycott. Although the impact of the boycott upon the United States may be more indirect, the impact is considered to be just as vital to an overall shift in the Middle East power balance since the United States has been Israel's one staunch and overwhelmingly important ally.

But the Arab blacklist of companies doing business with Israel has been in existence for many years. Why has the question of the boycott suddenly become so critical? One answer is that in the past the size of the Israeli market compared somewhat favorably to that of the Arab market for many consumer goods as well as for heavier industrial production. But with the influx of petro-dollars, the relative importance of the two markets changed abruptly. Suddenly, American companies recognized that if they were forced into choosing one or the other, the Arab market carried with it much greater opportunity for profit and expansion. Israel thus increasingly became of marginal commercial interest mainly because of its small size and trade potential.

Antiboycott efforts in the United States have a latent capacity for sharp influence on corporate trading patterns. If the punitive tax legislation against companies complying with the Arab boycott were fully implemented, American oil companies doing business predominately with Arab countries, for example, would find themselves at a strong competitive disadvantage. Without U.S. tax credits, American oil companies reportedly would lose about one-half their normal per barrel profit on Middle East crude oil, thus undermining their competitive position and strengthening that of the large foreign multinationals. But while the tax legislation if vigorously enforced might prevent the companies from doing business with the Arab countries, it could not force them to do business with Israel in the absence of adequate commercial incentives. Moreover, the boycott-sponsoring governments might respond by enforcing more strictly their own boycott provisions and by shifting the import of goods and services (a trade bill that may reach $10 billion by the end of the decade) away from the United States toward Japan and Western Europe.

While the Arab governments argue that in form the boycott parallels governmental boycotts of various countries including Cuba and Rhodesia, this assertion is not strictly correct. In the case of the Arab boycott, pressure is being placed on American companies, not on indigenous Arab companies, to curtail trade with Israel. For many Americans otherwise uninformed about the substantive aspect of the boycott, this effort to dictate to American companies is intervention in U.S. domestic affairs, which creates an immediate negative response. Thus, insofar as the boycott debate is carried on in terms of the *autonomy of U.S. commercial policy* rather than strictly in terms of U.S.-Israeli relations, the antiboycott effort may attract additional domestic political support.

On the other hand, it is also necessary to acknowledge that the boycott never has been very complete or free of leaks or uniformly administrated. While the Arab League has maintained one list of companies, individual governments have kept other, sometimes incompatible lists. Enforcement usually has been voluntary.The lists purposely have received little publicity so that they could be interpreted flexibly. Finally, dummy companies and other subterfuges have been used to get around official government policies.

What must be recognized is that regardless of outcome the boycott issue should not mask a much more fundamental economic issue facing Israel. That issue is whether Israel will be able to compete effectively over the long run with other Middle East governments as an attractive target for foreign investment and trade. Insofar as sufficient economic incentives exist, growth and commercial expansion will continue unimpeded by arbitrary international restrictions. If a sufficient profit potential exists, businessmen will tend to find it. But the larger problem for Israel is that, apart from boycotts and embargoes, the vigor of the Israeli economy may somehow fail to match the development and growth witnessed in other sectors of the Middle East. Ironically, the only way the antiboycott legislation can be effective is if it is totally inclusive, forcing other governments to accept all or nothing; yet the only way the legislation can get through Congress is by containing "loopholes" for the most important sectors. Thus the legislation will have symbolic impact but will scarcely affect trade patterns, which will continue to be determined largely on their commercial merits.

Assessing Israeli Leverage

In purely military terms Israel possesses two sources of leverage, one technological, the other political. On the technological side both the June war and the October war revealed a truism concerning military outcomes in the Middle East. The government with the technological edge in terms of air power, armor, or defensive capability has a decided advantage not-withstanding numerical superiority on the side of the opponent. In the June war Israeli armor was better attuned to desert fighting conditions than either the Egyptian or the Syrian. In the October war the advent of the Sagger antitank missile and the combination of conventional antiair-craft and modern ground-to-air missile emplacements took a tremendous toll on Israeli armor and aircraft, respectively, early in the war. Only the subsequent input of sophisticated electronic gear to enable Israeli aircraft to evade heat-seeking missiles and radar-directed equipment turned the air war in Israeli's favor. Seemingly small technological advances can tip the military scales. Hence Israel, with an increasing inferiority of numbers, must balance its fate precariously on the narrow ledge of such technologi-cal advances.[7]

A recent source of leverage for Israel is political. It exists outside the frame of obvious dependence upon the United States. While the Arabs have amassed $3 billion or so of arms in a single year, the Persian state of Iran has purchased over $5 billion of weapons, supplies, and services. Iran is, on paper at least, far more than a military equal of several of the sparsely populated oil-rich Arab kingdoms considered together.

The effect of Persian armament efforts on Israel is to divert pressure away from the Sinai, West Bank, and Golan heights areas. Following the diplomatic proverb that "the enemy of my neighbor is my friend," Israel can profit from Iranian ambitions for hegemony in the Gulf even though the Persians have nothing directly to do with Israeli security. Much of the Arab military buildup must be retained as a territorial safeguard against possible Iranian expansionist plans. Israel, of course, performs the same function for Iran, dividing and neutralizing much of the Arab military strength.

On the other hand, there exists some probability, however small, that Iran might join the Arabs in a Moslem onslaught against the infidel, as the Iraqi-Iranian bargain over the fate of the Kurds seemed to indicate might be possible. This union could occur for any of several reasons. Domestic political pressures for autonomy by the Arab population along the Gulf provinces of Iran could force the government's hand in foreign policy. Or the desire to hold OPEC together on political grounds in the face of in-creasing commercial pressures from the consumers could encourage Teheran to support the Arab cause. Finally, a coup d'etat against the shah could in-stall a radical government more willing to support Iraq and Syria than the current regime.

Notwithstanding these two forms of leverage, Israel is likely to find essential some sort of accommodation with Syria, Jordan, and the Pales-tinians as the capacity of the Arab world to exert direct military pressure and indirect economic pressure matures.[8] In the absence of the price in-creases, this trend could not so confidently have been predicted since the

Israeli GNP has been growing rapidly, large inflows of capital have regularly been received, and U.S. military aid has bolstered the Israeli military position. The price increases for crude oil have created a step-level function in the shift of power that was already slowly evolving. Another abrupt transition is likely to take place as well in the nature of warfare within the region.

Pressed very hard by Arab economic and military advances, Israel is likely for purposes of reinforcement to resort to nuclear weapons that can be produced locally and missile transport capacity that can be obtained from the United States. A missile like the Pershing carrying a nuclear warhead and possessing a 650-mile strike radius could transform the nature of Middle East war. It would mean that the relatively small, highly concentrated populations of Israel, Egypt, Syria, and Jordan all would become vulnerable to momentary annihilation. As the history of the last two Sinai wars teaches, the state with the advantage of surprise attack is the state with a large, possibly decisive, tactical advantage. In the absence of second-strike nuclear forces that could absorb a surprise attack and still deal an overwhelming blow to the aggressor (a force none of the Middle East states is likely to achieve), the deployment of nuclear weapons adds even further instability to unsettled political conditions. Deployment of a small number of highly vulnerable nuclear weapons puts a premium on striking first.

In addition, if and when Israel publicly reveals possession of nuclear weapons, immediate pressure will be placed upon the backers of the Arab states to supply nuclear weapons to them as well. While unilateral possession of nuclear weapons could be considered a comparatively stable situation for either party, assuming the weapons were used only for defensive purposes and then only if the governments were pushed into a situation involving major territorial losses, the existence of nuclear weapons in two or more countries on both sides of the dispute would likely aggravate fears associated with nuclear weapons spread.

Oil price increases have not created the threat of nuclear war in the Middle East. They have only accelerated the timetable for such war. Oil price increases have also directly contributed to shifts of power in the Middle East and indirectly fueled reorientations of policy by a number of important governments external to the region in Africa, Europe, and Asia. Even U.S. policy is no longer as autonomous as it was prior to 1973. Imported oil is at present critical to the U.S. economy, and the Middle East now supplies more than 60 percent of those imports. Until the trend of dependence is significantly reversed, foreign oil will count heavily in U.S. policy decisions.

By no means is the United States about to abandon its Israeli ally. But the terms of the special political relationship are likely to be drawn more tightly and accommodation with the Arab countries on territorial issues, political recognition, and rights of refugee populations, insofar as accommodation is mutually feasible, will obtain a higher priority.

While Israel, or U.S. foreign policy toward Israel, can in no way be held responsible for the major price increases beginning in 1973, the import of the price increases for Middle East politics is nonetheless profound. A short-term effect is that hostilities between Israel and her neighbors are eased because of Egypt's decision to accept the results of bilateral diplomacy and because all the Arab states are more or less deeply involved with the investment of petro-dollars. Whether this is a lasting condition or only a temporary adjustment cannot now be predicted. But regardless of whether or how soon the traditional quarrel again heats up, the political environment of the pre– and post–October war intervals is entirely different. While the actual course of the October war may have had something to do with the increased status of Sadat and his enlarged room for maneuver, the new Arab self-confidence, and the turmoil within the Israeli Knesset and the larger society regarding defense policy, none of these factors holds as much long-term significance as the upward tilt in oil prices. The oil price increases provide the revenue that is the lifeblood of Arab modernization. Regardless of how far industrialization actually proceeds in the Arab world, better trained and equipped militaries and large financial balances are shifting the regional balance of power.

Small states historically have played off major powers against one another and have eluded challenges by hostile neighbors. Eighteenth-century Prussia and Cavour's Piedmont come to mind as extraordinary examples of deft, high-risk diplomacy. Although neither Prussia nor, to a lesser extent, Piedmont could count on a powerful ally and patron such as the United States, neither government had to contend with the sea of religious and ethnic differences that surrounds Israel, an island in Middle East politics. But the danger in analyzing small-state diplomacy and Israel's prospects is to place excessive emphasis on the impact of war and too little emphasis on the changing dynamics of state relations, in particular, a theme as fundamental as the crescendo of oil prices.

From a purely military perspective Israel is likely to be able to continue to defend its borders against major foreign attack. Barring a mutually suicidal (and hence purposeless) nuclear war, Israel and its neighbors will continue to coexist. Israel will not be dismantled or "pushed into the sea." But at the same time Israel is likely to face grave pressure concerning such issues as the political status of Jerusalem and the fate of the Palestinian refugees. In part because of the oil weapon, the Arab countries have obtained more leverage over their own affairs and over aspects of policy external to Israel that nonetheless affect Israeli interests. Denial that the West Bank and the Gaza joined in a new mini-state are plausible alterna-

tive solutions to the Palestinian problem is becoming more and more difficult in the face of mounting criticism in the United Nations and foreign
attempts at ostracism and commercial strangulation.

It shocked some Israeli supporters to discover that the nobility of the
Zionist ideal, a homeland for Jews worldwide, a place of freedom, security,
and union, is not shared by critics who instead emphasize expansionism,
exclusivity, and dominance as themes to be associated with the Zionist
cause.[9] Just as the critics fail to understand the positive aspects of Zionism
and the historic needs of many in the Jewish community for identity so the
Israelis themselves fail to perceive how the image of Zionism is actually being interpreted by many concerned observers abroad.

Emergence of the oil weapon has shifted the axis of debate and transformed the diplomatic atmosphere that prevailed in the post–June war in-
terlude. But for the Arabs to benefit fully from this new atmosphere, a
willingness to moderate claims, to bargain, and ultimately to recognize the
permanence and sovereignty of Israel in exchange for fundamental concessions is paramount.

Honor, respect, reparation, and a homeland for Palestinians, satisfactory
administration of Jerusalem, recovery of occupied territories—all of these
objectives are real and feasible for Arab states. But despite the weight of
oil, none of these objectives is practical without endless, violent, and probably futile confrontation unless the institutional and territorial security of
Israel is also respected. Israel in no way has been responsible for the oil
price increases, but should the moderate Arab leadership employ the oil
instrument judiciously, oil will have in contrast a long-standing impact on
Middle East politics.

III

Obscene Corporate Profits:
The Myth of Exploitation

AT THE HEIGHT of the oil crisis during the winter of 1974 an outcry arose against the oil companies concerning profits, with echoes heard today. The oil companies seemed to be flourishing at a time when the government was urging cutbacks in such activities as car travel and neon lighting, when the cost of gasoline and heating oil was climbing, and when long lines of frustrated motorists were waiting for service at retail gas pumps. Anti–oil industry sentiment ran deep in the United States. In the following pages we analyze the origins of the "obscene" argument and its socioeconomic appeal, as well as the significance of the larger issue of viability of the industry in the overall context of consumer-producer country relations.[1]

UNDERSTANDING THE CASE FOR THE OBSCENE PROFITS ARGUMENT

Part of the criticism of the oil companies stems directly from their size. Of the ten largest corporations in the world, five are multinational oil companies. Exxon, the largest of the oil firms, has displaced General Motors as the world's biggest single corporate entity. But oil companies pervade the list of top companies at all echelons. Indeed, an oil company based in the Third World, the National Iranian Oil Company (NIOC), ranks forty-third among the world's corporate elite, and other Third World energy companies are rapidly growing.

Naturally, the size of the oil companies makes them highly visible despite conscious low-profile strategies. Incomes of the largest companies dwarf the national incomes of many of the countries in which they operate.

47

The average incomes of oil company employees exceed by a large margin the average incomes of citizens in the host countries. Ineluctably the image of the oil company becomes that of wealth, exclusiveness, secrecy, and dominance.[2]

Because of the scope and importance of energy, some aspect of an oil company's operations impinges upon the livelihood and life-style of each individual. Of late, contact with the energy sector has grown increasingly unpleasant for the average citizen, regardless of who is responsible for this condition. Not only does he breathe air and drink water polluted by refineries and petrochemical plants but also he drives to work everyday along freeways choked with car exhaust fumes. Combined with the environmental problems he has only recently begun to fear (and face), he is now forced to acknowledge a rise in the price of gasoline and the cost of home heating and cooling. Against this background of energy-related anxieties, any increase in profits received by an energy company is likely to be perceived by the average citizen as outrageous and unacceptable, an inequity compounding his plight.[3]

But in the United States the skepticism with which the energy corporation is regarded is seated in a deeper sociocultural tradition. Populism and the attack on bigness is a recurring theme in American social history. Opposed to the Hamiltonian bias favoring federal solutions and mercantile (corporate) participation is the Jeffersonian view of decentralization, noncommercialism, and rural virtue. Underlying the great agricultural reform movement of the late nineteenth century was a resurgence of faith in rural virtue and belief in the moral depravity of the commercial sector. Spilling over into the Progressive movement and the era of trustbusting under Teddy Roosevelt, populism continued to hold attraction for many American politicians, with its mixture of emotion and concrete purpose, fantasy and hard action. Throughout most of this period big oil was an inviting target of the reform spirit.

During the freewheeling days of early industrial growth in America, the image of the oil magnate as the robber barron left an imprint that the anonymous leadership of the industry today has yet to erase. Cosmetic changes of corporate nomenclature have had no more positive impact on the public consciousness than the far more significant revolution of multinational expansion and purpose. John D. Rockefeller's name is as closely associated with the image of big oil today as were his methods for conglomeration and sales in 1900. Combined with the Rockefeller–Standard Oil reputation for growth and uninhibited expansion was the image of massive political power harnessed by lobbyists through congressional patronage. Bigness in the oil industry came to be thought of synonymously with political leverage in government. Recent revelations of large-scale illegal campaign contributions to the leadership in both parties by oil companies as well as other large firms has done little to change attitudes of public distrust.

However, neither the absolute size of the oil firms nor the tradition of populist reform in America is sufficient to explain the appeal of the obscene profit argument in the absence of a third factor—the fear of business collusion. Beginning with the Sherman Antitrust Act (1890), which attempted to prohibit all monopolies and all combinations or conspiracies in restraint of trade, and the Clayton Act (1914), which prohibited price discrimination, certain kinds of horizontal integration, and interlocking directorates among competitors, the U.S. government has attempted to promote free industrial competition through legislation and judicial review. Perhaps as a result, industrial concentration in the United States has traditionally been much less pronounced than that, for example, in Germany or Japan. While the government can point to success in the prevention of overt industrial cartel formation, in actuality very little has been done through legal enforcement to reduce the effective power of trusts in most industries.

Moreover, the history of government intervention into markets is by no means of one-sided impact. The impact has often been to *negate* competition rather than to support it. Erosion of competition via government intervention often stems from attempts to achieve other desired objectives. Created to halt the wasteful overproduction of oil and gas and to encourage a degree of conservation through prorationing, the Texas Railroad Commission implicitly promoted price maintenance through production restrictions, a form of noncompetition. By defending the exclusive rights of holders of technical patents, the government discourages competition among the corporations applying the technology. By protecting the consumer against safety hazards and fraud, the government often prevents certain companies from entering the market, thus reserving it for a few. By allowing labor special privileges, agriculture price supports and subsidies, and academia the tenure system, government creates a series of legal barriers to entry that in effect limit the freedom of the marketplace by denying access to smaller or younger members.

Yet despite the relative impotence of past antitrust procedures, the trend in most capitalist democracies for a variety of interventionist reasons is to dictate increased governmental control. The overall result is by no means certain. But the trend is perhaps as likely to lead to a decline in efficiency as to an increase in competition and productivity. Since most competition at the level of the large corporation historically has come from pressures outside the borders of the country, governmental intervention in the domestic marketplace can as easily upset the national welfare as uphold it.

Curiously, the 1975–1976 upsurge of enthusiasm for divestiture in the

oil industry was catalyzed by Senate hearings that produced no evidence
of wrongdoing by the oil companies during the 1973 oil crisis (indeed,
additional examination suggests that they performed the buffer role between producers and consumers rather well). Neither the Subcommitee
on Multinational Corporations of the Committee on Foreign Relations
chaired by Senator Church nor Senator Henry Jackson's investigation of
the oil embargo turned up any evidence that the oil companies had created
the crisis or the subsequent oil shortage. Both Church and Jackson enhanced their positions as presidential aspirants in the battle with the
corporations, and the public impression of major corporate guilt was con-
firmed. Opinion data reveal the depth of public faith in oil industry culpa-
bility.

In two separate surveys nearly 30 percent of the respondents, the largest
single category, pointed to the oil companies as most responsible for the
energy shortage.[4] Only half as many people believed the federal government was to blame. Of the remaining targets for criticism, Congress, "the
Arabs," and "environmental groups" each polled less than 6 percent. Although the studies were conceived separately and covered different samples
of respondents, the results were strikingly similar. Hence the reliability of
the findings is not likely to be challenged.

Perhaps more disturbing for the oil industry and the government, some
68 percent of the Opinion Research Corporation sample was not satisfied
with the industry's efforts to relieve the crisis. Yet 55 percent of the respondents in the same sample doubted that the energy crisis was really a
"long-run problem." On the one hand, the public was dissatisfied with the
performance of the industry in rescuing the nation from the energy shortage, but on the other hand the seriousness of the nation's energy problems
was questioned in a way that suggests little willingness to support a costly,
long-range energy program. In this opinion climate, credibility of the principal actors in the energy arena is so poor that any energy program is likely
to fail.

A further interesting finding of these studies was that the allegedly
more educated and knowledgeable segments of the sample tended to blame
the oil companies most vigorously. While respondents in the lower income
households held the federal government responsible for the nation's energy
problems, the higher income brackets blamed the oil companies. Men
were more likely to blame the oil companies, too, than were women. If
these results indicate a permanent shift of attitudes, a possible interpretation is that the oil industry has lost favor with important leading sectors of
American opinion, creating a potential future loss of mass and elite support for the traditional role of the industry.

Hostility of large segments of American society to the oil industry and
to its role in the energy crisis was borne out by these data. But in considering the origins of this hostility, we must make a comparison with the

perspectives of other cultures. Although most other countries have antimonopoly laws with provision for heavy fines and other penalties, the purpose of this legislation seems to be to regulate foreign corporations with home offices in the host state more than to regulate oil companies that are locally based. If constraints on trade are perpetrated by multinational corporations located abroad having branches in the host country, these corporations are likely to be subject to regulation. In contrast, national oil companies are likely to meet with indirect governmental financial support and other political favors rather than legal prohibitions on expansion. British Petroleum (Britain), Petrobras (Brazil), CFP (France), and ENI (Italy) all, for example, have benefited from preferential treatment within the territory of the home state. Thus other societies appear to view the issue of regulation with far more ambivalence than do Americans.

One could argue that antitrust regulation broadly implemented is the luxury of a nation fortunate enough to have a huge domestic market and a number of major oil companies with home offices on its territory. Restrictions on the market behavior of these companies and upon their expansion could perhaps thus be construed as beneficial to the competitiveness of the industry and to its productivity both at home and abroad and thus in the national interest. But one does not find the Japanese government, for example, discriminating except in favor of its indigenous energy companies. Quite in contrast to the United States, other societies seem to perceive the oil industry in global terms, not expecting much competition among the price leaders but attempting to foster a competitive edge for their own national oil corporations.

As the world oil industry becomes more competitive, the dominance of American oil companies in the industry is likely to continue to decline giving foreign companies room to expand and integrate their operations where political conditions favoring concentration are more propitious than those in the United States. Economies of scale exist in many areas of the petroleum industry not just in marketing. If temporarily hindered, concentration will recur but perhaps in another, entirely different, national setting. Likewise, the benefits of large-scale enterprise under these circumstances may well pass to others. Americans—because of the unique dominance of their own corporations in the world energy field, because of their sociocultural interpretations of the proper role for the private sector, because of their historic fear of collusion—have not been able to see this perspective.

ACTUAL PROFITS IN RETROSPECT

Having discussed the attitude of the American public toward oil industry profits, we now turn to examination of these profits. To what extent was there a change in profits in the recent period that could have elicited unfavorable opinion? How justified were Americans in their criticism of oil company revenue and profit? In order to answer these questions we must consider the profit picture for the industry over the past two decades. We must for the same period also compare these profits (relative to equity investment) with those earned in other industries. Through our analysis of profit and investment data, a number of points become rather clear.[5]

First, the data in Figure III–1 reveal that the ratio of aftertax profit to stockholders' equity in the petroleum refining industry has vacillated in the post–World War II interval from a high of over 15 percent to a low of 8.7 percent. Profits were higher in general in the 1950s than in the 1960s. Profits moreover were at a *historic low* in 1972, one year prior to the OPEC takeover of market control. Any movement of profits upward from the

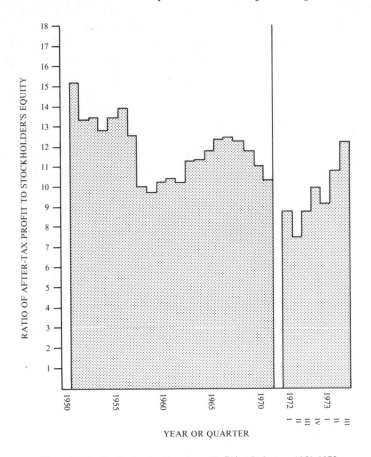

Figure III-1. Profits in the Petroleum Refining Industry, 1951-1973

Source: Federal Trade Commission and Securities and Exchange Commission, "Quarterly Financial Report for Manufacturing Corporations."

1972 low to the normal levels of prior years could thus have been regarded by the less than broadly informed observer as an unprecedented increase; indeed, if one focuses upon change rather than absolute levels of profit (as the stock market, for example, tends to do), the improvement in the oil industry's profit position in 1973 and 1974 was unmatched in any prior postwar year. The catch of course is that in terms of absolute levels the 1975 and 1976 profit figures were very near the historical average of just a little over 11.7 percent.

Beginning in the third quarter of 1972, oil company profits began to recover from the recession, buoyed no doubt by the general increase in petroleum prices worldwide. Thus, oil company profits were improving (although still below the postwar average) well in advance of the 1973 crisis of October and November. Indeed, profits reached a peak in the midst of the Arab oil boycott—at about the time that rationing of gasoline began. By 1975, partly because of loss of the depletion allowance, nationalization of petroleum interests abroad, increased taxes at the wellhead, and lagging demand, profits had returned to subnormal levels. But as far as the American consumer was concerned, the profit upsurge of the oil companies had coincided with the fear and hardships associated with the oil boycott. New higher gasoline prices reinforced the consumer's belief that the oil companies continue to be the beneficiaries of the increases. Had they been calculated, these circumstances could not have been better timed to induce consumer misinterpretation.

When we compare the profit levels of the petroleum refining industry to those of other industries in the nondurable category (Figure III–2) we reach similar conclusions regarding the normality of profit behavior. For the postwar period as a whole, oil company profits were not spectacular. They were somewhat higher than the average for the category as a whole (11.7 percent as opposed to 10.7 percent for total nondurable goods) and considerably higher than for a group such as food products, with a 9.5 percent profit rate. But other groups such as chemicals and allied products did substantially better than the oil industry with an aftertax profit rate of 12.8 percent. Moreover, profits tended upward for food in this twenty-year period, while exactly the opposite was the case for the profits of the refining industry. Thus, this index of oil company profits reveals important short-term profit movements but no spectacular ripoff of the American consumer that might justify the obscene profit label.

Second, turning to profits of the foreign oil industry in comparison to other foreign industrial groupings, we observe a similar pattern. Before 1957 the foreign oil industry enjoyed unparalleled returns to direct investment as large as 30 percent. But profits plummeted in the 1960s, and by 1964 mining and smelting was a much more lucrative area for investment. By 1969 the rate of profit in the foreign oil industry dipped beneath that of the manufacturing industries to the 11 percent level. Given this level of

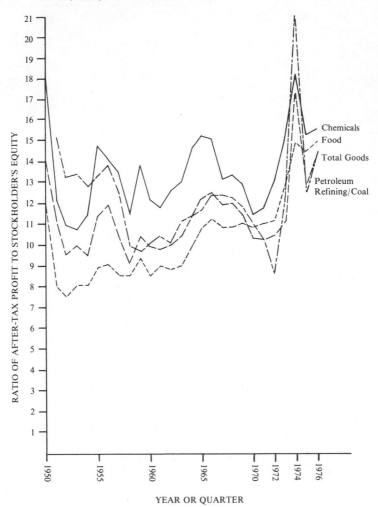

Figure III-2. Profits in Petroleum Refining and Other Non-Durable Goods Industries

Source: Federal Trade Commission and Securities and Exchange Commission, "Quarterly Financial
Report for Manufacturing Corporations."

return, foreign oil investments were less attractive than many areas of domestic investment within the consumer countries. What may have been
characteristic of oil profits at the beginning of the post–World War II era
was by no means valid twenty years later. The foreign oil boom had clearly
turned sour, at least for multinational corporations and the consumer
countries.

One further set of data supports a third conclusion regarding the oil
company profit situation: significant structural changes within the industry
accompanied the two-decade profit decline. Figure III–3 compares the
foreign capital expenditures of the majors, that is, the seven largest oil

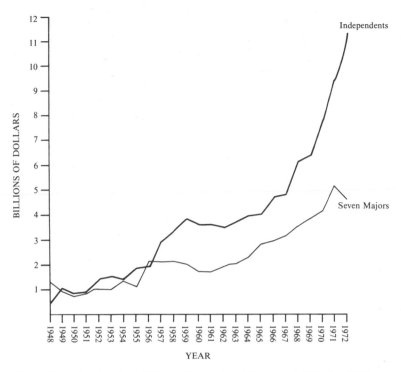

Figure III-3. Foreign Capital Expenditures of the Majors and All Other Oil Companies, 1948-1972

Source: Neil H. Jacoby, *Multinational Oil* (New York: Macmillan, 1974), pp. 249-250.

companies, and the so-called independents. A striking trend began after 1956, the year of the Suez Canal closure—the independents began spending far more and growing far faster than the majors. Indeed, in the period 1948–1972 the majors increased their total foreign capital expenditures only by about a factor of four. In the same period the other oil companies increased their expenditures more than twenty fold. While in 1948 the seven largest companies were spending three times as much as all other oil companies combined, by 1972 the situation had so reversed itself that the majors were spending only half as much abroad as were the independents.

The upshot is what economic theory predicts. Initial high profits attracted vigorous competition from the independents, some of whom themselves became sizable and highly integrated. Increased competition helped drive profits down until 1972, with the activity of the independents at an all-time peak, profits for the industry as a whole reached a nadir. Weakened in market terms, the majors were in a poor position to confront the producer countries politically. In a period of rapidly growing petroleum demand, control over prices in the short run passed from the majors and the consumer nations to Riyadh and Teheran.

A principal casualty of the profit debacle was the level of oil exploration. Discoveries of new oil and incentives are roughly correlated. Despite lumpiness in the rate and magnitude of new discoveries, oil drilling activity is a function of market conditions and profit levels suitably corrected for substantial time lags in the investment process. With the average of oil industry profits down below that of many other industries experiencing smaller risks, the rate of drilling activity outside OPEC during the late 1960s and early 1970s was not as high as it would otherwise have been had more normal profits prevailed. Lower profits also meant less capital availability at a time when offshore drilling and deep drilling were requiring larger and larger investment outlays. Low profits (combined with political and commercial uncertainty and societal hostility toward industry investment) acted as a drag on new non-OPEC discoveries, which, in an era of declining U.S. oil production after 1970, further contributed to the shift of market power from the Texas Gulf to the Persian-Arab Gulf.

Against this background, the profit bubble of 1974 becomes more transparent. Like the football player who is small but slow, the 1974 increase in oil profits was ill-timed but brief. Occurring in the midst of the temporary oil shortage, the brief profit surge caused indignation among American consumers but did little to restore genuine market power to the industry or to the consumer governments. In terms of public relations, the oil industry suffered another blow largely not of its own making, this time from an overdue improvement in profits (poorly distributed across time), which nonetheless would be widely misinterpreted as to cause and significance.

Let us now turn to a fuller examination of the structure of the oil industry and the pattern of market behavior as it has emerged in the post–World War II period, concluding with an assessment of how these changes in industry relationships affected the nation's welfare and, conversely, of how Americans have perceived these changes.

THE OIL INDUSTRY AND THE PRODUCER-CONSUMER BALANCE

Analysis of the international political role of the oil industry is clothed in paradox. On the one hand, the petroleum consumers, largely the advanced industrial states, accuse the industry of profiteering at their own expense and of collusion with the governments of the oil producing nations. The petroleum producing countries on the other hand advance exactly the opposite thesis. They accuse the companies of profiteering at the expense of OPEC interests and of bias in favor of the consumer orientation, particularly that of the United States.

Faced with these opposing theses, the analyst must get beneath the rhetoric of bargaining and diplomatic maneuver. A number of positions are theoretically feasible. Perhaps the consumers are correct that the multinationals have exploited them. Or perhaps OPEC is justified in its view that the industry has ignored producer demands. Or perhaps the oil industry has adopted an intermediate posture that is a compromise pleasing to neither governmental coalition. Or, finally, in dynamic terms, combinations of these positions may more accurately depict industry-government relations depending upon the market, political factors, industry conditions, and the historical interval in which these forces operated.

Historical Balance in Favor of Consumers

Without much difficulty one can build a case for the view that in the early post–World War II interval the oil industry tilted in favor of the advanced industrial countries.[6] The industry held this orientation for a number of reasons.

First, the home offices of the multinationals were located in the consumer countries, either the United States, Britain, Holland, or France (depending upon whether the French national companies are included in the same category with the private multinational companies). Proximity facilitates communication and mutual reinforcement of attitudes. Residence in a country alone does not guarantee socialization of corporate attitudes in support of that society, but other things being equal residence creates such a predilection.

Second, the multinationals are staffed by the nationals of the consumer countries. The higher the office, the more likely that the officeholder is a citizen of an advanced industrial country, probably the country in which the home office is located. An executive of a company is naturally prone to place interests of the company ahead of other interests, but he also is likely to perceive events through a lens colored by his education, citizenship, military experience, and family ties—all of which are normally associated with one or more advanced industrial countries.

Third, stockholders, insofar as they exert an influence on corporate leadership, are almost exclusively drawn from the ranks of the consumer countries. Profits made on oil produced in the Middle East or South America thus are transferred to stockholders living in Europe and the United States. In this sense the oil corporations represent a particular class of shareholders in an advanced industrial country who themselves are often members of the dominant decision elite of the country.

Fourth, and here we turn to much more dynamic factors, the large profits on foreign oil investments for much of the early postwar period coincided with relatively low per barrel prices for crude oil. Insofar as these profits were due to artificially low sale prices for crude, the transfer of these profits to the advanced industrial countries amounted to a subsidy paid by the producer nations. As demonstrated by the discussion in Chapter I, it is however probably impossible to determine a fair price for crude oil. But if the substitution price of alternative energy forms is conceived as an upper bound, then surely the posted price of crude was pegged substantially beneath this limit. Just as clearly, the producer countries were attempting to push the price of oil upward while the corporations opted for price stability and moderation. Consumer countries were the net beneficiaries of these multinational policies.

Fifth, a buyer's market for oil over much of the period strengthened the hand of the multinationals in their attempt to keep prices down. An apparent glut of oil in 1960, for example, brought about an actual dip in prices. It was possible for the multinational to argue that supply was outpacing demand and that to raise prices under these circumstances would be to invite loss of sales. Whether such arguments remained convincing to the oil producing countries or not, they were unable to challenge the pricing arrangements until the middle 1970s, a circumstance that of course meanwhile benefited the consumer nations markedly.

Sixth, the multinationals implicitly assisted the consumer nations by maintaining control of prices at the wellhead. By ownership of concession rights and by keeping producer taxes on crude at a minimum, the multinationals were able to transfer large profits directly to shareholders. But the real impact of this whole set of multinational policies was to keep the producer nations divided so that they could not themselves control decisions. Lacking sufficient information concerning even the extensiveness of their own petroleum reserves, the producer countries were hardly in a position to unseat the multinational corporations, upon which they depended for virtually their entire revenue. Since isolation meant the impossibility of governmental collusion and since isolation was in good part a function of the secrecy of corporate policy, it follows that the multinationals had an important hand in maintaining the political and commercial status quo. So also the consumer nations (often unknowingly) were enjoying precarious advantages provided by the multinationals.

In sum, for two decades after World War II the multinational oil corporations pursued their own profit interests, interests that to a remarkable degree coincided with the interests of the consumer countries. Both for the fairly static reasons of location, personnel, and administration and for the more dynamic reasons of market, political control, and profit optimization, the multinationals seemed to be acting as an instrument of the advanced industrial world. Meanwhile, however, the pillars on which such policies rested were already beginning to crumble.

Industry in Crisis, 1969–1973

Perhaps more than any others, two forces explain the crisis facing the oil industry after 1969. These two forces converged upon the multinationals with an intensity and a suddenness that the theorists of transnational relations had not anticipated. The two forces were the transformation of commercial conditions from that of a buyer's to that of a seller's market and the erosion of the political and market power of the major oil companies. Neither trend in itself is sufficient to explain the fourfold price increase achieved by OPEC in 1973, but together the two trends precipitated a revolution in oil politics.[7]

With occasional reversals the demand for oil outpaced supply in the late 1960s, leading to warnings of actual shortages during the extremely cold winter of 1972. Rapid economic expansion at the close of the Vietnam war also contributed to above normal consumption of petroleum products. Environmental protection measures encouraged many electric utilities to convert from high-pollution fuels such as coal to low-sulfur petroleum such as that found in Libya. In general, demand for petroleum worldwide was growing at a rate better than 4 percent per year, while in a number of industrial countries demand was growing at twice this rate.

Oil production was also expanding rapidly worldwide but could not keep up with the surge of consumption. A major blow to production came with the downturn in output from the Texas oil fields, a loss of more than 1 million barrels per day by 1975. As the Texas oil fields were gradually pumped "dry," this absolute decline in American production would have to be made up elsewhere by OPEC countries, Canada, or some other combination of producers. OPEC's unwillingness to expand production still further under the old rules aggravated the disparity between rising demand and lagging supply. The consumer countries would however by and large blame the oil corporations rather than the producers for the shortages. Emergence of the seller's market meant that the majors had to compete vigorously with the independents and the national companies for oil purchases. Under these circumstances, the leverage that the majors in particular held over the producer countries regarding price and terms of sales began to weaken. The Teheran pricing decision of 1971 (in which posted prices were adjusted sharply upward and escalators were included to compensate the producers automatically for inflation and for freight rate fluctuations) was evidence that market pressures had driven prices upward as economic theory would predict in a situation of relative scarcity. But the majors would not have lost control of the market entirely if it had not been for a second set of political and commercial forces.

Following the Libyan coup of 1968 against the monarchy, the revolutionary government headed by Gaddafi established a new pattern of industry–producer country relations. Ever since the Russian Revolution and the Mexican expropriation of foreign interests, nationalizations of oil have occurred. But Gaddafi rewrote the textbook on nationalization. It was the threat of the nationalization of corporate assets in the producer countries that ultimately—to use a phrase current in the Middle East during the period—"broke the back of the majors."

Against the background of the seller's market for oil, Gaddafi methodically undermined the control of the industry. He first threatened the independents such as Occidental and Bunker-Hunt, which had the bulk of their foreign oil investments located inside Libya and thus were particularly vulnerable to pressure from that government. Gaddafi demanded that they give up majority control of production interests. Having achieved capitulation, he turned to the majors which could be much tougher because of their worldwide operations. Gaddafi bluntly informed Continental and Shell, for example, that unless they yielded to the demand for majority contol in production decisionmaking and enlarged the returns from the sale of so-called production crude he would give their production shares to the independents, which because of the tightness of the market could be assured of adequate sales. This situation was watched carefully throughout OPEC and upon its outcome rested the whole future of corporate–producer government negotiations.

At this point three high-level representatives of the oil industry led by John J. McCloy met with President Nixon to explain the dilemma of the industry. If the corporations capitulated to the producers, decision power regarding production levels, rates of return, exploration, and sales would shift to the producers. Whether Nixon and his secretary of state fully recognized the danger of such a shift at a time when government was preoccupied with Vietnam withdrawal and the presidential campaign is not clear. Surely the magnitude and coordination of producer demands within the next two years had not been thoroughly comprehended. Whatever the reasons for the decision, the Nixon administration concluded that it could not at that time openly assist the oil industry in applying pressure on the Libyan regime. Only a combination of such pressure and stiffening of corporate ranks could have withstood the shrewd and continuing demands of the Libyan government, of Iraq, and ultimately of all the members of OPEC for control of the market.

Underlying the second set of forces that upset the producer-consumer market balance was a trend of some duration within the oil industry. Concentration had declined. Hundreds of independent oil companies and operators took advantage of the rapid expansion of the industry as a whole and of the escalating demand for petroleum and petroleum products to claim a share of the market. Increasing competition meant that the producing countries would learn to play off the independents against the majors, as Gaddafi eventually did.

Awareness of how such manipulation was possible came slowly because of the lack of skilled management within many OPEC countries and because of the awesome technical complexity of the oil industry. But the very capital-intensive nature of the industry became its greatest political weakness. By making a relatively few decisions at the top, a handful of managers could control the technicians who in turn operated the fields and plants on a day-to-day basis. If the industry had been more labor-intensive, more skilled managers would have been necessary from the developing world. Once control shifted at the top of a capital-intensive industry like oil, however, technical skills could be hired back from the companies. The difference in the new relationships was that OPEC, not the oil company executives, made the final decisions on prices and quantity of crude extracted.

OPEC proceeded carefully in the first year of control, 1974, as data on the pattern and terms of "buy-back" oil indicate. Buy-back oil is that amount of crude production proportional to the degree of direct ownership of production assets by the government. The government had the responsibility for marketing this oil, but about 90 percent was sold directly back to the major companies, indicating the lack of OPEC confidence in its own ability to market on such a large scale. This decision to sell to the same companies that had extracted the oil in the first place also indicates that the high vertical integration of these major companies remained an important market consideration. Nonetheless, over time, the temptation will be strong for OPEC to sell to national companies and independent oil corporations with retail outlets if they offer higher prices or better terms than the majors are capable of offering, the same companies that historically have operated concessions and are now on service contracts.

A reasonable overview of the crisis in the oil industry is that the major oil companies have lost control of the market perhaps temporarily, perhaps, permanently, to the OPEC governments. In the process the identity of interests between the consumer governments and the companies has been broken. Backed against a wall, the largest oil companies found themselves functioning in a new relationship with the largest oil exporting countries. For the time being, OPEC recognizes that the coordination provided by the largest oil corporations remains critical to price stability and smooth functioning of export markets. As long as OPEC needs technical skills, downstream facilities, and transport and marketing assistance and is unable to supply these services through indigenous operations, the present sinecure of the companies will remain uncontested. But unless a strong buyer's market for crude emerges, the squeeze will be on the industry as soon as the producer countries begin to absorb downstream petroleum functions.

If the majors are, as some observers have put the new relationship, "in bed with the producer governments," the corporations got there not by gentle seduction but by a process more analogous to a punishable criminal offense. The oil exporting nations demonstrated the effectiveness of organization in providing leverage over the multinationals. In the absence of support from the consumer governments, the corporations had little choice but to succumb. Among other things, the oil crisis had indicated the myth of the invulnerability of transnational corporations to national sovereignty. Indeed by 1975, the balance of industry weight shifted from what had previously been a remarkable correlation of consumer/corporate interests to one of rather close producer/corporate association. How long the new industrial role can prevail is quite dependent upon the global resource balance of power, an equilibrium which we can now tentatively begin to assess.

Where Does the Industrial Balance Lie?

From one political perspective the oil industry would prefer to remain as autonomous from domestic governmental activities as possible. Each firm pursues this ideal to varying degrees. Unpleasant consequences of overinvolvement with a particular party regime, or political leader may haunt corporate decisionmakers long after the original participants have left office. A corporation must use a low-discount rate in considering the merit of perilous political associations if the firm contemplates an extended residence in a country, for societal memories are understandably long.[8]

On the other hand, a second political perspective demands intense political interaction in each society in which the multinational operates, especially at the highest elective and bureaucratic levels. Political interaction holds out the promise of corporate security, ranging from tax matters to the physical safety of workers and executives. Political interaction also creates commercial opportunities which would otherwise go to a competitor. Hence the ideal of autonomy often gets lost in the competition for survival and expansion.

In theoretical terms the oil industry acts as a buffer between the oil importing and exporting countries, providing an interface which reduces the abrasiveness of government relations. Such a buffer works most efficiently when the interests of the industry leadership are in fact located midway between those of the producer and consumer nations, somewhat in the fashion depicted in Figure III-4. But as we have seen in the foregoing sections, the interests of the industry are seldom so neutral.

During the early post–World War II period the foreign oil industry tended to favor the consumer orientation. A buyer's market for oil prevailed during much of the period despite the abrupt closure of the Suez

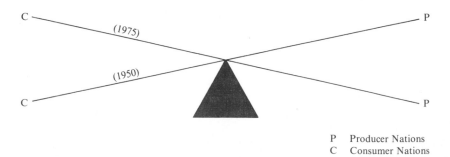

P   Producer Nations
C   Consumer Nations

Figure III-4. Politico-Commercial Orientation of the Oil Industry Leadership

Canal, an action which precipitated the use of larger, more efficient oil tankers and hence little tightening of the market. Fear of antitrust action by consumer governments as well as punitive tax legislation, combined with a natural coordination of interests and easy access to an adequate supply of crude, tended to tilt the industry toward the orientation of the advanced industrial consuming nations.

During the crisis of the oil industry (1969–1973), the balance shifted in the other direction toward the oil exporting countries at a time when a seller's market prevailed. We should emphasize however that market conditions were definitely not the only factors contributing to this shift. If the market alone determined prices, one would be hard pressed to explain a fourfold price increase in crude accomplished in a five-month period and set against a historical background of quite minimal price fluctuations and substantial excess producing capacity within OPEC. Political leverage over the industry, this time exercised by the producer governments, in the form of tax increases and nationalization certainly reinforced market tendencies.

Concentration within the oil industry is another critical element of the changing commercial balance of power among the actors. High concentration within the oil industry catalyzes association between the industrial leadership and either the consumers or the producers. Such concentration is perhaps not necessary for association and it is surely not alone sufficient. But high concentration enables the price leaders to offer a significant degree of market discipline to either the producers or the consumers in the short run, depending upon whether demand outstrips the supply of crude or, vice versa, whether supply exceeds demand.

Conversely, low concentration does not guarantee loss of market power for either the producers or the consumers. A decline in concentration may undercut the ability of either the consumers or the producers (depending upon where the balance of market power lies) to assist in maintaining price stability or in increasing prices, respectively. But this is true only if the producers or consumers themselves fail to provide sufficient coordination of their own interests through organization, dispersal of information, production or consumption share agreements, price arrangements, and penalties (pecuniary or other) for failure to observe agreements. A decline in concentration within the oil industry could thus occur with virtually no impact on prices or the quantity of oil extracted if certain industry functions were transferred or assumed by either a tight producer or consumer coalition.

But a decline in concentration clearly will reduce the influence the industry *itself* exercises on the market in any event. Nevertheless, the analyst must not jump to any quick conclusions concerning who might benefit, producer or consumer, from such fragmentation. While reduced concentration would force the industry to adopt a middle or neutral position (a position that it might otherwise adopt as well), lack of concentration means that the industry cannot act effectively as an independent third force between producers and consumers. The industrial leadership could not place its weight behind producer or consumer policies because the large number of small firms would threaten this association. Obviously, the degree to which concentration exists or does not exist throughout the entire integrated structure of the industry becomes an important element in determining the extent to which the industry is likely to act convincingly as an offset (or buttress) to the producers or the consumers.

Usually, five to seven years is required in the oil industry for significant market changes to make themselves felt throughout the industry. Enormous lag times, abetted by nonpecuniary political factors, condition shifts of investment. Discoveries are lumpy. Since risks are so high (although eased by limited liability arrangements) and alternative energy resources are so dependent upon technological innovation, major shifts within industrial structure take place either slowly or, where rigidities exist, erratically. The present orientation of the commercial balance is not immutable nor is it secure from attrition by market forces. Yet in a field in which economies of scale are so pronounced in both product and marketing and in which competition will always be far from perfect, calculated shifts in the role of the industrial leadership warrant examination, perhaps more than they normally have received.

FUTURE STRATEGIC OPTIONS FOR INDUSTRY LEADERSHIP

In the aftermath of the energy crisis 1969–1973, the industry must chart a new course for itself since the energy crisis wrought important changes in market structure, behavior, and corporate outlook. At least four strategic options are available to the majors in the next decade: a crystallized producer-industry alliance, a return to consumer-industry partnership, a renewed battle for market share and the search for autonomy with emphasis on petrochemicals. A brief discussion of each option and its advantages and drawbacks follows.

Crystallized Producer-Industry Alliance

Making permanent virtue of short-term necessity the majors may seek to build on the situation into which they recently found themselves thrust. They may seek to form a a lasting alliance with OPEC. Assuming that the oil exporting countries do not spite themselves by discouraging this sort of association and assuming that the largest oil corporations are assured of satisfactory profit margins and reasonable prospects for growth, the companies might pursue further OPEC allegiance. Saudi Arabia, the country with the largest oil exports, and Exxon, the corporation with the greatest influence within the industry, are likely in particular to find advantages through coordination that are mutually attractive. OPEC in turn would benefit from access to technology and managerial skills and a large, integrated retail network. The marriage could be consummated if OPEC member countries could buy into the retail network of the companies, much as Iran attempted but failed to do with Shell American, in return for a guaranteed supply of crude at the market price. But before this marriage of convenience is seen to be ineluctable, let us consider a number of possible obstacles.

For one thing, the current structure of the oil industry is no longer as highly concentrated as it once was. Accordingly, the majors must compete rather vigorously to hold on to what is left of their market share at each level of the industry. Not only do they face incursions from the independents, which are likely to try to drive hard bargains with members of the producers' cartel that may be dissatisfied with their revenue, but also the large producer countries are themselves likely to become competitors of the majors in the areas of refining and transportation. Despite resulting inefficiencies in the tanker trade and processing, the producer countries can always require that their own bottoms and refineries be used rather than those of the oil companies.

For another, OPEC has a strong incentive to reduce industry profits so as to keep non-OPEC exploration down. Since Saudi Arabia alone possesses 25 percent of the known oil reserves, with the upper Gulf region contributing another 16 percent and Iran 9 percent, and since further oil discovery within OPEC is perhaps easier than elsewhere, overall constraints on exploration are not particularly painful to the cartel. Indeed, such constraints on external development are necessary if OPEC is to maintain control of the oil market.

Third, the majors must consider the response of the consumer governments to such activity, avoiding punitive legislation designed to break up associations with foreign governments. Regardless of whether antitrust legislation, for example, has any real impact on the durability of OPEC, proponents in the consumer countries may *think* that it has such an impact. Meanwhile, such legislation could have a very measurable negative impact on the size and welfare of the largest oil corporations.

Finally, whether OPEC recognizes this situation or not, the companies will no longer so dramatically be held hostage once nationalization of their foreign assets proceeds to completion. Set free, the companies may reconsider their options, concluding that permanent association with OPEC countries (with the possible exception of Saudi Arabia) in a period in which a buyer's market is gradually returning and in which a number of attractive new investment areas are opening up is not in the best interests of the companies. Thus, for reasons of competition, consumer retaliation, and corporate self-interest, the crystallization of the producer-industry alliance may never fully take place.

Return to Consumer-Industry Partnership

Nostalgic observers in Britain and the United States may ask whether it is possible to get back to the grand days of the 1950s, when oil company profits were at a peak and the interests of the advanced industrial countries and the industry seemed in parallel. With OPEC firmly in command of prices, it is difficult to see how the foreign oil industry can do more than earn a minimal income on service contracts. This income can be monitored and varied according to the needs of the OPEC employer. With an excess of oil rigs in the fields and OAPEC anxious to move downstream with investments in all aspects of the product markets, it is hard to visualize control returning to the industry. But following a massive new find in the South China Sea not under the authority of a government in the cartel or following the tacit rules of the cartel, the industry might regain part of its lost influence. Such a discovery, if it occurred, could however as easily fall under the jurisdiction of a communist regime with rigid guidelines for extraction. Once out of the bottle, the genie of foreign political control could not be returned merely by replacing the cork.

Foreign oil corporations, provided they retain their lead in technology and their margin of efficiency especially in marketing, are not likely to be disenfranchised. But the degree to which they are needed by OPEC is relative and changing, and OPEC is not likely to facilitate corporate profit levels that would weaken its control. A return to the condition of market dominance by the oil corporations, even if possible, will not come easily.

Renewal of the Battle for Market Share

Facing new future commercial and political pressures from both producers and consumers trying to retain market control, the largest oil corporations may have to contemplate as well an even greater internal industrial struggle for market share. Falling profits in the 1960s did not seem to drive out small, marginal firms or raise the costs of entry. On the contrary, there were more small companies in each phase of the industry in 1970 than there had been in 1960. Lacking close political association with either the producer or the consumer governments, the majors may experience an even more vigorous challenge from the independents, particularly at the retailing end, as OPEC governments seek to sell their oil much of it already refined, directly to the consumer governments or to the independent retail chains.

What form is this struggle likely to take and how will the industrial hierarchy respond? Independent companies are responsible for the bulk of the natural gas discovered within the continental United States and a large fraction of the total crude oil discoveries. Eventual decontrol of gas and oil prices in the United States, combined with certain tax exemptions for the independents, is likely further to spur competition within the domestic oil industry. Despite a tightening of the retail gasoline market during the embargo, larger quantities of refined gasoline available to independent retailers could reduce concentration at the marketing end once again. High costs of deep drilling and offshore drilling may, however, retain advantages for the biggest enterprises capable of obtaining capital more easily.

Abroad the situation is somewhat different. There the national oil companies, not the privately owned independents, provide the greatest competition to the principal oil corporations. Two fields in which the national oil companies of the producer countries are likely to wrench control from the private corporations rather quickly are transport and refining. In a period in which recession has caused thousands of tons of transport capacity to be placed in drydock, the producer countries are rapidly buying up excess tanker capacity with surplus funds that would otherwise be vulnerable to inflation and exchange control. Similarly, in a period in which environmental reforms and market uncertainties have discouraged the construction of new refineries among the consumer countries (despite the economic advantages of locating crude processing installations near retail outlets), the national companies of the producers are encouraging refinery construction at the wellhead in part to stimulate the growth of secondary and tertiary industry. A consequence is that much of the vertical integration previously associated with the power of the majors is being chipped away. How are they likely to react to these market incursions?

Market share attrition in these areas is likely to be met only through the emergence of a new understanding between the majors and the producer governments. If the OPEC governments recognize the significance of two factors, then the battle over market share may dwindle to a mere skirmish. First, OPEC will have to acknowledge that it cannot do all things simultaneously and equally well. The private oil industry will retain those functions such as high-cost exploration not easily assimilated by the national oil companies of the OPEC members. Second, for the majors to salvage their market shares, the OPEC leadership must recognize the advantages to itself of continued price stability and a modicum of market discipline provided through uninterrupted vertical integration. Truncated integration is likely to lead for them to some erosion of market control unless all functions are assumed by the procedure themselves. The majors in turn are likely to bargain for long-term agreements regarding the sale of gas and oil at negotiated prices. Should the mutual benefits of this approach not appear transparent to OPEC and should the short-term advantages of sales to independents and to national companies in the consumer countries become more appealing, then concentration in the world oil industry will diminish even more rapidly than it so far has, with corresponding damage to OPEC interests.

Hence, in the market share struggle, either OPEC must rely on the industrial leadership to cooperate or OPEC must replace all of the functions that that leadership has provided in the past in order to generate adequate market controls of its own. The awkwardness for OPEC of getting from the former to the latter position is the margin of commercial safety allowed the traditional industry leadership.

Petrochemicals and the Search for Autonomy

Given the pressures of head-on collision with the independents and the national companies and the problems of a return to the status quo associations of the 1950s, the majors may instead opt for a reorientation of the business toward its most profitable sector. Over the past two decades petrochemicals have outranked other sectors of the petroleum business in profitability. Petrochemicals have other advantages for the majors such as a research emphasis that can make use of their substantial research capability. Because of the diversity of the petrochemical field, its growth prospects, and its dependence upon technological innovation, it is a field in which the OPEC countries are not likely to obtain early dominance. As petroleum becomes more expensive over the next two decades, less and less of it will be used for fuel purposes and larger fractions for petrochemical end products, a field that is likely to grow far more rapidly than the oil production and distribution phase of the industry.

On the other hand, not only must the majors seek growth and profitability but also they must avoid increasing government controls in the home countries, which perhaps eventually may amount to direct ownership participation. Autonomy of the private sector in the United States is rapidly disappearing in an era in which so much of the total sales of many industries is government related. While not everyone in the petroleum industry would strongly resist reduction to the status of a government-regulated utility, the desire for commercial autonomy among many of the multinationals is still high. Although most of the large oil corporations already have an interest in the petrochemical field, a larger emphasis might raise eyebrows in Washington, much as has tighter horizontal integration in alternative energy fields such as coal.

Furthermore, greater simultaneous focus on petrochemicals by a number of the larger firms could lead to overproduction and profit declines in spite of spectacular expansion of petrochemical demand. Predicting the size of the petrochemical market is complicated by the decision of many producer countries to get involved at least on the periphery of the market (for example, in fertilizer production). Hence, although innovation of petrochemical technology is yet beyond them, Saudi Arabia, Venezuela, Iraq, Nigeria, and Iran are all capable of purchasing the technology for large-scale commercial operations, adding uncertainty to what in the next decade may turn out to be an overcrowded business.

On balance, however, the petrochemical field holds significant investment appeal. Many of the new discoveries in the areas of housing, medicine, nutrition, and environmental safeguards must come from petrochemicals, making the field glamorous and respectable. Its importance and respectability, combined with its inherent growth prospects and profitability, continue to make petrochemicals an attractive option for the largest oil corporations.

Conclusions: Disappearance of Profits and the Rebellion of Public Opinion

Two contravening trends mark the fate of the petroleum industry in the period 1955–1975. On the one hand the profit boom of the early 1950s has disappeared, probably never to return. On the other, the industry has lost credibility with the American public to an alarming extent, worsened by the brief and ill-timed upsurge of profits in 1974. Ironically, in an interval in which the industry is facing its greatest challenges abroad, it also has the least support among the advanced industrial countries. How can this turn of events be explained?

A possible explanation rests in the dynamic of public opinion and in the formation of popular ideology. Mannheim wrote in 1936 of the peculiar inability of each ideology, cogent and useful as it may have been at one time, to keep up with the flow of political events. Likewise in the analysis of public opinion regarding U.S. foreign policy, a debate separates those analysts who find public opinion to be a "wise counselor" and those who find it to be a hindrance to the formulation of intelligent foreign policy.[9] One of the conclusions from this debate seems to be that in a democracy, the government must (and does) heed public opinion on broad policy issues. But the more specific one becomes concerning the details of policy and the more one considers means in foreign policy conduct, the less public opinion has to offer. This is so because the public does not have the information needed to make sound judgments about details nor perhaps the training and experience necessary to guide the implementation of its judgments. Regarding issues in which secrecy necessarily prevails or new complex forces are at work, misinformation and misinterpretation are more likely and the limitation of opinion as a policy instrument becomes more glaring.

Such is the case with opinion regarding the oil industry. The myth that current profitability is at an all-time high is but a myth; yet the public is ignorant of this fact as well as the international forces that have transformed market behavior. Public opinion today regarding profits may accurately reflect the situation in the early 1950s, but it is a generation behind the rush of contemporary developments. Similarly, the plea for trustbusting comes at a time when concentration within the industry has already declined and is much lower than it is in comparable industries such as aluminum, steel, and computer technology and at a time when the actual "trust" is no longer a group of corporations but a group of nations organized beyond the legal reach of the American government. The adage of the barn door and the horse is appropriate here: closing the door after the horse is gone, however, may have an important psychological function.

This psychological function is the second reason explaining the anomoly of the public opinion–profit relationship. Opinion often requires a scapegoat. Anger against the companies can be seen largely as a displacement by Americans of anger at themselves as a nation for allowing petroleum policy to fall into the OPEC trap. Some of the anger is pointless since the oil fields in Texas, Louisiana, and California were bound to become exhausted eventually. Part of the anger results from recognition that attempts at fairness and perspicacity failed because price controls on domestic oil and gas and the actual incidence of certain environmental reforms, laudible in themselves, turned out to have devastating implications for energy policy.

The dilemma for the industry was that even when it did argue against certain policies on the ground of energy sufficiency, its credibility was so low that no one listened. Institutional credibility is one of the principal themes that the whole issue of oil profitability and the rebellion of public opinion ought to raise. Those who have important information to provide the government and the public cannot get a hearing either because of past actions no longer attributable to them or because of legitimate conflicts of interest. Consequently, those who have to make tough policy choices in Congress and in the executive branch either do not have adequate information to make reliable decisions or experience little public support when uncomfortable decisions are to be made. In such an atmosphere profit myths gain utility in the battle to shift responsibilities and to defuse pressures that cannot lead to an immediate and effective energy program.

Battered by political developments both internal to the United States and external, the oil industry is only beginning to reexamine its posture and prospects. A new definition of its commercial identity and societal role is likely to emerge out of the crucible of the OPEC market takeover. Profit myths undoubtedly will influence how that new industrial role and identity are perceived in the United States and how flexibly the industrial leadership in turn is able to respond.

IV

Divestiture: Myth of Salvation Through Regulation

Objectives of Divestiture

As some voters, most congressmen, and all members of the oil industry know, divestiture is a contemporary term for trustbusting, or the breakup of large industrial firms. But what is not widely known is the political thought that lies behind and justifies divestiture. Only after discussion of these political objectives can one fairly evaluate the merits of divestiture whose treatment seems often largely to be the monopoly of lawyers and microeconomists.

In order to determine the political objectives associated with divestiture, set against three-quarters of a century of antitrust efforts, one must consider three factors: choice of industry, scope of the industrial target, and time point. It is of much historical political signficance that divestiture has been directed at members of the American oil industry in the period following the 1973 energy crisis. It is also interesting that at least in the initial proposed legislation divestiture has not been limited to a single company accused of exercising monopoly controls but has been directed at the entire industrial leadership. We have already dismissed excess profits in the oil industry as a possible motive for divestiture (Chapter III). Other industries such as steel, automobiles, computers, and aluminum, moreover, are far more concentrated than petroleum. Then why should petroleum receive more regulative attention than industries showing far greater sales concentration? And why should the oil industry be the target of consumer government attack precisely when the industry is reeling from the loss of most of its upstream assets to the producer governments? Is regulation em-

71

ployed now because weakness in the global oil industry makes the principal firms more vulnerable to attack? Perhaps divestiture is being used as a subtle threat to keep the majors in line at a time when OPEC is also exercising leverage over the oil industry. Yet, as is later developed, the diffused base of pluralist regulative concerns and the congressional backing versus State Department opposition to divestiture reduce the likelihood that this later explanation has much validity.

Attempt at simultaneous regulation of an entire industry is also an important indicator of current antitrust intent. In one sense divestiture must address the activities of several American firms at once because not much difference in size separates the industrial leaders. But could regulative attack on the industry as a whole also reveal a purpose not normally associated with antitrust efforts, a purpose perhaps at least implicitly external to the bounds of monopoly regulation but central to energy politics?

From the perspective of international politics, the timing, the scope of divestiture, and the identity of the industrial target all acquire special meaning. Divestiture is largely being thought of by some proponents as a *weapon to undermine OPEC and to destroy its market power.* Thus, it is the external political and commercial implications of divestiture that seem to explain its timing and characteristics best. Whatever traditional merit deconcentration of industry and firm may have in the context of the present debate, this objective is decidedly of secondary interest in the context of oil. Since OPEC success has been so spectacular and the United States seems to possess so few diplomatic instruments to counter this success, divestiture is construed as a means of destroying the new alleged link between the producer nations and the oil companies. We reserve for a subsequent section a more extensive discussion of how divestiture is calculated to accomplish this objective of depriving OPEC of the privileges of vertical integration. Our task here is simply to note that conventional justifications for antitrust actions seem insufficient in the framework of divestiture and that likewise much of the conventional legal and economic analyses of monopolistic behavior must be enlarged and refocused to incorporate the new international political and commercial implications of divestiture.

The scheme of this chapter is as follows: in the first section we present the case for divestiture both in theory and as applied to oil, both in terms of what we define as efficiency arguments and in terms of strategic and commercial arguments that have appeared so compelling to the proponents of divestiture. Before treating the special case of horizontal divestiture (restraints on ownership of other energy resources by petroleum companies), we focus on the new theoretical meaning beyond that of monopoly that divestiture has acquired. In particular we address first the central question of whether divestiture can in fact weaken OPEC. Next we analyze the further international political implications of divestiture for security and the balance of power.

By the first question we mean to explore the commercial assumptions underlying the link between the large oil companies and the producer nations. We shall probe the logic of a weakened OPEC shorn of a guaranteed market for petroleum and petroleum products. We shall weigh the extent to which a disruption of the American market will have worldwide market effects and the extent to which divestiture can add an increment of competition to an industry long characterized by expansion and economies of scale. Finally, we shall ask whether divestiture policies can sustain division within the industry or whether reintegration will instead wipe out temporary benefits.

By the second question we intend to discuss the implications of divestiture for American security and for the shifts of political power occurring within and between geographic regions. We shall also ask whether dominance of the world oil market by American companies yields any political and commercial dividends to the United States and whether a different future composition of the industry might alter these dividends. Divestiture is thus placed in a broader analytic context than is normally true of debate over the merits of antitrust actions. In the end, as we shall see, the debate will be decided not in the more conventional setting for antitrust discussions, the domestic legal realm, but in the international realm of politics.

THE CASE FOR DIVESTITURE

Perhaps the prevailing antitrust viewpoint among economists is that the appropriate test is whether a firm possesses market power resulting from monopolistic market *structure* rather than from monopolistic practices.[1] An alternative view is that a "rule of reason" should be applied in each situation regardless of how much of the market a single firm dominates.[2] According to the latter criterion, judicial opinion need demonstrate only that competition "might probably" be reduced by a particular corporate action to warrant dissolution. Yet legal and commercial evidence of constraints is difficult to compile, and the former doctrine is generally conceived to be harsher if also less selective.

Divestiture and the Market Structure Doctrine

According to the theory of regulated monopoly, firms have a prima facie interest in obtaining a monopoly price that is higher than costs justify or than freer (i.e., greater) competition among firms would permit. This higher price facilitates the generation of "excessive profits." Excessive profits in turn mean that income distribution may be worsened (assuming preferences for greater income equality) as monopoly profits enrich the monopolist at the cost of the poorer consumer. Excessive profits also may mean that the consumer is paying too high a price for the quantity of

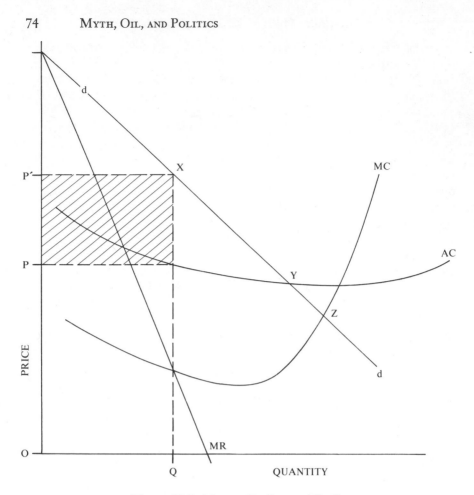

Figure IV-I. Monopolization and Profit

goods he receives. And the amount of labor that goes into the production of those goods may be more than is efficient from society's viewpoint.

These theoretical arguments, which undergird the market structure doctrine, are perhaps clearer in the form of a graphical presentation.[3] Figure IV–1 depicts the relationship between price and the quantity of goods traded for the monopolist at X, who maximizes his profits, for the monopolist at Y, who had accepted a regulated price, and for the firm at Z, which is producing at what society might regard as an efficient price, the marginal cost price. The respective graphs are to be interpreted as follows.

Marginal revenue MR, the revenue obtained from selling each additional unit of product, is derived from the demand for that product dd. Marginal revenue drops more rapidly than demand when the quantity of a good offered increases; that is, marginal revenue reflects the *change in the product of price and quantity* as determined by the slope of the demand curve. Average costs for a firm theoretically decline and then rise again as optimal size is exceeded. Marginal costs respond more quickly to these changes. The best profit point for the monopolist is that point at which marginal cost equals marginal revenue at E. (Above or below that point profits decline.) The shaded area reflects the monopolist's special profit bonus. If the government is able through regulation to depress profits to Y, society supposedly enjoys a price situation closer to equilibrium. The price the consumer actually pays for the product conforms more to the utility or value that he receives from it. Because of decreasing costs, the firm would operate at a loss if the price were pushed downward all the way to Z, the theoretical point of optimal efficiency, and would require some sort of governmental subsidy to continue production at this profit level, a solution with manifest practical complications.

Set against the logic of these theoretical arguments regarding market structure is a set of questions about the impact of size and vertical integration on efficiency. For one thing there exists much disagreement about how quickly the cost curves level out and begin to rise. The argument that a continually falling marginal cost curve would lead to eventual monopoly by a single firm is challenged by a whole series of practical constraints upon expansion to that point—constraints including national barriers to competition, countervailing power at the levels of factor inputs and across the product mix, and obstacles to the aggregation of sufficient capital. In short, economies of scale may be much more prevalent than is often realized, although there are many political and commercial barriers to their capture.

For another thing, the theoretical presentation of regulated monopoly fails to demonstrate how several small firms, each possessing higher marginal costs than a larger firm having greater market control, *necessarily* would sell at a lower price and lower profit margin than the larger firm; divestiture of larger oil firms, in other words, might lead not to lower profit margins but instead to higher margins for the resulting smaller firms. This observation is made even stronger if one assumes that the larger firms, fearing antitrust action, may set their prices not at the profit maximizing point, where marginal cost equals marginal revenue, but at some lower profit point allowing the firm the privilege of diminished governmental visibility and a better chance of long-term political survival.

However, accepting for the moment the outlines of the market structure argument, how does the oil industry fare under these criteria? Is there a prima facie case for divestiture based on the structure of the oil industry in the last quarter of the twentieth century? On the contrary, in terms of the conditions established by the market structure doctrine, the oil industry in its current format is a quite unfeasible target of antitrust legislation. Briefly let us note the evidence for this contention.

First, as argued in a previous chapter, profits cannot be defined as excessive for the oil industry by the standards of profitability observed for other industries. Moreover, profits in the oil industry have followed a long slide, from a high in the period immediately after World War II, when the industry did correspond to an oligopoly of the majors, to today's level at which profits for some firms are indeed subaverage.[4] Except for the untoward profit bulge in 1974 during the interval of post-OPEC price adjustment, oil company profits have remained at a normal level. A monopoly profit is being earned on oil, but this profit, or "rent," is going to the true cartel, OPEC, which absorbs approximately forty-four times the level of profit earned by the companies. Since 1973 the companies' aggregate profits have fallen off by more than 25 percent, a level that is likely to stabilize as the new era of service contracts and offtake arrangements becomes established.[5] If "excessive profits" is the linchpin of the market structure antitrust argument, then the oil industry is currently able to pass this test.

Second, the oil industry is composed of hundreds of companies, many quite small and unintegrated. But the degree of concentration enjoyed by the twenty or so companies that are vertically integrated is not unusually large by industrial standards.[6] Concentration of firms in aluminum, steel, and automobiles, for example, exceeds concentration in the oil industry. If the objective of divestiture were to promote efficiency per se through increased competition and deconcentration, then the place to begin would not be the oil industry but elsewhere in the corporate world where firms would have much more difficulty in passing the market structure test.

Third, concentration in the oil industry has been falling off as the grip of the Seven Sisters weakens and more and more companies achieve a measure of vertical integration. This trend is likely to continue as national oil companies in the producer countries gain access to the market and begin to compete with the large multinationals. In many cases this competition from newer firms is fostered politically and even subsidized, thus putting greater pressure on the industrial leadership than exists in fields of less interest or "national security" importance to the national governments. If the producer governments continue to press for fully integrated firms of their own, it is hard to see how the trend toward greater competition will be thwarted.

Fourth, tacit divestiture has already occurred in the oil industry. Foreign assets of the American firms in production and exploration have disappeared following nationalization. When control of the operations passed to the OPEC governments in at least a de facto sense, a critical link in the chain of integration from wellhead to retail gas pump was broken. As long as the remainder of the chin stays intact, market power will not disappear entirely for the corporate leadership especially in a period of supply plenty. Loss of upstream assets, however, indicates how quickly and how far "divestiture" has proceeded unaided by American governmental initiative.

In short, from the perspective of the market structure doctrine, the

American oil industry seems to be no more a candidate for antitrust legislation than other industries and in view of recent changes in concentration and market control perhaps much less a candidate. But if the market structure doctrine fails to apply, is the oil industry vulnerable to divestiture claims according to updated rule of reason notions upon market *conduct* and *behavior?* While antitrust law is not always entirely clear about which behavior is considered acceptable or unacceptable, one can with some ease note those practices that have contributed to price stability over the years.

Rule of Reason Doctrine

At least eight separate practices—some considered legal, others defined as illegal by the Sherman Antitrust, the Clayton, or the Celler-Kefauver Antimerger Acts and numerous Supreme Court decisions such as that in the Cement Case (1948)—tend to limit competition and to contribute to market discipline when employed.[7] The diversity and number of these practices suggest the difficulty of obtaining any broad-ranged relief from oligopolistic controls through the rule of reason approach. Part of the explanation for why many of these practices do not provide a foundation for antitrust action is that their implementation throughout the capitalist world is so widespread that the rule and the transgression of the rule have become equally pervasive and almost indistinguishable. Another part of the explanation is that the practice, though in some ways a constraint on competition, is also in other ways a contribution to growth and efficiency. Joint ventures, for example, surely limit competition but they also reduce the enormous risks associated with exploration. Such ambivalence makes the practice a poor candidate for antitrust legislation or action.

A quick survey of several of these practices in the context of the petroleum industry may provide some insight into how the industrial leadership has been able to survive as long as it has.

1. *Foreclosure of Market Shares.* Supposedly this practice is one of the implicit advantages (and dangers) of vertical integration. Once integrated, a firm that was previously autonomous might refuse to do business with competitors. Competitors thus have lost access to part of the market or have had it "foreclosed." While foreclosure is illegal,[8] it may go unreported or unprosecuted for a variety of reasons. So many conditions can be placed on the former business relationship with competitors, for example, that they voluntarily yield profitable association. Since they are vulnerable to other market leverage, they may not report what is in any case a seemingly ambiguous instance of foreclosure. But foreclosure strengthens market control by the industrial leadership.

2. *The Squeeze.* According to the Federal Trade Commission the major oil companies "have engaged in conduct . . . squeez[ing] independents at both the refining and marketing levels." [9] Allegedly, the companies limited the supply of crude oil to the independent refineries to the point

where their profits dwindled. Squeezing occurred in the opinion of the
FTC because the integrated majors exploited the advantages of import
quotas (which were abolished in 1973) and the oil depletion allowance
(which was abolished for large companies in 1975). Supposedly, the import quotas, which went only to existing refineries, enabled the majors to
buy crude at the cheaper world price and to sell refined products at higher
domestic prices. Likewise, the majors were supposedly able to exploit the
22 percent oil depletion allowance by seeking high crude prices, decreasing
refinery profits arbitrarily, and making a reasonable profit overall while the
lower refinery profits of the unintegrated independents tended to drive
them out of business.

Evidence seems to suggest that neither argument explains the very real
squeeze on independent refiners and marketers in the mid 1970s.[10] The
Mandatory Oil Import Quota Program granted the small, independent refiners far larger proportionate shares than the majors. Moreover, most of
the majors would have found unprofitable profit shifting in the way the
FTC has described it because the majors themselves were not self-sufficient
in crude oil and had to buy from independent suppliers.

A better explanation for the squeeze on independents, both refiners
and marketers, is that they had grown up on the fringes of the industry
during the oil glut of the 1960s. When supplies of petroleum became short
in the 1970s, the independents were the first to feel the pinch because they
were not as capable of riding out a low-profit period as the larger firms enjoying the benefits of economies of scale, access to capital, and the greater
durability accompanying size. In a curious way the energy crisis demonstrated as no artificial example could the advantages of vertical integration
and the importance of "security of supply."

3. *Employee and Director Exchange.* Without doubt, the practice of
employee and director exchange (restricted by the Clayton Act but not destroyed), found throughout modern corporate relationships, results in the
transfer of information regarding price and markets that is valuable to companies establishing and delineating the same.[11] On the positive side, such
exchange of personnel across supposedly sovereign and autonomous corporate lines provides decisionmakers with a breadth of managerial experience upon which to make better judgments. On the negative side, from
society's viewpoint crosscutting directorates *through numerous intermediary
institutions* such as banks, accounting firms, law firms and even foundations provide opportunities for information transmittal that in effect reduce the amount of competition prevailing in the market.

4. *Joint Ventures.* Because of the enormous cost and the low probability of success associated with oil drilling, joint ventures among several
companies limit liability by spreading risk. But joint ventures significantly
interfere with competition, too, by eliminating some of the uncertainty regarding whether one firm will obtain a major breakthrough at the expense

of the others. Hence, the incentive to press the exploration effort as hard as ideally might be the case is similarly reduced.

On the other hand, if the government chose to ban all joint ventures in an era in which offshore drilling and deep drilling are becoming more costly and perhaps less reliable, the decision would probably have two effects: first, American firms would be at an immediate disadvantage relative to large Japanese and European firms; second, the amount of exploration activity might fall off if capital suppliers were unwilling to assume the added investment risks. For these reasons joint ventures are likely to continue despite their depressing impact on some more ideally constituted form of competition.

5. *Parallelism.* It is possible to illustrate the effects of parallel price decisionmaking on competition through a rather elegant graphical formulation (see Chapter VI on price administration). The upshot is that oligopolistic firms are forced into cooperation with the price leader, ultimately accepting a second-best profit situation to avoid ruinous price wars and market share battles. Parallelism certainly exists in the oil industry as in other industries. Only after the price leader initiates an action are the other large firms likely to follow suit. But parallelism is so diffuse and yet so widespread that even its effectiveness as a price control technique is not easily challenged by fiat. Indeed, monitoring such behavior and *fairly* enforcing prohibitions would probably be more costly than acceptance of its consequences.

6. *Collusion.* While collusion is prohibited by the Sherman Antitrust Act (1890) and successive legislation, selective application of this practice probably still occurs. In particular, collusion is a workable technique in situations in which a government invites sealed bids and in which the bidders are few in number.[12] Where rebidding is not allowed (thereby encouraging one bidder to undercut the others) and where all bids are revealed (thus embarrassing cheaters), collusion is particularly successful. Government lease sales would seem to be an unusually attractive target for this practice.

Curiously, collusion may be a much more significant practice abroad for members of the oil industry than it is in the United States, where surveillance is rather constant. The U.S. government could easily get into a situation in which it forbade a collusive practice at home but overlooked or positively encouraged the same practice used on the part of oil companies abroad. Iran, for example, has long held that the Consortium, encouraged by the State Department, has conspired against it to hold down the amount of petroleum exported at the discounted OPEC price.

7. *Research Cooperation.* As with other "noncompetitive" practices, research cooperation is open-ended and very troubling in its effects. On the one hand, joint research among companies could become an unfortunate conduit of technical, statistical, and strategic information reducing compe-

tition if not properly monitored. But on the other hand, independent research by several corporations can be redundant and wasteful of resources. Failure to communicate findings can be a greater obstacle to technical progress than transmittal of usefully collusive information can be a hindrance to competition. Indeed, one can argue that any legal impediments to joint industrial research should be removed immediately since there are already so many incentives for companies to act as competitors in spite of oligopolistic industrial tendencies, keeping really important industrial secrets to themselves for as long as possible or trading them for significant market concessions. Here again firms seem to be acting simultaneously as oligopolists and potential free market competitors.

8. *Barriers to Entry.* No other constraint on competition in some phases of the oil industry is more prevalent than barriers to entry, and none is more ambivalent. The key issue is the extent to which the barriers are contrived, and even this issue is essentially irresolvable. Because of the huge cost of building a refinery, for example, most potential investors are eliminated. But surely the technical cost of an installation is not contrived and the barrier to entry is genuine. Other examples are not so transparent.

Much useful information is transmitted through trade journals that are in theory available publicly in libraries to all scholars. But the high annual subscription rates of some of the best trade publications puts them beyond the acquisitions budget of most public libraries. The cost for the members of the industry is trivial, and naturally the journals charge whatever rate the market will bear. The practical effect is however to keep much of this information out of the public domain.

Likewise, the government unwittingly shores up the barrier to entry by auctioning off prime drilling areas to the highest bidder. One effect of these auctions is to tie up substantial amounts of money that might otherwise be employed to cover drilling costs themselves. A potentially more serious problem for society is that only a large firm, or a combination of the largest firms, is able to acquire the choicest areas. The higher the bid price, and the greater the variance among prices, the more efficient the competitive model may seem. But likewise the higher the price, the smaller the ring of companies capable of paying it plus the added costs of exploration and drilling. High auction prices thus would appear to be in the interest not only of the U.S. government, the recipient of this type of tax revenue.

9. *Government Regulation as a Market Constraint.* Perhaps the most important single source of price stabilization in the oil market prior to 1973 was the entirely legal activity of the Texas Railroad Commission, the state governmental body responsible for determining production quotas for the Texas oil fields. In periods of excess production capability the effect of setting the "allowable" production was to ensure that the price of oil was not driven down through "wasteful" competition. Once annual crude oil

production began to decline in the United States, however, the functions of the Texas Railroad Commission in this regard became redundant and its influence over price shifted to power centers within OPEC.

Having examined some of the practices that tend to limit competition, whether legally or illegally, and that contribute to "orderly" markets and price leadership, the question again arises as to whether these practices in the aggregate constitute according to the rule of reason doctrine a justification for divestiture. Our contention is that a convincing case has not been and probably cannot be made on those grounds. The reasoning is pragmatic.

First, if certain practices such as crosscutting directorates through intermediary institutions were to be banned in the oil industry, they would have to be banned across all industries in which they abound. Thus, insofar as the objective is to focus on the oil industry alone, such antitrust action is not specific enough. Conversely, if the oil industry were the sole target of the legislation or decision, it could legitimately complain of discrimination because the same practices for which it was being penalized prevail throughout the corporate world.

Second, insofar as sufficient information can laboriously be gathered on many of these separate practices and insofar as they can be demonstrated *in each instance* to inhibit competition, the separate effects would be relevant to the behavior of individual firms but often not to the industry as a whole. However, divestiture is a policy that is being prescribed for all the top firms in the industry despite evidence in market structure terms that no single firm dominates the industry in the classical antitrust sense.

Third, the focus on individual market conduct or performance is piecemeal and therefore unsatisfactory. Competition, in practice, is quite heterogeneous and variable. In an area like the innovation and development of oil drilling equipment, for example, competition currently is extremely vigorous. It is very difficult, moreover, to create an overall index of competition in *behavioral* terms that adequately captures this heterogeneity. The market structure approach is superficially more satisfactory because it is conceptually simpler—if one is willing to make the intuitive leap from structure to imperative behavior. But without simplicity of conceptual measurement, the rule of reason, behavioral approach to the justification of divestiture is much less compelling.

Fourth, although some of the previously discussed practices may help catalyze *vertical integration* and divestiture is designed to break up vertical integration, it does not follow that the presence of certain noncompetitive market conduct (assuming that it exists) *justifies* a radical solution such as divestiture. Why not? Vertical integration also provides advantages and efficiencies that even some of the small firms can enjoy. One of these is a reduction in transaction costs. If purchasing and sales staffs at each of the several levels of the industry are eliminated, much unnecessary bureaucracy and paperwork is avoided. Likewise, long-term contracts that contribute to price rigidity also provide security of supply. In the refinery industry, for example, any amount of downtime or unnecessary subcapacity operation at a billion dollar installation rapidly erodes productivity and profits. Vertical integration in its several manifestations tends to smooth out market vacillations. This is in the interest of the owners of the refineries and also, perhaps, depending upon the importance of constancy of supply, in the interest of the ultimate consumer of petroleum products. Insofar as vertical integration exploits the logic of economies of scale to their fullest, these efficiencies ought to be preserved and noncompetitive practices ought to be treated by methods other than divestiture or radical reconstitution of the industry.

An analogy to noncompetitive practices in the oil industry is the case of frostbite. While most physicians would agree that frostbite is undesirable, one who works outdoors in cold weather inevitably will suffer from this condition from time to time. Amputation may cure the malady; however, it also will adversely affect the victim's future efficiency and task performance. Other treatments for this condition might have less drastic consequences. It is just as dangerous to recommend inappropriate cures as it is falsely to identify symptoms or to underestimate the seriousness of the illness that symptoms indicate.

In sum, when considering both the market structure doctrine and the behavioral rule of reason approach as a basis for divestiture of the oil industry, the analyst must weigh an important trade-off. The analyst must contrast the possible *efficiencies* associated with vertical integration and the *inefficiencies* attendant upon potential price manipulation by the largest firms, for which vertical integration is a key to size. It is probably not feasible to suppress all of the latter inefficiencies while benefiting from the former. Divestiture would tend to eliminate both.

We label this phenomenon the *paradox of uncapturable efficiencies*. Vertical integration is of potential benefit to society. It could result in greater cost savings and efficiency by eliminating bottlenecks and transaction costs. But the paradox is that larger firms employing vertical integration to the fullest have greater control of the market than smaller, more competitive firms, and with this control they avoid trimming their operations (e.g., getting rid of the golf courses and fat expense accounts); since profits are a somewhat arbitrary accounting phenomenon and also are greatly influenced by the price leader in the industry, they may not fully reflect the efficiency or inefficiency of a firm's operations.

The upshot of the paradox of uncapturable efficiencies is that while vertical integration probably creates measurable cost savings, these savings may never reach the public. Forces of market concentration and size counterbalance to some extent, though probably not completely, the salutary impact of vertical integration in that efficiencies of integration may not all be passed on to society.

Since the proponents of divestiture are aware that divestiture would not resolve this paradox but rather destroy the potential efficiencies as well as the market concentration (which as demonstrated earlier is quite low for the oil industry), we conclude that the real basis of the movement to break up the largest oil companies must rest with other objectives. Given the weakness of the classical antitrust position in support of divestiture, other stronger arguments must exist. These other arguments are somewhat more novel and somewhat less founded on equilibrium and free trade market notions and have perhaps too long been slighted.

Strategic and Security Arguments

Divestiture becomes explicable as a political and historical phenomenon only when discussed in terms of strategic and security arguments. Then the timing of divestiture, its encompassing industrial focus, and the selection of the oil industry as a target obtain meaning. At least three broad arguments establish the case for divestiture according to this perspective.

First, assert the proponents of divestiture, OPEC could not remain intact without the commercial and strategic functions provided by the majors.[13] Divestiture is therefore justified *not* primarily in terms of direct efficiency arguments, which are the domain of classical antitrust procedure, but by the indirect effect divestiture would have on the fragmentation of OPEC. The argument is subdivided into two further contentions. These contentions are quite self-contained. Each is complex, politically grounded, and demanding of careful review.

On the one hand, the vertically integrated marketing network of the majors is alleged to be critical to the satisfactory distribution and sale of petroleum. Without the capacity of the majors to dominate refining, pipelines, and retail sales outlets, OPEC would have to rely on a splintered market. Competition among OPEC countries within this fragmented market of many smaller companies would drive prices downward as each country tended to underbid the other in order to sell its oil. Lacking its own vertically integrated channel for the distribution of oil, OPEC, according to this viewpoint, would be the prisoner of competition in downstream operations. By increasing competition between the producers and the buyers of crude, the proponents of divestiture hope to force OPEC to give up the advantages of market control, which they assert the majors now provide. On the other hand, they continue, divestiture could supposedly undermine OPEC from another direction as well. As long as there is no production agreement among the OPEC members, the majors act as a lawyer or broker, making production decisions for the countries, and thus as a buffer for OPEC members. According to this contention, OPEC cohesion rests directly on the ability of the cartel to employ a skillful "lawyer" who through finesse and low visibility is able to determine for the producer countries what is in their own best interest and then convince them of this fact.[14] Constraint on the flow of oil is essential to sustain prices, but, in this view, cheaters who wanted to increase production and thus drive down price or expand market share at the expense of the other cartel members could not escape detection and subsequent commercial and diplomatic pressure because of the pervasive presence of the majors. In a market with many smaller competing units at each level, cheating would be hard to detect and OPEC cohesion would falter. Thus, according to this latter contention, divestiture would foster confusion and ultimate dissension in the OPEC cartel by destroying the mediation role of the largest oil companies.

A second large set of strategic arguments underlying divestiture focuses on the assertion that OPEC and the oil companies have formed an alliance composed of mutual interest, making the integrated oil industry a threat to American welfare and security.[15] Just as vertical integration helped to keep prices down in the pre-1923 era by strengthening market control and sustaining U.S. imperialism so, this argument runs, in the post–1973 era vertical integration helps keep prices up and sustains the dominance of OPEC. Since the majors and OPEC have a common interest in high prices and the United States does not, the United States should recognize, following this logic, that vertical integration is one of the factors harmful to its commercial and security interests.

Similarly, since the consumers can no longer trust the loyalties of the oil companies, why should the governments continue to provide them fiscal and diplomatic support? Some advocates of divestiture urge an end to all subsidies to the companies in the form of tax credits for foreign losses or extraordinary payments to producer government.[16] Such credits made sense only in a period in which they strengthened control of oil prices at a favorable level. Today, according to these critics, the payments are merely a subsidy to the companies for behavior that is irresponsible.

A further extension of this thesis is that the oil companies should not be the ones entrusted by the United States to industrialize the producer countries. Divestiture would open up the investment market to a larger number of competing companies. The near monopoly of business that the four American oil companies attached to Aramco enjoy should be opened up to every one so that no single corporation becomes dependent upon the Saudi government for lucrative investment contracts, ultimately undermining the responsiveness of the company to the American national interest. It is just as possible in this view to create corporate dependence on the import side as it is to foster dependence on the oil export side. Freer competition allowing non-oil companies a greater share of these contracts, assert the proponents of divestiture, will reduce the element of this risk to the U.S. economy.

Furthermore, since long-term price arrangements between producer country and firm and "participation" agreements that enable the companies to buy back a fraction of the oil produced by the governments are in reality a way of keeping the oil companies dependent, these practices should be destroyed. They simply are devices conceived by OPEC to keep the firms bound to it, according to divestiture advocates, and breakup of the large multinationals will eliminate the attractiveness of this control technique for the producer nations by increasing the number and flexibility of separate contracts.

Third, the proponents of divestiture seek to illuminate the contradictory interests that the oil companies presently display in pursuing that which is in the consumer interest, namely, a reduction in prices and an end to cartel cohesion. The interests are contradictory in part, it is said, because the companies have huge domestic petroleum reserves in the United States; a high world price for oil safeguards profits on these reserves. By pressing for a drop in prices, the companies risk loss on investment inside the United States especially since the cost of deep drilling and drilling on the continental shelf is so high that the profit margin is already thin. Divestiture would break up companies into domestic and international segments for the legislation would have no authority over foreign companies and the American companies would separate their foreign from their domestic assets. According to the divestiture viewpoint, breakup of the large multinational corporations would permit a resolution of contradictory interests. Resulting smaller foreign corporations would not have the same objections to oil price declines as the multinationals because price declines would not threaten all of their assets in the same way.

As if to support the logic of the divestiture argument, OPEC governments express fear that breakup of the major oil corporations would damage cartel interests. While scarcely based on extensive analysis, at least as revealed in public statements, this fear would seem to reinforce the logic of divestiture advocates that fragmentation of the oil industry is genuinely in the interest of the consumers. Yet deeper analysis could, and in fact does, reveal otherwise, and possible alternative conclusions do exist.

In sum, the theorists of divestiture see OPEC cohesion much like a three-legged stool propped up by the current policies of the producer nations, the past overconfidence and inaction of the consumer governments, and the new pro-OPEC strategies of the multinational oil companies. By kicking out the leg representing the multinational oil companies, the proponents of divestiture hope to make the stool topple, ending the domination of OPEC. How realistic this analogy is regarding the present oil situation and how relevant divestiture is to a solution of consumer problems are the subjects of the remainder of this chapter.

Can Divestiture Weaken OPEC?

Our task now is to assess each of the strategic arguments favoring divestiture, since these have weighed so heavily in the genesis of divestiture legislation, attempting to discern the plausibility and impact of divestiture on these grounds. In this section we deal primarily with the potential impact on OPEC, while in the next section we consider the impact on U.S. national and commercial interests.

Vertical integration provided by the major oil companies is, according to the proponents of divestiture, essential to the ability of OPEC to transport and market petroleum. How essential to OPEC is this ability to distribute oil through vertically integrated channels? And, if it is essential, how necessary is the contribution of the majors per se to OPEC plans? Is another form of vertical integration feasible and perhaps ultimately as attractive to OPEC, or is the commercial universe strictly limited to a single form of vertical integration?

Vertical integration surely provides OPEC with several important advantages. At a time when many of the producer governments are attempting to train and locate their best young executives in the newly created planning agencies and in the production end of the oil operations, the added burden of having to worry about transport and marketing would be troublesome. Long experienced in the mechanics of monitoring and scheduling sales of petroleum, the majors also are able to maintain a high level of efficiency in these operations. The majors also probably are still capable of exercising enough discipline in the market such that price vacillation is kept to a minimum, thus easing the task of planning and projecting budgets for the oil-rich countries. But a number of observers have asked whether vertical integration is really *mandatory* for OPEC sales. If divestiture suddenly broke the old trade channels apart (which incidently might require a period of years that would see extensive litigation), the OPEC countries would not *stop* selling petroleum. OPEC is not that constrained by administrative shortcomings and restrictions. OPEC could sell directly to a variety of smaller companies that in turn would handle other marketing responsibilities downstream. Practical administrative problems would not be much greater were a hundred entities involved than were twenty or so.

The real question, however, is whether the *market discipline* offered by the majors through their integrated hierarchies is essential in marketing. Surely OPEC, with its enormous financial reserves, could survive increased price vacillations of the kind observed in other commodity sales. OPEC has an advantage because these large reserves were created in advance of any possible fluctuations caused by more competitive market conditions. Indeed, the producer countries would probably be much better able to survive market instability than many of the consumer countries having very low financial reserves relative to income or actual balance of payments deficits.

But would increased competition among smaller firms each dealing directly with OPEC drive the price of oil downward and force a collapse of the cartel? Divestiture could very well have the opposite effect. Divestiture would tend to increase both the mean profit levels of firms within the industry and the variance in profit levels because risk is greater for the smaller firms. Without vertical integration they would also tend to be less efficient and costs would rise. More important, as long as OPEC preserved its unity it would have an easier time setting prices because the market would be more divided and less capable of challenging its decision. If twenty major companies have little leverage with OPEC, a hundred smaller companies would have even less. Organization in the face of disorganization has power on its side.

Another market outcome of divestiture is just as likely, however—*reintegration*. Insofar as vertical integration is a commanding structural phenomenon (the impetus toward reintegration following the breakup of the Standard Oil Trust in 1911 is an example), the logical response for the oil industry would not be to do without vertical integration.[17]

The logical response would be to reintegrate outside the United States. Inasmuch as the United States is the largest single market for petroleum, reintegration could not be as complete in some respects as it currently is. The U.S. market would remain fragmented. But outside the United States reintegration might be very complete, albeit no longer under the control of companies based on U.S. territory.

Thus, if vertical integration really were essential to OPEC for marketing purposes, this chain might reemerge along new lines. Alternatively, if no one else sought to reintegrate the industry (an unlikely possibility), the largest oil producers might attempt to achieve this goal themselves either through use of entrepreneurs already operating from within OPEC countries or through incentives to foreign management to accomplish the task for OPEC. Either way, the industry would scarcely remain in a state of commercial anarchy for very long.

Let us turn to the second contention of the proponents of divestiture, that the majors are performing an indispensable function of broker and setter of production levels for the cartel. It is probably true that the major companies provide the OPEC countries with much market information. It is also true that OPEC has so far been unable to agree on production limits based on reserve-to-production ratios, capital absorption levels, per capita wealth, economic importance, some other criterion, or a combination of these. But it is a mistake to assume that the companies *themselves* determine production levels without the support of at least the largest producer, Saudi Arabia. And if Saudi Arabia is needed to sanction production level decisions, then the role the companies play may indeed be a very secondary one of providing information. Information can be obtained from a variety of sources, including a more centralized communications structure within OPEC, a single large company presently operating external to the United States, or a reconstituted firm displaying properties of vertical integration.

What makes OPEC price maintenance work is that Saudi Arabia is adopting prudent decisions that can be backed up through production changes and that so far have been accepted by the other OPEC members even when the decisions have not pleased them. Very clearly, the companies are not deciding the respective production levels of each OPEC country in the absence of support from the largest oil producer. What is critical in this argument is not the vertical integration of current firms but the role of Saudi Arabia.

Since Saudi Arabia is interested in price stability (defined as price increases at the rate of world inflation), as are the largest oil companies, there may be an advantage in leaving the decisions with this institutional combination for the present. Prices will not decline until either non-OPEC supply increases drastically and/or demand is reduced drastically, a much more difficult achievement. But in the interim, if price and production decisions were instead determined by an OPEC panel of governmental representatives, much greater attention for political reasons would be given the clamor for sharp price hikes. By keeping information closely held and by working primarily with the largest and most conservative oil producer, the price leaders in the industry backed by some market control through vertical integration recently have been able to slow down the upward tilt in prices. Furthermore, the prospect of government intervention is enough to keep the consumer interest within sight of the industry. The largest firms realize that to disregard entirely either the consumer interest or the OPEC perspective is to place their own institutional existence in peril.

In response to the criticism that foreign tax credits should be abolished, one must consider the effect of these credits on the overall policies of the firms regarding exploration. If there is no relationship between the tax credits and the level of exploration, then the credits are not buying the consumers very much. Some producer nations are anxious to see greater exploration in their countries and are seeking to encourage the companies in this direction. Other countries, perhaps the bulk of them, seem to feel that exploration will not be hurt if incentives are removed. This policy is rational only for countries that have either very large proven oil reserves or very little hope of finding new reserves. For the consumers, any disincentives to exploration are a disaster, and the foreign tax credits must be evaluated in this light. In any case, divestiture is an awkward method of deciding the merits of the tax credit issue.

Similarly, the criticism that the oil companies should not be entrusted by the United States to industrialize the producer countries is scarcely an issue to be decided through divestiture. It may well be that Saudi Arabia uses Aramco for development purposes because the government wishes to establish additional ties with the companies that export its oil. It surely is the case that it will deal closely only with firms that it trusts. But destruction of the vertical integration that characterizes the firms formerly a component of Aramco will neither hinder Aramco's effectiveness nor open up the Saudi market to a larger number of non-oil American firms. On the contrary, divestiture could destroy part of this market by transferring Saudi allegiance to large European or Japanese firms anxious to do business in both oil and industrial goods.

To some extent the producer countries will naturally be the ones to choose who will do business with them. Firms that are large and fully integrated and capable of both marketing petroleum and handling investment contracts are probable business partners for the OPEC countries. Divestiture can make some American firms less attractive to OPEC, but can divestiture make other, smaller, nonintegrated firms more attractive? Unfortunately, the answer is likely to be negative.

Divestiture may also disrupt the long-term contract arrangement and make participation agreements less feasible—but to what purpose? Long-term contracts cause a firm to become dependent on a particular crude supplier only to the extent that the terms of the agreement are favorable. No firm can be forced to conclude such an agreement against its will when other options are available. In a period of rising prices such as the current one, long-term contracts favor the buyer rather than the seller of petroleum and for this reason are likely to be broken, if at all, by the seller rather than the buyer.

Only in a period in which the buyer of petroleum faces downside price possibilities are long-term contracts a disadvantage, and if the possibilities are great enough the contracts will probably be renegotiated just as they were repeatedly during the 1971–1975 period on the upside. Long-term contracts probably do take some of the short-term fluctuations out of prices, which may or may not be in the consumer's interest. But long-term contracts also reduce transaction costs and provide some security of supply, which may benefit the consumer if passed along.

Participation agreements generally are thought of as interim arrangements to enable the producer governments (or members of the family elite owning shares of production) to become familiar with the market. The more "participation" crude sold on the open market, the more likely that competition will increase, with whatever price benefits this may bestow on the consumers. To the extent that participation crude was forced into the channels of the vertically integrated firms, the multinational oil companies were thought to be able to exercise leverage against the producers. If divestiture denies the firms the capacity to control this fraction of the market, then the producer nations will have obtained even more leverage over the consumers and will be in an even better position to dictate terms of trade.

Proponents of divestiture who argue that fragmentation of the large American oil firms is dictated by a conflict of interests between low prices for foreign oil and high prices (and therefore large profits) on their domestic American holdings are similarly confused about the powers of divestiture. Not only the large oil firms with domestic oil reserves but also the United States itself is cross-pressured on the price issue. High world prices for oil enable the society to pursue innovative research in alternative energy sources and exploration for high-cost new oil. Lower world prices for oil would cost the American consumer less but also would afford less expansion of production while stimulating consumption of oil even further. Does it follow, then, that the United States should be penalized because it is of two minds about whether oil prices should be raised or lowered? Divestiture would no more reconcile these opposed interests for the United States than it would for the oil firms. The conflict of interests remains and must be dealt with by other techniques.

Clearly the United States should adopt two measures that would have a positive effect on oil company production and exploration activity in the United States without the negative and futile effects of divestiture. First, the United States must allow the price of oil to rise to the world price, thus accelerating domestic exploration. Second, it must build a price floor under the production of energy from new sources so as to remove the risk of investment to the entrepreneur. If proper tax constraints on certain kinds of energy consumption are legislated, the imbalance between the nation's consumption and production of energy can be brought into line. But the apparent discrepancy between desiring a low world price for consumption purposes and a high domestic price for purposes of production will remain.

Even after divestiture it is not clear that the foreign segment of the American oil corporations would prefer *lower* oil prices. Fragmentation of vertical integration might reduce the company's ability to defend price stability, but it would not erode the company's desire for better earnings and higher profits. Thus, divestiture appears to be a futile instrument in pursuit of a reconciliation of foreign and domestic energy perspectives.

In reviewing the general impact of divestiture on OPEC cohesion, one can observe the following. Vertical integration is probably not essential to the marketing, distribution, and processing of crude and crude products. But if it is essential, a reintegration of the oil industry is likely to occur in the wake of divestiture, providing the OPEC producers with access to markets. Divestiture could lead to an interval of some market uncertainty and chaos in which smaller firms bargained directly with OPEC producers. But whether greater competition in downstream operations would lead to price declines depends very much on whether OPEC retains institutional cohesion. Institutional cohesion in turn is very much a function of *general supply and demand conditions* for petroleum. A tight market favors continued cohesion regardless of whether divestiture is implemented.

Divestiture is also not likely to destroy the OPEC cartel by abolishing the mediation role of the majors. If there ever was a time when such destruction by this technique was possible, that time has probably passed and Saudi Arabia has learned to exert its leadership successfully as the largest producer within OPEC. This leadership relegates the majors vis-à-vis price and production decisions to a very subordinate role. While an adequate production formula has yet to be determined, OPEC in effect sets price and determines production levels, not a group of American companies, integrated or atomistic.

Under these circumstances the answer to the question "Can divestiture weaken OPEC?" seems in the longer run to be answered in the negative. If divestiture were both sudden and complete, OPEC might in the short run have to make more rapid adjustments than it would prefer. But in the absence of these conditions, and within a somewhat more extended interval, OPEC is likely to escape much of the potential political and commercial impact of divestiture. Can the same be said for the international strategic position of the United States?

INTERNATIONAL POLITICAL IMPLICATIONS OF DIVESTITURE FOR THE UNITED STATES

Insofar as the United States (not the other consumer countries) is contemplating divestiture, the analyst has the obligation of examining the proposed industrial changes in the light of their international strategic and commercial impact upon the United States. It is one thing to observe that divestiture is not likely to achieve its principal objective of weakening the producer cartel. It is another, stronger indictment to demonstrate that divestiture may have further negative side effects for the country that itself initiates the program of industrial reorganization. In exploring this possibility we examine first the evolving politico-commercial relationship between the United States and OPEC, second the question of oil industry leadership among the consumer countries, and third a view of divestiture as the failure of confrontation politics between trade blocs. We will attempt to show that divestiture has perhaps its largest impact in terms of these international strategic considerations.

Stimulus to Downstream Integration by OPEC

No doubt divestiture would shock the infant planning and coordination apparatus within OPEC and the petroleum and finance ministries within the Saudi Arabian government. Divestiture would appear to threaten the link with the multinational corporations at a time when these corporations are beginning to recognize a communality of interest with the producer nations. Divestiture would appear like some infestation of termites eating away the foundations of a new industrial-governmental relationship that is working with surprising efficiency.

Very soon, however, OPEC, which has absorbed so much rapid change already, may come to recognize that divestiture is less a danger than an opportunity, an opportunity that the generation of surplus petro-dollars could exploit to the long-term advantage of the producer nations. Most of the capital-rich OPEC countries face a development choice. They can focus on either petroleum-related or non-petroleum-related growth. Diversification of the industrial base obviously is attractive, especially for those countries like Iran with quite finite petroleum reserves. When the oil runs out, other industrial processes must shoulder the responsibility for capital generation. Conversely, the petroleum industry in its current condition is scarcely a glamour stock; its technical complexity and uncertainty raise investor doubts; its capital-intensive nature creates relatively few jobs; political constraints on oil investment in the consumer countries frighten off some of the richest potential investors in the Arab world; and, finally, indirect investment efforts through the stock and bond markets have been discouraging for some countries like Kuwait that have explored this option. Yet notwithstanding these debits, divestiture could force OPEC to move more rapidly than it had originally planned in the direction of downstream investment in the petroleum industry—and with very positive results for the producer nations. Countries with the largest financial surpluses—Saudi Arabia, Kuwait, the United Arab Emirates—do not have as many investment opportunities as others with larger populations or more varied natural resource bases. Petroleum-related development offers these countries great opportunities because the industry is capital-intensive, not labor-intensive, and because these are the nations having the longest time horizons for petroleum reserves. In addition, concentration in downstream petroleum operations will provide the Arab producers with further political leverage in time of potential supply interruptions.

Thus, divestiture could accelerate the process of translating the refinery industry and the petrochemical industry from the Gulf of Mexico to the Persian-Arabian Gulf area despite possible inefficiencies associated with locating these industries near the source of production rather than the source of consumption. Divestiture would accelerate this process for two reasons: first, it would cut off capital to the American industry now fragmented and less able to acquire financing for large projects; second, OPEC itself would be forced to play an increasing role in downstream activities abandoned by the private oil industry. Divestiture would also reinforce the industrial management in the view that the consumer governments were less than serious about remaining in control of downstream petroleum operations, thus providing the corporations with a political signal that the best investment opportunities for them lie with joint projects in OPEC countries.

Evidence that this investment trend has already commenced exists for the period 1976–1977. A decline in petrochemical projects planned for the

United States and Europe matches a large increase in proposed installations, many of them very sizable, for the Middle East and North Africa.[18] A similar case study of how public policy in the consumer nations can have an impact on gross investment patterns is in refinery construction. Environmental legislation, much of it desirable in itself, combined with uncertainty regarding feedstock supply and cost factors, has caused a flight of the high-technology refinery industry out of the United States toward the Middle East.[19] Public policy decisions probably do not "cause" these trends as much as that they "catalyze" or accelerate trends already occurring.

Beneath these commercial trends is a very significant shift of political power as well. Governments less able to provide for their economic needs domestically and efficiently are more vulnerable to foreign constraints on their security and welfare. Embargoes and boycotts are only the crisis manifestation of a much broader and more incremental shift of power away from the older industrial centers.

Divestiture thus may be an awkward decision for OPEC in terms of timing and adjustment. But its ultimate strategic effect could be quite salutary at least for the largest and richest oil producers. From the American perspective it is hard to see how divestiture can offer the same politico-commercial advantages even when viewed largely in a free trade sense. While the United States might retain a comparative advantage in the manufacture of high-technology equipment and installations, it will have lost its capacity to trade the lucrative secondary and tertiary processing of petroleum for the crude it no longer possesses in abundance. Accompanying this loss of value added processing is an increased capacity on the part of the OPEC countries to set and maintain price and production levels through greater downstream integration. Hence, divestiture, which was conceived as a strategy to relieve the consumers of foreign dependence, could instead rebound against them.

Shakeup of Industrial Leadership among the Consumer Countries

Divestiture would also not leave untouched the order of the international petroleum hierarchy. Two foreign companies, British Petroleum and Royal-Dutch Shell, among other smaller firms would certainly benefit from the industrial organization. Although it is true that both British Petroleum and Shell have large American assets and that assets would probably be sheared off formally and made more legally autonomous than is currently the case, Exxon, the largest American company, would suffer the most damage and would have to relinquish its position as the number one firm in the industry. A glance at the profit picture for Exxon relative to that of the other multinational oil companies over the past twenty years reveals the advantages of being number one, and the price leader, in terms of returns to equity. Insofar as this income is remitted to the United States, some of its citizens and perhaps the polity as a whole benefit. But other, more political factors are also at stake with respect to the identity and hierarchy of the industrial leadership.

A single large corporation that leads an industry and establishes broad policies that other corporations will tend to follow has far greater international influence than four or five separate, competing entities in an industry dominated by a large foreign corporation. Uneasiness over the size and vigor of American corporations in Europe could readily be replaced after divestiture by American uneasiness at the ascendancy of European or Japanese oil corporations. One of the great problems with divestiture, then, is that it would not apply broadly enough to include all the large multinational companies equally; instead, it would rearrange the industrial hierarchy so that the corporations with a base in the United States would operate at a disadvantage in terms of the benefits of vertical integration, giving foreign companies an edge in relative production shares. Increased competition is purchased at the cost of United States interests alone. Some of the foreign assets previously owned by American oil companies might seek to reintegrate outside the United States under the auspices of a "benevolent" industrial government such as Japan or the Federal Republic of Germany. In any case the United States would lose influence within the petroleum industry and through that industry in the wider arena of international affairs. Similarly, the United States would have to forsake income from divested foreign assets that were reintegrated abroad.

National security implications should follow from the present discussion of reorganization in the oil industry. Critics of the multinational corporation who may knowledgeably bemoan its lack of responsiveness to the national interest will perhaps moan only more loudly if the charter of that corporation disappears from national control entirely. In practice the multinational oil corporations led by Exxon have a rather good record in meeting national needs during war and international crisis such as the imposition of embargo. While it is allegedly true that the Sixth Fleet was told during the 1973 crisis that American oil companies could not guarantee to supply it with adequate amounts of fuel, how much more likely would such a response be if the industrial leadership were under foreign control and limitations of supply forced even more serious differential cutbacks among Western allies? Proper coordination between the industrial leadership and the State Department during crisis is essential to the prevention of the precipitous use of force by the United States as much as by a panicky foreign government. But if that leadership not only faces increasing pressure from OPEC but also has divided national loyalties, only the most sanguine analyst would predict a high likelihood of equitable treatment for the American interest if for no other reason than that the extent of U.S. political leverage over foreign corporations abroad is minimal.

One should not assume that a multinational oil corporation whatever its national base and current commercial orientation would purposely and vindictively disregard the interests of any nation during crisis. Commercial survival is too precarious for malicious intent. Likewise, one should not automatically assume that the presence of the home office of a multinational oil company on a nation's territory will obtain for that nation an increase in jobs, welfare, and security: too many variables such as tax policy and asset distributions intervene to reduce the correlation in interests. Yet over long time periods the shift of concentration away from the enterprises of one nation toward those of others implies a subsequent shift in political influence for that nation. On this observation (if not on the related normative question) both the critics and defenders of the modern multinational oil corporations tend to agree. An ambiguous indicator of this observation perhaps is that both the Defense Department and the State Department have opposed divestiture on strategic grounds. A possibly better indicator is the actual shift in corporate influence away from the United States in the four years following the 1973 energy crisis (and the international political interpretation that this shift beckons).

Divestiture as the Failure of Confrontation Politics

From a certain analytic distance, divestiture perhaps can best be seen as an attempt at a quick, unilateral effort by some members of Congress to save the American strategic position through domestic regulation when confrontation politics in the international realm seems to have failed. It is almost axiomatic that the oil companies alone were not going to prevail against both market conditions and OPEC's political resolve. A concerted response by the consumer governments in support of the multinational bargaining position would have been necessary in November 1973. Despite the Justice Department decision of 1971 authorizing a waiver of antitrust legislation so that the multinational oil companies could negotiate collectively with the producer governments, the firms were not completely united in policy objectives. More seriously for the consumer position, the consumer governments were neither in agreement regarding energy vis-à-vis OPEC nor willing to provide the companies vigorous diplomatic support. Thus, the proponents of divestiture were correct that confrontation politics had failed in part because the tactic had never really been tried.

But both divestiture and confrontation politics have in common the objective of forcing a retraction of OPEC prices *without* first changing the background of petroleum demand and supply conditions. Divestiture in addition carries the burdens of indirectness, isolated commercial impact, and associated negative side effects with respect to the U.S. leadership role. Supposing, however, that divestiture were successful in placing pressure on OPEC (again in the absence of a fundamental change in the amount of new non-OPEC energy produced or a substantial drop in world energy demand), three further strategic outcomes of confrontation must receive consideration.

First, confrontation with OPEC since enriched with large financial reserves could invite increased political tensions—not so much war as disruption of supply. Although the consumers might consider increased political tensions a necessary price for relief from the high cost of imported petroleum, these tensions can scarcely be disregarded. New International Energy Agency regulations notwithstanding, the capacity of the consumers to surmount constraints on supply is still perhaps less than the capacity of the producers to do without revenue for a time or to do with reduced revenue. Unless the consumers resorted to force, commercial confrontation could lead to eventual commercial capitulation.

Second, and conversely, a tumultuous confrontation with OPEC could unseat conservative political regimes in Saudi Arabia, the United Arab Emirates, and Iran, thus complicating the implementation of U.S. foreign policy. Some analysts may consider concern over the impact of bargaining on regime ideology within OPEC nations as gratuitous. But to trade commercial gains in terms of oil price reductions for a political radicalization of the Middle East accompanied by all the implications for foreign policy change is scarcely a net benefit. Fear of political revolution in the Arab world should not preclude tough bargaining and effective long-term economic planning, but such planning should also not ignore possible undesirable political consequences of rash commercial actions.

Third, and more probable, confrontation with the OPEC producers could force on OPEC a type of cohesion against a hostile external threat that it does not currently display. If the producer governments cannot now agree on a production share formula, thus running the risk of internal battles that could damage price coordination, confrontation with the consumer governments could induce OPEC members to settle differences and place a higher priority on unity. Divestiture might thus force OPEC to take planning steps that have been left to the multinationals, with some small dividend to the consumer nations as a result.

But of all impacts, perhaps the most likely consequence of divestiture would be facilitation of the shift of commercial power to OPEC, accelerating certain trends, and causing OPEC to grasp the reins of production, transportation, refining, and marketing a bit sooner than the cartel could easily manage. Saudi Arabia, in particular, has an interest in fostering a new pattern of vertical integration subject to its needs. All of the OPEC countries are of course dependent upon foreign technology supplied by the private sector. Reorganization of the petroleum industry might temporarily complicate these communications and coordination efforts. Alone it would not, however, deny OPEC that which long-term demand and supply conditions favoring Middle East oil have brought into existence and which

Saudi commercial domination reinforces, namely, self-interested cohesion over the near term.

HORIZONTAL DIVESTITURE: A SPECIAL CASE

Vertical divestiture would break up firms into functional levels; horizontal divestiture would divide up firms according to type of energy specialization. A firm subjected to horizontal divestiture would produce and process only a single form of energy such as petroleum. The reason that horizontal divestiture is a special case is twofold: horizontal concentration by oil companies in several areas of energy production is not a very real current problem but is an important *potential* problem; consequently the term "divestiture" perhaps does not really apply to necessary policy action in this problem area, but some type of preventive administrative action in the public interest may be recommended.

Horizontal integration can in theory limit competition between fuels in a serious fashion. A large firm or group of firms with substantial interests in two or more fuels could seek to keep a cheaper form of energy off the market until their interests in another fuel had been fully exploited at satisfactorily high prices. Naturally, rather strict assumptions have to be met regarding price, profitability, elasticities of demand, and degree of concentration.

In the history of international oil matters, a parallel situation has arisen in which governments have argued that the oil industry has held certain concession areas off the market for years because there was insufficient political pressure by the host government to develop these areas. It has been argued that areas along the Oman coast, in Iraq, and in Iran at various times all were subject to such discrimination. In contrast, because of the open access policy of government and the limited time dimension associated with concession rights, development proceeded with astonishing rapidity in Libya during the late 1960s. One must recognize, however, that many factors such as geological accessibility, quality of crude, transport distances, and political stability also determine which exploration areas are likely to be developed first. Libya was strongly favored by these factors during the mid-1960s. Nonetheless, if the oil industry were able to restrain development in one area while giving preference to other areas, the reality of this ability suggests that it could operate across fuels, given appropriate market structure and conditions, just as it seems to some extent to have operated across petroleum exploration areas.

Stating a principle and demonstrating its practical validity, however, are two quite different things. In general, large crude oil producers are also large natural gas producers. Concentration within the uranium industry is

higher than that within other fuels. But most of the large coal and uranium companies are *not* owned by the multinational oil firms.[20] Concentration across fuels is probably *lower* than it is within most of the individual
energy industries.

Despite this evidence of low horizontal integration, there is also evidence that concentration has increased since 1955 (particularly among the
top eight firms) and is likely to continue to increase. Increased interfuel
concentration will occur as petroleum companies invest more heavily in
uranium and coal reserves. Yet there is an important available constraint
on this trend. The U.S. government still owns the largest fraction of coal
and uranium reserves. By controlling the manner in which these reserves
are distributed and by monitoring mergers and exchanges, the government
can prevent excessive interfuel concentrations without resorting to divestiture.

Horizontal integration is thus a special case both because it is a potential future problem and because it can be controlled through proper administrative action other than divestiture. The United States will nonetheless
have to pay a cost in keeping the concentration ratio down in interfuel
terms. That cost is the possible loss of development capital made available
by a petroleum industry increasingly looking elsewhere for profitable investments. But society cannot have both maximum investment flows into
new energy sources and maximum competition among fuels. In any case,
since current concentration ratios are low, the problem of the investment-
concentration trade-off is a future one but one that should receive study
and administrative attention.

CONCLUSIONS

In this chapter we reviewed the grounds for divestiture and considered
whether divestiture is capable of achieving the aims proponents outline.
We also sought to determine whether the aims of divestiture themselves
seem justified in larger political and economic terms. We were especially
conscious that the selection of the oil industry as target, the post–energy
crisis timing, and the industrywide focus of divestiture suggest that this attack on oligopoly is not an ordinary antitrust endeavor.

By dividing conventional antitrust arguments into two groups, those
supported by the market structure doctrine and those indicated by the rule
of reason (or behavioral) approach, we were able to draw revealing conclusions. In market structure terms the oil industry is one of the least likely
industrial targets for divestiture because concentration therein is low by
contemporary standards. Profit levels are also not abnormal. Alternatively,
turning to the rule of reason we found that some noncompetitive forms of
behavior probably do exist within the oil industry, contrary to the claims

of some of its more strident defenders. But two problems emerge in trying to use this information as a basis for divestiture. Each act of noncompetition would have to be proven in specific cases and then somehow generalized to the industry as a whole, a very difficult, long, and probably not very fruitful way of getting at industrywide divestiture. Second, most of the criticism of the petroleum industry focuses on practices (regardless of how theoretically unattractive) prevalent in modern capitalist enterprises. Why, then, should oil be singled out as the sole target of divestiture?

These interim conclusions suggest that the divestiture legislation must in fact have been stimulated by other, stronger arguments. The logical foundation for these divestiture arguments is in the international strategic and commercial area: as a device to weaken OPEC; and as a method to further U.S. welfare and security aims. Upon examination, however, the two principal contentions underlying the first argument—namely, that divestiture would cause OPEC to fail because OPEC must have access to the majors to market its petroleum and that divestiture would destroy the broker function of the multinationals, which allegedly allows the producers to reach agreement on production shares—seem to carry little weight beyond the very short run. True, OPEC does not favor divestiture since its management tasks are already large. But, in our view, should divestiture occur, OPEC would merely be forced to take on responsibilities sooner than would otherwise likely be the case. Similarly, divestiture far from adding benefits would probably have some additional very negative side effects in terms of U.S. national interest.

Given these conclusions, partially qualified in the special instance of horizontal integration, divestiture looks like a technique for destroying the efficiencies of vertical integration without replacing them with corresponding advantages. The myth of energy salvation through regulation appears to be a wistful shortcut beset by more risks and dangers than prudent gains for the country implementing the legislation.

V

International Energy Agency: Myth of the Collective Consumer Response

EVOLUTION OF CONSUMER SOLIDARITY

"A principal purpose of consumer cooperation," said Henry Kissinger, is "to prepare substantive positions for a producer dialogue to ensure that it will be fruitful."[1] Behind this delicately worded statement and others made by the president and members of the State Department lies the answer to why the International Energy Agency was created. International in membership, the organization is nonetheless an American idea. Hence, in measuring the success of consumer solidarity, one must ask what purposes the American architects of the new IEA had in mind.

At one extreme the purpose of the agency could have been merely to promote a comfortable image abroad of mutual progress on tough energy problems and of unity among the industrial democracies. Regardless of real organizational achievement, the image of unity would be useful at a time when great uncertainty unsettled the electorates of each industrial nation and at a time in the aftermath of Vietnam and Watergate when the foreign policy leadership of the United States was seriously being questioned. In a period of crisis, international symbols of unity and leadership serve the nation-state well.

At the other extreme the IEA could have been conceived as the spearhead of an overall effort to solve the global energy problem. In this context the IEA could have been envisioned as the fulcrum of the American energy program with coordinated policies on each of several levels—a genuine organizational response to the producers' phalanx, OPEC. Such a purpose would entail a degree of unity matching that of OPEC, enabling the industrial countries ultimately perhaps to purchase petroleum collectively at negotiated prices, balancing monopoly (a unitary seller) with monopsony (a unitary buyer).

Systematically reviewing the actions and statements of government officials for this period, one comes to the conclusion that IEA was meant to exceed the former minimum purpose but not to achieve anything like the latter objective of direct purchase and sale of petroleum.[2] As Kissinger pointed out, IEA was to convince OPEC that it had to deal candidly with the industrial nations, which had the capacity to coordinate their energy programs in a way that could put downward pressure on the oil price and that could prevent the negative political and economic consequences of another oil embargo. In order to achieve OPEC respect, IEA would have to initiate and implement a series of specific energy proposals; declarations of principle would not be enough. Upon enactment of these proposals, IEA would then be in a position to bargain collectively with OPEC for presumed concessions in a number of areas. It has always been a principle of postwar American diplomacy to negotiate from strength if possible. Political unity could buttress strength. But to appreciate how difficult the task of consumer solidarity was going to be, and how imperative, one must consider the nature of the diplomatic setting in late 1973 and early 1974.

Diplomatic Setting of the Washington Energy Conference

Panic is the best way to describe the attitude of some of the leading democracies at the close of the October war. In the wake of successive cutbacks in oil production of 9 percent and 25 percent, respectively, the price of oil skyrocketed. A practice of "leapfrogging" took place whereby France, West Germany, and Japan attempted to outdo one another in an effort to assure adequate supplies of petroleum at ever increasing prices. News from Baghdad, Teheran, and Riyadh constantly spoke of huge arms contracts and programs of technological transfer exchanged for agreements to sell specified amounts of petroleum at the "market price," a price that the consumer governments appeared determined to bid upward. A first task of the Washington energy conference scheduled for February 1974 was to coordinate consumer buying behavior so as to dampen the effects of leapfrogging. In other words, the first job of consumer solidarity was to get the consumer governments to tighten the reins on their own purchasing activity.

An irony of this first tactical objective of solidarity was that the market was behaving very normally indeed and that within a short time sufficient petroleum would be sold so as to make many of the wild-eyed initial contracts look ridiculously priced. It was the desire on the part of producers like Libya, Iraq, and Iran to exploit the upsurge in prices (which for all anyone knew was temporary) that caused prices to level off not the remonstrances of economic leadership within the coalescing IEA.

A further irony of this early phase of diplomacy was that the United States now indulged in precisely the bilateral bargaining that it had protested, a bit belatedly perhaps but with a greater vigor and magnitude than the Europeans and Japanese combined. It was in the United States, after all, that the greatest technological plums, both military and nonmilitary, were to be obtained, and it was the newly created bilateral commissions with Iran and Saudi Arabia that became the cornerstones of American Near East diplomacy, notwithstanding American interest in furthering consumer solidarity through the IEA.

An additional characteristic of the diplomatic setting in January and February 1974 was that political uncertainty and animosity vis-à-vis OPEC remained high. A consideration that made calling the Washington energy conference more difficult was the emanation from Riyadh of threats to continue the embargo if the consumers made any effort to form a bargaining bloc. Washington tried very hard to convince its allies, on the one hand, that IEA was essential to a strengthened bargaining position relative to OPEC and, on the other, that should the embargo remain in force (an unlikely event in the American view) the United States would come to the aid of its allies through whatever means necessary. France in particular doubted the American resolve to safeguard its allies, pointing to the declining American domestic oil reserves, the huge American domestic demand for petroleum, and the entangling American defense commitment to Israel as reasons for an attitude of placation toward OPEC. At the same time this French strategy appeared to Washington to epitomize French policy since de Gaulle, a policy that simultaneously sought one foot inside and one foot outside any alliance with the United States. The very harshness of the bargaining line that the United States initially pursued through IEA left France the intermediary between the consumers and producers. As the benevolent intermediary, Paris could hope to obtain favorable assurances from the producers, especially Algeria, regarding oil supply at the expense of the consumer coalition. To the French, however, this policy of independence enabled them to play an important role as buffer at the interface of pressures between the north and the south of the world system.

In short, the diplomatic setting on the eve of the Washington conference was complicated by external threats, commercial enticements, and internal fragmentation. That the conference took place at all is credit to the rather masterful diplomacy emerging from Washington, the more so considering that it was under weight of commercial pressure not experienced in magnitude perhaps since the international monetary decision to devalue the dollar in the earlier Nixon years.

Membership and Political Structure of the IEA

At the Washington conference twelve other industrialized nations and the United States agreed to form an organization that nine months later would become the International Energy Agency: Belgium, Canada, Denmark, Sweden, the Federal Republic of Germany, Ireland, Italy, Japan, Luxembourg, the Netherlands, Norway (an associate member), and the United Kingdom. Five more states joined—Austria, Spain, Switzerland, Turkey, and New Zealand—for a total of eighteen, with France conspicuously absent.

On paper IEA is even stronger procedurally than OPEC because the former organization has established formal voting rules whereas the latter still requires unanimous decisionmaking. But as the May 30, 1976, meeting of OPEC in Bali indicated, "unanimous decisionmaking" can be a euphemism for Saudi domination of procedures and outcomes, just as the American veto within IEA would ensure defeat of binding energy decisions in the latter organization.

According to the outline set forth in Kissinger's National Press Club speech on February 3, 1975, the structure of the IEA was to evolve in three phases:[3] The first largely involved development of measures to protect against emergencies. Both the cutoff of oil and the manipulation of petrodollars were seen as the potential cause of such emergencies. Second, IEA would attempt to reduce the consumption of imported oil so that demand would fall, bringing the price with it. This was the period in which Secretary of Treasury Simon, for instance, expressed considerable confidence that conservation measures combined with the effects of the recession could shake if not "break" the cartel. Despite warnings from members of the oil industry that had made careful studies of the "capital absorption capability" of the leading OPEC countries, particularly Saudi Arabia, and that had concluded that conservation would have little impact, there was hope in government circles that market conditions could be "transformed."[4] It was known, for example, that Saudi Arabia could in 1975 survive on as little production as 3 million barrels per day, or one-third of the 1973 production rate. Such phenomenal latitude stemmed from the unusual Saudi financial reserve situation, which enabled the government to weather lean periods without hardship. Nonetheless, plans to impact the market were widely discussed in Washington during the early days of IEA. Third, IEA had the obligation to "meet with the producers to discuss an equitable price, market structure, and long-term economic relationship." Throughout the planning sessions the commitment to cooperative discussions with the producers was very clear. This commitment from the United States was necessary in order to get some of the more reluctant members of IEA to proceed with planning. They correctly perceived themselves to be in a much more vulnerable import position than the United States, which had only recently peaked its domestic production of oil and still imported only a minority fraction.

But while Kissinger promised future talks with the producer governments, he had something different in mind from that which many of the

European governments and Japan envisioned. By "fruitful dialogue" he meant significant concessions on the part of OPEC; by "preparation" he meant grinding out a mutually acceptable set of IEA proposals that could provide sufficient leverage in future discussions with the producers. Always he reminded his audiences that only once the consumer nations had taken the "essential steps" would the dialogue with the producers take place, not before. Timing and degree of solidarity thus became critical issues in the evolution of IEA and in the measure of its policy success, topics that we shall subsequently explore.

Assessing the Policy Objectives of IEA

IEA policy falls into roughly four categories, with early success experienced in the first categories and uneven achievement in the latter ones. We will attempt to explicate each policy from the IEA viewpoint and then discuss its impact on global energy matters.

Boycott and Embargo Deterrence. Although the 1973 oil embargo was by no means universally effective, its effectiveness had increased greatly over the embargo attempt in 1967, and in the opinion of some observers prospects seemed good for even more visibly punitive supply interruptions in the future.[5] In many ways the oil embargo is the model diplomatic instrument, coercive yet nonviolent, relatively controllable yet possessing enormous scope and shock value. Insofar as use of the oil boycott does not induce the target states to employ force, a boycott or embargo threat, unless otherwise countered, is likely to offer the OPEC states incomparable leverage. The IEA leadership decided to restrain this leverage as a first priority.

According to deterrence theory derived from the nuclear weapons field, each level of force must be countered by a deterrent at the same force level for maximum effectiveness. Subversion, for example, is not offset by threatened use of nuclear weapons. Such a threat would not be credible. No one would believe that the threat would ever be carried out since the response is so incommensurate with the size and gravity of the original act. In addition, the perpetrators of the original act of subversion in all probability could not even be targeted by weapons of such huge size. Instead, subversion must be thwarted by the very government that faces the insurgency, assisted by aid and training from a major ally.

Likewise with an oil embargo the way to offset its effectiveness is not through reliance on military force alone, which would risk escalation to major war perhaps with the Soviet Union, but rather on techniques that would negate the commercial effect per se of embargo. Such techniques would have to be easily implemented and to possess a high degree of reliability. Facing these credible responses to the oil embargo, OPEC members would be less likely to risk an interruption of supply since by previous calculations it could be seen to fail. A government might still take that risk but the probability of such a decision has been lessened. Also, use of force always remains a last resort if it appears that commercial deterrents are not working.

First among the embargo deterrents is a commitment on the part of the members to increase their emergency reserve stocks of oil, which in some cases presently are nonexistent, to satisfy requirements for ninety days or more. By rationing or other controls, these stocks could be extended through an additional reduction of demand. These stocks are very expensive to store above ground, are vulnerable militarily, and are subject to loss through fire or other hazards. Hence, the United States is employing salt domes in south Texas that have large capacity and that are unlikely to leak. Petroleum in large quantities will be readily available for transport to nearby refineries in order to meet the nation's needs primarily for gasoline and heating oil.

A further much discussed aspect of this embargo deterrent is that, properly designed, it might contribute to a weakening of the cartel.[6] The logic of the assertion is this. If petroleum is purchased from the smaller producers, which are much more in need of revenue than Saudi Arabia or Kuwait, the IEA membership should be able to buy these large quantities of oil at a discount, thus eliciting competition within the cartel and putting downward pressure on price. But the difficulty with the assertion is twofold. First, this purchase of petroleum in no way supplants petroleum that would *otherwise* be acquired through conventional channels. It is petroleum bought under special contract that is withheld from the consumer for emergency use. Thus, the purchases of this additional, stored petroleum can almost be thought of as part of a separate market. The effect of the additional demand may not *raise* price under these conditions, but it will certainly not lower price either. Second, even assuming that OPEC as a whole has excess production capacity that would enable it to meet these large purchases, the governments like Venezuela and Indonesia that might most likely be willing to make the sales are also for a variety of reasons the governments with the *least* excess production capacity and the highest cost production. Saudi Arabia, with the largest excess capacity, certainly is not likely to comply with this IEA strategy and indeed probably has warned the other cartel members against cooperation with IEA. Thus, prospects are not bright for a price break via storage purchases *in the absence of a change in overall demand and supply conditions.*

A second fundamental deterrent to boycott is an agreement among the IEA members that in the event of supply interruption the members would share the available supply. In effect, this is what the oil companies themselves did for the governments in 1967 and 1973 but are probably not in a position to do in the future. Oil sharing has two attractive political characteristics. First, in theory at least, it suggests that societies better off in oil terms because of domestic production or alternative energy sources would help those societies that are poorer or more vulnerable. Whether this principle would ever come into effect is open to some question, given the hysteria and greed that the 1973 partial embargo seemed to trigger. On the other hand, the principle of sharing according to need is a worthwhile goal and contributes to an ideological unity within IEA. Second, and probably more important, oil sharing discourages the attempt at selective embargo addressed at specific IEA members. It creates the image of a solid front. An attack on one member is an attack on all. This is the concept that underlies all alliances and represents the type of commitment that may add strength to international endeavor in parallel activities.

Selective embargo is not a mere speculative possibility. It is one of the most serious threats to IEA unity. In 1973 the Arab producers attempted to isolate Holland and the United States while treating differently other industrial consumers that favored a presumably different foreign policy toward Israel. Since the oil companies still enjoyed a large measure of autonomy in their patterns of distribution, they were able, often through subterfuge, to reallocate the burden of the very real production cutbacks.[7] But with loss of decision autonomy and with larger entry by the producers into the tanker trade, such balancing of burdens will increasingly have to be performed by the consumer governments themselves.

The reason the selective embargo is in theory such a powerful instrument is as follows. In order to hurt the industrial consumers as a group, a majority of the OPEC producers would have to hold back production, creating problems of coordination and compliance. But in order to hurt a single isolated economy, Saudi Arabia alone, for example, could reduce production sufficiently—assuming the other OPEC members did not increase production to a corresponding degree—to strangle the nation's welfare. If selected embargoes worked, and the IEA did not demonstrate solidarity, each industrial consumer would become highly vulnerable to even small fluctuations in OPEC supply. Hence, oil sharing has its greatest benefit in offsetting limited embargoes directed at specific countries.

To create a third deterrent, IEA has committed itself to assume *equal percentage cuts in consumption* in the event of a boycott.[8] The political advantage of this approach is that it is uncomplicated and easily monitored. The difficulty with the approach is that it may be quite inefficient. Britain, with large oil and gas reserves of its own in the North Sea, may discover that cutbacks are much easier for it than West Germany, which must import a higher margin of foreign oil. Equal percentage cuts in consumption may also, for example, impinge more heavily on transportation in a large country where space is a problem and in an economy more dependent upon the automobile. But from the perspective of public credibility, the equal percentage cutback concept probably is more understandable and thus more acceptable than other, more subtle approaches. Under any circumstances the cutbacks are voluntary and self-imposed and provide at least a guideline for concerted action in future emergency.

Fourth, and finally, IEA has created an embargo deterrent in another area, that of international finance. One of the fears of some policymakers in the spring of 1974 was that petro-dollars would accumulate in OPEC coffers, causing huge balance of payments deficits in the consumer countries. Pessimists doubted that importers, businessmen, and investors could recycle earnings from petroleum sales quickly enough to avoid a breakdown of the international financial machinery. Having demonstrated that this scare was misplaced, the consumer leadership identified another financial concern, namely, possible future manipulation of international monetary reserves by high-surplus OPEC countries. In contemplation of this last fear, IEA agreed on a $25 billion fund to protect members against deficits caused by oil shortages or from arbitrary shifts of funds by producer nations.

How real is the fear of monetary manipulation by governments with large balance of payments surpluses on capital account? On the one hand, the temptation would be great to use an apparently easy source of leverage such as the decision to move dollars into yen or marks or vice versa as a means of obtaining foreign policy objectives. Again, the technique is nonviolent and extremely focused. On the other hand, for a government like Saudi Arabia to play games with the international monetary apparatus is like fiddling with the fireplace until the house burns down. Saudi Arabia more than any other country in the system is in a sense vulnerable to tremors in the international monetary arena. It has a far higher ratio of financial reserves to GNP than other states and thus is, for example, much more subject to negative effects from devaluation. Most OPEC countries are financially conservative and with good reason. They cannot afford a loss of confidence in the international monetary system. Hence the $25 billion fund is good insurance against a hypothetical but not very probable risk. The greatest risk would come from large independent investors that might choose to speculate on governmental actions.[9] But real or not, the risk of financial manipulation has been satisfactorily covered by the creation of the IEA insurance fund.

Together these four embargo deterrents—oil storage, oil sharing, proportionate consumption cuts during emergency, and the financial reserve fund—all serve to discourage interruptions of supply or the use of petro-dollars for destabilizing financial purpose. Since each deterrent reduces the likelihood that an embargo would be successful, the deterrent also reduces the likelihood that the embargo will again be attempted. Unfortunately for the consumers, if an embargo is again applied, potential effectiveness of its implementation has also increased for certain reasons previously discussed, thus making the embargo more attractive to the producers, other things being equal. IEA deterrents are designed to ensure that other things will not remain equal and that supply interruptions will continue to be high-risk endeavors for OPEC policymakers.

Acceleration of Alternative Energy Sources.   Most IEA countries recognize that large increases in energy supply can emerge only from new non-OPEC oil discoveries or from the development of alternative energy sources such as coal, fission, or, in the long run, fusion. In order to accelerate the development of energy sources other than petroleum, IEA has adopted a set of principles that are to facilitate the execution of joint energy projects, the provision of capital, manpower, and technical skills, the identification of constraints in specific energy sectors, and the cooperation and coordination of national research and development programs. So far, it is fair to say, however, much more has been done on the national level than on the international.

Why has there been reluctance to proceed jointly on these broad, mutually beneficial research and development programs? Several explanations are evident on the political and economic sides.

First, progress has been slow within IEA in the alternative energy area perhaps largely in contrast to achievements regarding the emergency measures. Emergency measures were possible for several reasons. Most democracies are *crisis oriented* rather than *process oriented*, and the fear of embargo is more real to governments than the slower diminution of energy supplies. Moreover, several of the emergency measures required only pledges of future action or steps such as increased storage, which the governments already had planned independently to take. Most of the embargo deterrents were also quite specific, limited instruments that the governments could justify easily in political terms. Action in the realm of alternative energy sources requires more than this level of commitment.

Second, the scale of the capital requirements is enormous in developing new energy sources such as fusion. With the Western oil industry alone planning to invest nearly $250 billion of new capital over a decade, the acquisition of so much funding is a problem even for the richest industrial states.[10]

Third, the uncertainty of investment direction and payoff creates a kind of inversion of the norms of conventional democratic politics. Current administrations are expected to pay for that which will benefit future administrations. Yet the current government leadership receives no immediate gratification that can be transformed into votes, only the unattractive responsibility of having to find the necessary investment funds. Since the research payoffs are nebulous by the standards of democratic politics, policymakers are reluctant to choose coal liquification over solar energy, for example, or fusion over breeder reactors, preferring to spread the risk by pursuing all research leads simultaneously. But the effect of this decision is vastly to increase the cost of research and development. Not fully aware of the benefits that economies of scale and the learning curve can bring to a variety of projects in the energy field, many legislators in the Western industrial states argue that the prudent course is to wait until the "natural process" of scientific and technological innovation points to the "correct" option. But because of the lag times involved in such developments and the centricity of dwindling energy supplies to the modern economy, this latter course does not appear feasible.

Fear of risk is definitely at the heart of the inertia associated with long-range energy planning at the international level. IEA has wrestled with one aspect of development risk, suggesting a solution that has been poorly understood in the United States.

Creation of a Price Floor for Petroleum. Reasoning behind the IEA price floor concept epitomizes the blend of political and economic thought in the field of energy.[11] Since OPEC had the power in a favorable demand-supply setting to raise the price of oil, IEA policymakers conclude that the price is somewhat arbitrary and could be lowered at will by OPEC through an expansion of production.[12] A high current price for crude oil supports high-cost production of energy from alternative sources such as coal. But large quantities of energy from alternative sources would at some future time flood the market, driving down the price of OPEC crude. IEA planners suspect that the OPEC leadership might therefore try to prevent this collapse of the market for crude oil by subverting the production of energy from alternate sources. The easiest way for OPEC to protect the petroleum market would be to drop the world price for petroleum. This action would eliminate entrepreneurs in the high-cost energy sector unable to compete with the cheaper crude oil. Even the *threat* of this strategy by OPEC would keep many investors out of the alternate energy field. In order to stop OPEC from trying this strategy of market subversion and in order to give confidence to private investors in the consumer states, IEA devised the notion of the price floor.

According to the price floor idea the investor in alternate energy production would be guaranteed at least a $7 per barrel minimum return regardless of how low the world price for petroleum dropped. With the investor's downside price risk eliminated, many more entrepreneurs should be encouraged to pursue alternate energy projects, some of which might become very efficient and profitable.

A great misunderstanding associated with the price floor idea, however, has been that IEA is in effect trying to guarantee a high world price for oil—in effect rewarding OPEC for its decision to raise the price of crude. But the IEA proposal in fact does not reward OPEC at all; it does the opposite. It encourages downward pressure on the world price of crude by inducing new volumes of production from other sources. And it achieves this goal at very little real cost to the IEA consumer.

The technique proposed by IEA is to place a tariff or quota on the amount of crude imported from OPEC at a price below $7 a barrel. Above this threshold the market operates as usual. Below this threshold price, the consumer of imported oil would in effect have to pay the consumer government the equivalent of the difference between the lower world price for oil and the $7 minimum. But the consumer government would then be able to use these tariff proceeds for whatever purposes might be in the larger interest of the society. Alternatively, the consumer could purchase energy from the domestic nonpetroleum energy source at the $7 per barrel equivalent price and pay no tariff. The critical point, however, is that the OPEC price might continue to drop under the pressure of additional energy from the new sources, while the investor in the consumer country developing the high-cost innovative processes would be protected.

A criticism of the IEA proposal is that it would reward high-cost inefficient output from the alternative sources. This criticism would be potentially solid if two further conditions were also true: one, innovation and development represented essentially a static process in which no new ideas emerged to lower costs over time; two, OPEC really had the capacity and the intention of lowering the price of crude for whatever reason. While the infant industry argument is often used falsely to justify tariffs that seem to remain in perpetuity, in a highly innovative area such as breeder reactor technology cost savings over time would seem plausible and the threshold price itself should probably not become an obstacle to further increments of efficiency.

Regarding the second and perhaps more important point, there is good reason to believe that Saudi Arabia, for example, would face extreme opposition from high-price preference states within OPEC if it attempted to lower prices precipitously. Why, then, the need for the price floor concept? A price floor is needed to convince entrepreneurs that this analysis of OPEC behavior is genuine. If this assessment of OPEC behavior is indeed correct, the investor would of course have nothing to fear for the next seven to ten years from lower world crude prices anyway. But the price floor concept has cost nothing. And it has provided one very important strategic element: insurance to the investor in the consumer country against improbable but certainly not insignificant price risks.

Given the logic of the minimum safeguard price concept and its trivial cost in the context of the present market, why has the IEA membership been hesitant to endorse the idea? Three specific explanations seem to underlie the resistance.

First, some governments may feel that the minimum safeguard price would allow very aggressive low-cost innovators excessive profits since for them the spread between the $7 support price and their own cost would be wide and widening. Second, other governments may perceive that regardless of their own participation in this IEA initiative, the entrepreneurs that will make the program work and that will contribute to their nation's employment and income will be located in a few of the large industrial states like Germany, Britain, France, Japan, and the United States. Migration of the technology and enterprise to the other IEA members may, in the estimation of some governments, be slow indeed, leaving them as barren of energy sources in 1990 as they are of petroleum fields today. Third, a majority of the IEA membership may feel that the United States, as the richest of the high-technology countries and the one perhaps most concerned about energy dependence, will go ahead with a support program on its own. Thus, they would be able to enjoy the benefits of the low world price for crude (assuming the price were either driven down by additional energy supply or consciously reduced for strategic reasons by Saudi Arabia bent on subverting the alternative energy program) without having to support expensive research programs and without enforcing the price floor plan. Their industry would then obtain a competitive advantage over our own, which would be stuck with $7 a barrel oil.

In responding to each of these assertions, one must note that in the absence of the minimum safeguard proposal each of the IEA members is likely to be far worse off than it would be with the relatively small sacrifices it would have to make on behalf of the proposal. If, as in the first assertion, some companies become excessively profitable because of unforeseen breakthroughs, this "problem" can be handled through tax policy. If, as in the second assertion, certain countries fail to benefit immediately from the location of a portion of the new energy industry on their territory, they will at least benefit from the lower cost of energy available through the world market. If, as in the third assertion, the United States does have plans to safeguard its energy development industry regardless of IEA decisions, and if this creates competitive advantages for industry abroad, the situation is likely to be quite temporary; the more likely and more permanent effect will be a higher world price for energy and less sharing of the gains of energy research and production within IEA than would otherwise be true. Moreover, by not participating in the safeguard program, the IEA members run the risk of being locked out of some major breakthroughs that they might otherwise have enjoyed in the field of fusion research, for example. In the end the minimum safeguard price is a strategic instrument that will probably work effectively only if all the major energy consumers participate.

Mutual Programs of Conservation. In January 1975 President Ford set as an American goal a total saving of 1.2 million barrels of oil per day by 1977.[13] A month later IEA set as its goal a total saving of 2 million barrels a day by the end of 1975. Recession made the achievement of these goals seem perilously and deceptively easy. Indeed, a bad joke going the rounds of Washington was that whenever the price went up and the quantity of oil consumed went down, the EPA defined the savings as conservation.

But the task of conservation has not been so easy, particularly in the United States, which has the worst record of energy conservation in the

IEA. Over one-third of all energy consumed in the United States goes for personal use. About 10 percent is devoured by the ubiquitous automobile.[14] The scandal of waste in the nation's driving habits is so conspicuous (to everyone but Americans) that a retiring oil company president publicly recommended, in the face of the contrary interests of his own industry, that Americans pay an additional $.40 a gallon tax on gasoline to cut down on waste. Simply by switching to cars that get twice the present gas mileage, which could be accomplished within the normal turnover rate for cars of three and one-half years, the nation could save 5 percent of the energy it now throws away. Both Detroit auto makers and foreign car companies can easily meet this demand with current designs for somewhat smaller cars. Car travel would not be affected. Such savings could hardly be defined as sacrifice, nor would the growth rate of the economy, for example, be harmed by the changes.

From the perspective of international energy collaboration, demand for energy must level off if any consumer bloc is to obtain market leverage. As long as demand continues to outpace new non-OPEC supply, commercial unity among the industrial governments will be difficult to achieve and will have little politico-economic meaning because despite increasing costs each government will be desperately striving to acquire assured access to energy. The argument raised by some critics of conservation that the addition of taxes to already high gasoline prices is an admission to the producers that prices are not really as high as they should be is a weak argument. On the contrary, the ability to establish an impressive energy conservation program is evidence of two things of genuine interest to OPEC. A conservation effort indicates first that the rich industrial nations recognize the need to meet the producers halfway by eliminating waste and thereby prolonging the value of foreign oil reserves as well as their own. Second, it indicates that the industrial countries can regulate their consumption habits, thus warranting the respect that cuts in the demand for imported petroleum ought to earn in the context of new discoveries, energy from alternative sources, and consumer solidarity. Part of the reason that conservation has been so delayed in the United States by the standards of other industrialized countries is that the failure of the Project Independence report to provide plausible advice and projections left a shock wave of pessimism in its wake.[15] Members of the oil industry must accept part of the responsibility for this unfortunate result. They so convincingly pointed up weaknesses in the report that, although frequently countered by advertisements and statements of individual firms, they left a general impression of the hopelessness of energy conservation. While conservation alone is not likely to reduce the need for energy sufficiently to put much demand pressure on prices, it is nonetheless useful at the very least to decontrol oil prices in order to reduce a fraction of the gigantic bill for oil imports. But a leadership vacuum seemed to follow behind the collapse of some of the more ardent projections of Project Independence. This vacuum in turn has had a serious impact on the cause of international consumer solidarity.

From the perspective of other members of the IEA, there is a major gap between America's pronouncements and its performance. Energy conservation is a notable example. Other members with the same per capita wealth as the United States consume half the energy. Yet they, like the less energy prudent countries, are admonished to accept the American lead in a possibly damaging political confrontation over price and commercial terms with the producer nations. It is easy to see why the weight of American leadership within the IEA is not as heavy as the earnestness of the energy problem for the industrialized countries seems to justify.

In short, assessment of IEA policy suggests that to date progress has been much greater in the area of embargo deterrents and emergency measures than in the long-term programs of research collaboration and development or in energy conservation. As a consequence, the favorable impact of consumer solidarity on the *certainty of energy supply* has been far more noticeable than it has been on the *purchase of petroleum at lower prices.* Lags of seven to ten years are to be expected between the implementation of the long-range programs and the emergence of any effects. Hence, the analyst must limit his observations to proposed programs and probable results. Yet the disparity between the merits of the IEA emergency principles and proposals and the long-range price-related efforts of the agency at this stage is worth comment.

BROADENING THE DIALOGUE

Crisis in international oil matters has had two decisive impacts on Third World relations, neither foreseen prior to 1973. First, the OPEC price rise has drained scarce foreign exchange away from the poorest one-quarter of the world's nations. Increased foreign aid has replaced these losses only partially and selectively. Many Third World countries now feel the influence of the OPEC nations in financial and political terms and are beginning to look toward the cartel leadership for relief from the very conditions that the oil price rise has brought about. Second, and paradoxically, OPEC, the source of considerable financial strain in the Third World, has become an ideological model to emulate. Cartel formation is looked upon as a new model of how to deal forcefully with the industrialized countries. Dialogue between IEA and OPEC has quite naturally become embroiled in these larger international political matters. At the invitation of French President Giscard D'Estaing, IEA thus gradually has entered the broader debate regarding the new economic order through the Conference on International Economic Cooperation (CIEC) established in December 1975.

It is the widening of the consumer-producer dialogue and the clash between CIEC and IEA that preoccupy us in this section.

Before we explore the IEA-CIEC dialogue in detail, let us consider the background of American diplomacy that has shaped the institutional setting. Henry Kissinger championed consumer solidarity as a prerequisite to serious talks with the OPEC leadership. He was (jointly with former President Nixon) also the architect of the first real balance of power diplomacy at the highest nation-state levels since 1945, namely, the shift toward China, the Soviet Union's principal rival. But, as the modern Metternich, he became the target for criticism as one concerned more with state interests and power than with international "morality," and with great state politics rather than with Third World relations. This criticism emanated out of the Republican National Convention from Ronald Reagan, the Republican challenger for the nomination, from Jimmy Carter and the Democratic party, and from many Third World governments. Whatever the merits of the argument, Kissinger strove to erase the image late in his term in office as secretary of state through trips to Africa and South America and through a consideration of proposals to tie the producer-consumer dialogue to larger Third World concerns. In this decision, there was a certain defensiveness about participation. Concessions regarding timing, participation, and substance came slowly, and with some reason. That the American government accepted the convergence of energy issues and Third World concerns at all arose not so much out of immediate state interests but out of a combination of political pressures associated with the presidential election year and external diplomatic forces. As we shall see shortly, this convergence was indeed something of a Trojan horse ridden skillfully by the OPEC leadership with predictable effect.

IEA and the CIEC Connection

Following two preparatory conferences and nine months of difficult bargaining, the structure of CIEC finally emerged. It consisted of four commissions on energy, raw materials, development, and finance. Each commission had fifteen members, five representing the industrial states and ten representing the oil exporting and non-oil developing states. Delegates represented in all twenty-six states plus the European Community. Representatives from international organizations doing work in these areas also could observe the commission meetings. Each commission had co-chairmen drawn from each of the two principal groups of countries. The structure of the conference itself revealed something of the political dynamics underlying the debates.

Interestingly, Kuwait, Saudi Arabia, and the United Arab Emirates, states with per capita incomes rivaling and in some cases exceeding those of the industrial countries, were not represented by an autonomous OPEC grouping. Instead, the OPEC countries coalesced with the non-oil developing nations. The effect of this structure was to isolate the industrial countries and place them opposite a single bloc of developing nations composed of both poor non-oil and oil-rich societies.

A second aspect of the conference structure that indicated the direction of the dialogue was that IEA as an organization was not permitted observer status. Algeria argued that IEA was a "confrontational organization" (in contrast presumably to OPEC) and was not recognized by the OPEC group. IEA, it said, would emphasize too much the energy aspect of the conference. Unwilling to deny IEA observer status on the grounds that it was confrontational (as it and OPEC in truth are), the United States, Japan, and the European Community refused to accept this decision and allowed the preparatory conference to close without agreement. But the impact of these proceedings showed how deeply energy matters were buried in larger political considerations.

In order to try to channel the dialogue toward an energy focus, the United States stressed specific problems for the respective commissions to address. It outlined the need for careful analysis of energy supply, demand, and price questions and their impact on economic development. The argument here implied was that when the developing countries recognized the degree to which world economic recovery and their own hopes for economic growth were being damaged by proposed OPEC price hikes, they would begin to examine the political foundations of their relationship with the oil producers.

Second, the United States urged a quid pro quo for the transfer of industrial technology to the producer countries. Both the producer countries and the consumers should, it asserted, promote the development of new energy supplies. These supplies would benefit the global economy, and special effort would be made to locate energy-related technology in the non-oil developing countries.

Third, using the American proposals on raw materials submitted to the Seventh Special Session of the U.N. General Assembly in 1975, the United States was prepared to explore ways of maintaining long-term supplies of raw materials free of vacillations of price and on terms that were "remunerative" to producers and "fair" to consumers.[16]

Fourth, the United States sought to split the assignments of the Development Commission. On the one hand, the commission would attempt to recommend ways of accelerating growth for the poorest group of countries, partly through new financial arrangements jointly sponsored by both the industrial and the oil-rich countries. On the other hand, the commission would also have the goal of determining the cause of the large balance of payments deficits facing the non-oil countries of the Third World.

Fifth, the United States sought to allocate to the Financial Commission very general responsibilities of summary and coordination. But the United States also mentioned the need to study the condition affecting public and private foreign investment.

Each of these focuses suggests the orientation the United States and the other members of the IEA wanted to give to the conference. But these recommendations also indicate the distance separating the industrialized and the developing countries on most issues. It is instructive to interpret the diplomatic meaning underlying the proposals.

By seeking to obtain from OPEC a commitment jointly to develop new energy supplies, the United States sought two objectives simultaneously. First, it sought to get OPEC to help pay for some of the high-cost development of industrial technology, in return for which the oil producers would have access to the technology by the time their own oil fields began to empty. Second, the energy produced by the technology would both prolong the life of the oil reserves in the producer countries and help keep the interim price for oil down. Attractive though these benefits might be to OPEC, the cartel might still prefer to let the industrial countries pay for their own high-cost technology in the alternative energy field while enjoying high oil prices for as long as possible unimpeded by a spurt of new energy generation. The bait held out to the non-oil developing countries, namely, the transfer of this technology to them at some future time, was hardly attractive enough either to induce them to split their alliance with the OPEC nations or to exercise much influence on their rich allies. While the raw materials proposals were straight forward, they still left open the question of the level at which commodity prices would be stabilized. A commodity fund that sought to maintain price stability at mean price levels since 1945 would scarcely interest most commodity producing nations.

A better example of the strategy that the United States was pursuing at the CIEC involves the Development Commission, an organ of the conference that one might expect would be dominated by the proposals of the non-oil Third World countries. But by recommending both an exploration of joint financing arrangements with OPEC and a hard look at the cause of the current, increasing balance of payments deficits experienced by the poorest countries, the United States again sought to keep the conference energy aware. OPEC members could scarcely reject the joint financing arrangements without irritating their poorer non-oil associates. But if the OPEC countries rejected the joint proposal then some of the pressure would be taken off the United States and the other industrialized countries to increase their aid commitments in a period of slow recovery from the recession. Moreover, by linking the joint financing arrangements to an examination of the balance of payments difficulties of the poorest countries, the relationship between the oil price increases and the deficits should have become unmistakable. Again, the Third World governments, if they were honest with themselves, would have to question the degree to which their current allies were in fact increasingly responsible for their present financial and economic woe.

Forced into a dialogue that moved further and further away from the topic of energy distribution and supply, the United States therefore shaped its presentations so as to illuminate the problems high oil prices have created for the non-oil poor countries as well as the non-oil rich. Positions taken by the United States at CIEC did not necessarily reflect unwillingness to explore means of accelerating growth in the poor non-oil countries. What the positions did reflect was dissatisfaction with the way the conference had proceeded and the nature of the structural relationship within CIEC in which the IEA countries found themselves.

Let us now turn to a fuller discussion of the political bargaining and maneuver behind coalition formation within CIEC. In the process we shall attempt to shed light on the strategies of the respective blocs and on their decision options.

Strategies of the Bloc Partners. Earlier we argued that, for IEA, CIEC was a Trojan horse saddled by an OPEC rider. Inside that horse was a series of problems and issues that either could not be solved in the context of the energy debate or when left unsolved would embarrass the industrial countries to the advantage of the new oil-rich elite. In order to clarify this thesis, let us examine each coalition of states.

OPEC itself did not relish a dialogue with the industrialized consumer countries. The cartel was not anxious to test consumer solidarity or to give IEA greater international visibility. In fact, OPEC was not enthusiastic about entering a major international forum to discuss what it could do to assist the developing countries. There was always a risk that such a conference would backfire and that the poor countries would complain about their growing oil deficits. Within OPEC, opinion was greatly divided between the cautiousness of Saudi Arabia and Kuwait, which already had substantial assistance programs of their own, albeit very selective ones, and Algeria, which sought a world ideological role as the spearhead of the new international economic order. Participation in the conference created some internal dangers for OPEC as well. Members of the cartel range from extremely conservative, capitalist powers to states with the pretense of radical socialism such as Libya. The conference was likely to acquire a socialist flavor, thus causing discomfort for the most important oil states. Why, then, did OPEC embark on the CIEC course?

The answer is that OPEC had a choice and it selected the lesser of two evils. Either it could face IEA head-on at some later date, probably selected by the consumers after they had had a chance to complete their own internal negotiations. Or OPEC could attempt now to join the Third World campaign for a new economic order acting as the champion of the developing countries. Just as China had always been uncomfortable for reasons of political size as the vanguard of the Third World, now OPEC would feel somewhat uncomfortable in this role for reasons of wealth. But the opportunity to strengthen its strategic defenses through a political alliance with some of the most populous nations in the world, indeed the majority of the world's nations, was difficult to turn down. The association had the additional advantage of covering the OPEC flank by postponing a debate over the relationship between the oil producing countries and the non-oil poor. But the central advantage of this strategy for OPEC was that on the surface it met the IEA challenge for a dialogue, while preparing all kinds of diplomatic surprises for IEA once the conference began. The strategy blunted consumer solidarity without risking a frontal attack.

What were the options and interests of the Third World countries? Before sifting these in detail, let us note the governments representing the developing countries at the Paris preparatory conference. Brazil, India, and Zaire represented the developing consumer countries. Two of these countries are among the richer commodity producers; whereas the third, India, is one of the military giants of the world, ranking thirteenth in military expenditures, just after Canada and Iran. These governments are not so much representative of the poorest quarter of the world's population as they are representative of the most politically assertive of the developing states having the best prospects for becoming major regional and perhaps global powers.

As a group, the developing consumer countries faced an important strategic choice and the identity of their leadership affected this choice. Either they could accept the invitation of the United States to join the other consumer countries in a program to obtain compensation for lost revenues due to the oil price hikes. Or they could join with OPEC in a battle against the rich industrial nations. Neither choice was ideal, but one appeared to have higher long-term payoffs than the other.

If the developing consumer countries adopted the former course and got on the consumer bandwagon, they had a reasonable chance of correcting their balance of payments deficits due to oil and even perhaps of obtaining new financing arrangements or increased foreign assistance. But they would damage any chances of receiving OPEC assistance. This problem in itself was not large since the leaders—Brazil, Zaire, and India—were not receiving aid anyway for reasons of religion, political ideology, or wealth. More seriously, a shift toward the industrialized states would create one more fissure in the ranks of the Third World nations, separating previously important nonaligned states like Indonesia and Nigeria from other classical protagonists such as India. Finally, the option to join IEA looked to the Third World consumers more like a limited peasant uprising than a revolution to obtain broad objectives. Once the United States satisfied its energy dilemma, for example, its ardor to explore and further commercial concerns of Third World nations was likely to cool.

If, on the other hand, the developing consumer countries chose to ally themselves with the new-rich states of OPEC, they also ran the risk of being left behind. It is not at all clear, for example, that Venezuela or Nigeria or Indonesia or Iran wants to see regional rivals aided materially, and together OPEC covers most of the significant regions of poor countries in the world. An alliance with OPEC would also entail giving up any vociferous presentation of energy-related grievances to the producer nations. Moreover, if the cartel failed and prices tumbled, the Third World consumer countries would be back politically where they started.

Yet for several reasons a loose confederation of OPEC and poor consumer states was a likely event. In a way curious to the industrial countries, the poor consumer nations are very proud of OPEC. Like an ethnic boxer rising from the ghetto, OPEC has done what no other alliance or association of poor countries has succeeded in doing, that is, bloodied the nose of the rich nations while accelerating its own growth. Countries like Brazil and Zaire, furthermore, would like to see the cartel idea work in coffee or copper. Perhaps in jointly challenging the rich industrial countries, they hope, the magic of Aladdin's lamp will rub off on them. Long-term interests suggested to the Third World leadership that the leverage that only OPEC can apply on the industrial West and Japan will serve the objectives of many Third World countries better than an alternative alliance with the industrial consumers. Either way, desperation marks the efforts of the poor consumer nations.

From the perspective of the United States, the timing of CIEC was not satisfactory since solidarity was incomplete in IEA. But the United States had little choice. It had committed itself to dialogue with OPEC. Now OPEC had ensconced itself in CIEC, thus diffusing the issues and obscuring the questions of energy supply per se. If the United States refused to meet with the poor consumer countries and OPEC, it had to justify the policy both to the world and to the IEA membership arguing for a new interdependence and an end to confrontation. Taking a chance on the ability of IEA to hold together under bargaining pressure and on the capacity of the negotiators to keep the energy problem in front of the conference, the United States reluctantly agreed to broaden the dialogue, thus in effect forfeiting direct discussions with OPEC alone regarding price and purchasing adjustments.

Dependence and Cartel Politics. Dependency theory seeks to explain the poverty of Third World countries in terms of their subjugation to a core state or capitalist metropolis.[17] Dependency ostensibly emanates from loss of autonomy through private foreign investment and from unfair terms of trade that shift against primary commodity producers that must import industrial goods at inflated prices yet cannot control the market for their own produce. How does the confrontation between IEA and OPEC fit into this thesis of dependence?

For the orthodox dependistas, the OPEC price hikes must appear as a triumph for the free market since the dependency of the oil producing countries on the major oil companies and the industrial consumer countries has been broken. According to this view, IEA appears like a counter-revolutionary attempt by the consumer nations to restore the old imperialist controls; CIEC is seen as an attempt to extinguish the fuse of confrontation between the producers and consumers and steer the dialogue into more useful channels.

Another way of interpreting these events, however, is possible. If the oil producing countries were in fact politically and economically dependent upon the advanced industrial countries before 1973, the reverse is the case in 1977. The industrial consumer countries are at the mercy of OPEC oil policy today. But this raises the questions of how long oil markets will remain out of competitive disequilibrium and of whether dependency is a function of political power considerations or market supply and demand conditions, or both. In any case, dependency has been demonstrated to be reversible, and this demonstration will have further effects.

We may witness many attempts at repeating the demonstration in less profitable markets.[18] Moreover, under the prevailing conditions of dependency in the oil market, both the poor and the rich are dependent upon OPEC although for the rich countries this reliance may be balanced by OPEC dependence. The critical issue for CIEC and the Third World is whether in the current climate of confrontation the poorest quarter of the world's nations will benefit or will suffer additionally. An unfortunately high probability says that the "Fourth World" will in fact be worse off at the conclusion of the great oil dialogue.

COALITION FORMATION WITHIN IEA

Successful U.S. leadership within IEA is to some extent a function of the *cohesiveness* of the organization. A fragmented consumer agency composed of opposing coalitions of states is the antithesis of consumer solidarity. Regardless of its dedication, the United States is unlikely to be able to exercise leadership effectively if unity is lacking with respect to the central purposes of energy policy.

Cohesiveness of the consumer organization is in turn partly a function of how *similar* the member states are to one another in terms of *energy characteristics*. Unity is much more feasible in an organization in which all of the states, for example, share approximately the same degree of dependence on an external petroleum supplier. The more integrated the member states are in terms of foreign trade and the more similar they are regarding political and economic development, the greater the feasibility of consumer agreement. Similarity of energy and commercial characteristics is not sufficient for a unified energy outlook, but the absence of similarity

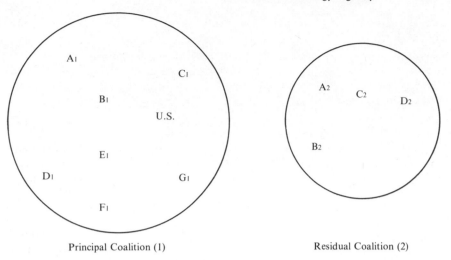

Principal Coalition (1)   Residual Coalition (2)

Figure V-1. Principal Coalition Model with U.S. Participation

diminishes the prospects of such a unified outlook. Similarity of cross-national behaviors and attributes may be thought of as the prerequisite of IEA unity and successful U.S. energy leadership among the industrialized consumer nations.

Models of Coalition Formation

At least three possible models of coalition formation depict the structural relationships within IEA: the Principal Coalition Model with U.S. Participation; the Principal Coalition Model without U.S. Participation; and the Decentralized Coalition Model.

In the Principal Coalition Model with U.S. Participation, the bulk of the states form a single coalition. The United States is a member of this coalition, thus facilitating leadership on consumer energy policy (Figure V–1). Other coalition members and the United States share a common set of energy characteristics. Perhaps less important than the nature of these characteristics is the fact of similarity and hence the potential congruence of energy outlook.

In the Principal Coalition Model without U.S. Participation, a single dominant coalition exists within IEA, but the United States is not a member (Figure V–2). The United States is isolated from the bulk of the other IEA members by a cluster of attributes and behaviors. This isolation hinders the formulation of a common basis for decisionmaking in energy matters. Rather than coordinate similar policy preferences, the United States must in this situation seek to create a common foundation for policy where there is none. When similarity of energy characteristics is lacking, a

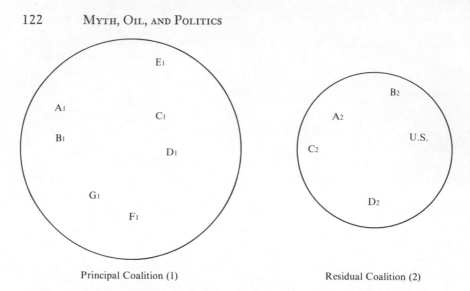

Principal Coalition (1)   Residual Coalition (2)

Figure V-2. Principal Coalition Model Without U.S. Participation

tendency emerges toward policymaking by hegemony instead of policy-making by consensus.

In the Decentralized Coalition Model, numerous small, fragmented groupings of states proliferate within the organization (Figure V–3). A condition of structural anarchy prevails. It is not especially important which coalition the United States joins because there is very little similar-ity between any single cluster of states and the others. The problem for

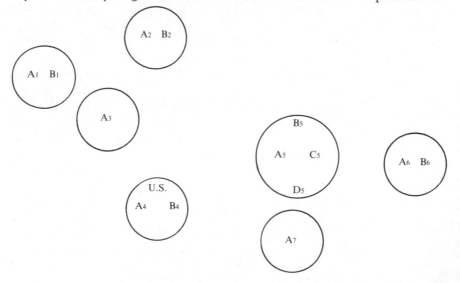

Figure V-3. Decentralized Coalition Model

the leadership is not so much that its energy interests and those of another important coalition are at odds—as in the previous model—but that there *is no* dominant set of interests within the organization. One can expect drift and political uncertainty to follow from such a decentralized coalitional milieu.

Q-Factor Analysis of State Energy Characteristics

By examining the similarity of energy characteristics across the IEA membership via a suitable statistical technique, we shall attempt to reject the null hypothesis of U.S. participation in a principal coalition of member states. Either absence of a principal coalition or absence of U.S. membership in such a coalition would technically meet the requirements of the test, signifying that the IEA is unlikely to follow the U.S. lead in energy matters on the basis of a communality of political understanding.[19]

A particularly suitable technique for this purpose is Q-factor analysis of the principal components type employing a varimax orthogonal rotation.[20] This technique has several attractive properties. It yields "factors," or coalitional clusters of states, that are statistically "orthogonal," that is, independent or uncorrelated. In this sense the clusters may be thought of as behaviorally autonomous. Second, the technique reduces the variation in data set to "simple structure." The *smallest number* of possible autonomous factors, or clusters of *states*, results from the analysis. Third, the comparative *weight*, or *importance*, of each resulting *coalitional factor* is indicated by the percentage of statistical variance explained by the factor. Fourth, the comparative *importance* of each *state* within each coalitional factor is measured by the factor loading, or coefficient, associated with each state. Fifth, calculation of factor scores enables one to determine the degree to which each of the original indexes such as crude oil imports is responsible for the creation of a particular coalition grouping of states. Thus, factor analysis supplies perhaps more useful statistical information regarding coalition structure than virtually any other technique.

However, use of the technique must be qualified in two significant ways. Unless the analyst begins with a clearly formulated hypothesis or other theoretical insight regarding the nature of the anticipated coalition structure, the approach may resemble an empirical "fishing expedition" rather than legitimate research. Furthermore, Q-factor analysis is excessively sensitive to gross variations in the range of the indexes employed. In order to counteract this tendency, the analyst must first "standardize" the raw data by using a method such as Z-scoring, which yields indexes displaying a mean value of 0 and a standard deviation of 1. Appendix I to this chapter lists the thirty-nine indexes used in this study to measure the economic, political, and energy characteristics of the IEA membership.

Turning to the empirical findings in Table V–1, we observe that the

TABLE V-1. Coalitions within the International Energy Agency

	Principal Coalition (Factor 1)	Residual Coalition (Factor 2)	Communality
Denmark	.990	.016	.980
Belgium	.986	.022	.973
Austria	.985	.057	.974
Sweden	.981	.032	.964
Spain	.978	−.034	.958
France	.978	.016	.956
Switzerland	.977	.067	.960
Netherlands	.967	−.032	.937
Italy	.967	.010	.935
Ireland	.963	−.075	.933
United Kingdom	.952	.181	.940
Canada	.926	.114	.871
Turkey	.885	−.185	.818
Japan	.885	−.008	.783
Germany	.854	.060	.733
United States	.019	.992	.985
% Variance	85.1	6.7	
Cumulative %	85.1	91.9	

null hypothesis of U.S. membership in the principal coalition has been rejected. Not only did the factor results yield a principal coalition and a residual coalition as predicted, but the principal coalition accounted for 85 percent of the variance and fifteen of the sixteen sample countries (including France, the government that had adopted the antithesis of the American energy position). Alone on the residual coalition, the United States revealed its isolation in energy terms. Japan, Canada, and Europe demonstrated much more affinity for each other than for the United States. Under these circumstances, leadership within the IEA is understandably difficult for the United States.

Indicating the extent to which the analysis captured the contribution of each state to the factor structure, the communalities varied from a low of .73 for the Federal Republic of Germany to a high of .98 for the United States. Despite generally very high communalities across the sample, Germany and Japan were partial exceptions, suggesting that some important variance in energy matters may have been missing from the data set, a point addressed in Chapter VII.

Interpretation of the coalition structure is perhaps more complete when discussed in the light of the factor scores (Appendix II to this chapter), which show the association between each index, such as oil imports, and each coalition of states. The United States appears to have fallen into the residual coalition because of a strong capital flow position, its organizational participation, its extensive lignite production, and a combination of a relatively high petroleum-to-total-energy ratio plus relatively low dependence on Middle East oil per se. While this dependence increased rapidly after 1972, the United States obtained most of its imported petroleum at that time from Venezuela, Canada, and North Africa—more secure sources of supply in the opinion of many IEA members. Similarly, the United States imported far more goods from Israel than the average IEA member and pursued a much more autonomous foreign policy.

In short, these empirical results reveal an extraordinary cleavage between the United States and its allies regarding energy characteristics. Our theoretical insight into the nature of IEA coalition structure has been completely reinforced by these empirical findings. Unable to depend upon a similarity of energy characteristics between itself and the remainder of IEA, the United States is not likely to be able to obtain a favorable consensus on energy policy. In the absence of such consensus, political domination would have to replace efforts at coordinated leadership, an option that itself is not very politically attractive.

THE MEASURE OF ACHIEVEMENT

Preparations for the Washington energy conference indicated that consumer solidarity faced strains of a commercial and political variety. Throughout the CIEC negotiations, these strains complicated the effort of the IEA leadership to maintain desired energy focus. France's unwillingness to join IEA first highlighted the lack of cohesion among the industrial consumers. But the nomination, by the European ministers, of the Organization for Economic Co-Operation and Development (OECD) rather than IEA as the appropriate forum to study joint energy policy showed that stress was more pervasive than many observers had expected. What is the impact of such organizational and structural cleavage on consumer energy policy?

Heterogeneity of Energy Interests

National energy policies are linked to state interests and these interests seem to vary broadly.

First, Europe, Japan, and the United States differ greatly in their dependence on imported energy in general and on OPEC oil in particular.[21] Japan imports more than 90 percent of its coal and oil. Europe is less dependent upon imports of total energy than Japan since some countries like the Federal Republic of Germany have sizable coal deposits, but since 1960 Europe more than doubled its imports of oil from OPEC sources. Prior to 1973, the United States imported less than a third of its petroleum requirements, but three years later that figure had increased to more than 50 percent. The general picture is clear: Japan is the most dependent upon foreign sources of oil and total energy, followed in turn by Europe, the United States, and finally countries like Canada that still produce large and increasing amounts of domestic oil.

Second, a great difference in the rate of increase in energy consumption separate the IEA members.[22] Prior to 1973 world demand for energy was increasing at about 4.5 percent. On the average, European demand increased at a slightly higher rate, but more important the rate of increase varied from a low of 2 percent for a country like Britain to 10 percent for Italy. The United States appeared to be on a curve of rapid increase in demand in the late 1960s because of the increased use of air conditioning and of electrical processes in industry and because of constraints imposed by environmental issues. Japan exceeded all members with an average annual increase in energy consumption of 12 percent. Thus, again, Japan was far more sensitive on the demand side to the energy crisis than other IEA members.

Conversely, since the United States consumed energy at a far higher level than other members such as Germany and Sweden with a corresponding per capita wealth, the United States had far greater opportunity to save energy through conservation. From the perspective of the other IEA members, the United States was both *increasing* its rate of energy consumption by a smaller margin than some members and consuming at a higher *level*, thus if necessary allowing a margin of constraint. This suggested—in conjunction with its lower fraction of energy imports—less foreign energy dependence for the United States. Less foreign energy dependence meant more room for diplomatic maneuver in dealing with OPEC policies than other IEA nations felt they enjoyed.

Third, the energy outlook was quite different for member states because of differing proposed strategies to solve their energy problems. At one extreme Canada was relatively energy independent (exporting natural gas to the United States) and benefiting from the oil price rise as an incentive for greater domestic exploration and production. Likewise, Norway and Britain, having large investments in high-cost North Sea oil and with the objective of becoming possible net exporters of petroleum in the next few years, continued to favor a high world price for oil. West Germany, in contrast, had to turn to its coal reserves and atomic energy to replace foreign oil. Japan, at the other extreme, continued to seek favorable deals with oil producers, exchanging technology and manufactured goods for assured access to oil at the market price. The problem with Japan's policy was that it could not afford to offend, or use leverage against, any of the oil producers because of its own extreme vulnerability to supply interruption. Meanwhile, the United States was vacillating between get-tough policies verging on threats of military intervention and promises of energy independence to pleas for consumer cooperation within IEA and "interdependence" with the producers. Failure even to decontrol the domestic price of oil and gas suggested that American energy policy was lukewarm about either ending its own energy disparity or leading a collective international response to achieve the same objective at the international level. Despite the rhetoric, the other IEA members have concluded that the United States favors collaboration with the producers rather than confrontation, and they do not want to appear to take a position tougher than the perceived U.S. position.

Lethargy of the Middle Classes

Petroleum myth has in part created the atmosphere where a change in energy policy requires a careful mobilization of support epitomized by Jimmy Carter's "moral equivalent of war." Throughout the industrial democracies, however, a deeper problem has been the unwillingness of the middle classes, long accustomed to comfort, extraordinary individual mobility, and cheap energy, to sacrifice or to adjust to the new energy situation. How else can we explain the resistance of the U.S. electorate (and through it the Congress) to decontrol of gas and oil prices in order both to save energy and to encourage new exploration, especially by wildcatters and independents. In order to support our assertion that it is the middle class and not the inner-city poor or the workers who are most opposed to a more rational energy policy, thus undercutting international efforts within IEA, let us review briefly certain patterns of energy consumption.

Slightly more than one-third of all energy consumed in the United States for example is for *personal* use for heating, cooking, operating appliances, air conditioning homes, and personal transportation.[23] Another large percentage is probably concealed in the choice of construction materials and in the production of energy-intensive consumer goods. The upturn in the rate of U.S. energy consumption since 1948 has for the most part occurred in areas that appeal to middle-class tastes: e.g., automotive horsepower, aluminum, active ingredients in detergents, plastics, and no-return beer bottles. The poor consume energy much less lavishly. Although the poor account for 18 percent of all households, they use only 5 percent of the gasoline. They own fewer cars and their cars get better gas mileage. They drive less for non-business-related purposes. They live closer to their places of work and they use public transportation more frequently.

A disproportionate percentage of blacks are poor, and black households use less than three-quarters the amount of energy per household than whites despite poorer home insulation and more inefficient heating and cooling systems. Much of the disparity in energy consumption between blacks and whites stems from the lower standard of living of the former group. But even for households at approximately the same income level, blacks tend to use less energy than the whites, who have been accustomed to luxury over a longer time period.

But the fact that the poor consume less energy, partially for income reasons, partially out of a habit of thrift, does not mean that the incidence of conservation programs is easier for the poor. Since the poor have less disposable income than the rich, energy price increases hurt the poor disproportionately. It does not seem plausible to penalize those segments of the population that are already the most thrifty. In order to promote efficient energy use as well as equity, various schemes of income protection, tax rebates, or direct subsidies could correct the effects of inequities when the price of energy rises. But the middle class will have to support such legislation and so far it has shown small inclination to do so.

The difficulty the Carter administration experienced in gaining acceptance for the stand-by gasoline tax of up to 5 cents per gallon annually shows the reluctance of the middle class to admit to the earnestness of the U.S. oil dilemma. It is a reluctance founded foremost on the desire to retain comfort and luxury since the cost of the tax could easily be overcome simply by driving smaller, more economical cars. The inability of the United States to achieve a balanced, comprehensive energy policy has created a credibility gap at the top of the IEA leadership.

Circle of Fragmentation and Loss of Market Control

Market conditions have much to do with the probability of success for the IEA. From the political perspective IEA unity is most needed, and is in some sense most feasible, when the member states face an immediate common threat to their welfare. Current conditions ought to favor this type of unity. But from the economic perspective the opposite is the case. Loss of market control contributes to the dissolution of consumer solidarity or prevents the emergence of that solidarity. Market control and fragmentation vary inversely. The greater the market control of the member states, the less the fragmentation of their own consumer solidarity, and vice versa. Thus, the circle of division must be broken, under present economic conditions of OPEC dominance, by political resolve among the IEA members, much as division among potential military allies is overcome through recognition that the collective security of the unified alliance is greater than the summed securities of the individual parts. Politics must supplant the countercurrent of economic insufficiency.

Another way of looking at the circle of *consumer division* is in terms of the balance of organizational forces. The sequela of OPEC's cohesion and success is IEA's fragmentation and failure. There is no necessary, or deterministic, relationship between producer unity and consumer disunity, but there is a *tendency* for the relationship to obtain. As long as demand and supply conditions continue to support unity within the producer cartel, the cartel is in a position to promote division among the IEA members. This can be done through the creation of an auctionlike atmosphere in which the consumer governments, or the intermediaries, the companies, must bid against one another for petroleum contracts. As long as OPEC keeps its production levels low enough and as long as consumer demand continues to grow at a superior pace, OPEC can discourage a government like France from joining a cohesive consumer association through a combination of commercial inducements and the veiled punitive action of supply interruption should the government vigorously support consumer solidarity.

Thus the circle of consumer division is itself an obstacle to IEA success. The greater the loss of market control on the consumer side, the more the fragmentation of IEA in commercial terms. So far, a strong OPEC and a lack of sufficient political cohesiveness among IEA members have contributed to the IEA inability to formulate vigorous, binding policies capable of influencing price.

SUMMARY: BILATERALISM, MULTILATERALISM, AND THE FUTURE

IEA has built a foundation to cope with commercial emergencies. There can be little doubt about the reality of its accomplishments in this area. It has not, however, been able to surmount a national consumer policy of bilateralism. *Multilateral negotiation* with the producers through IEA has not changed OPEC strategy or obtained concessions because so little truly multilateral bargaining has occurred. All of the really significant exchanges of technology in return for guarantees of market access, for example, have been bilateral—and all consumer governments, including the United States, have participated in this activity.

Some slight tendency for government-to-government sales of petroleum circumventing the major companies has been noted, for instance with Iran in 1976. Unhappy with the quantity of oil purchased by the Consortium, the shah instructed the National Iranian Oil Company itself to sell oil directly to consumer governments, and with some success. This behavior could increase competition within the oil market, driving prices down somewhat, but the practice has little to do with IEA unity. IEA unity is in no way responsible for this development within the world oil market and would not necessarily contribute to or benefit from direct government-to-government petroleum sales.

Summing up the attitude of OPEC toward the current institutional threat presented by IEA, the magazine the *Middle East* observed,

The West has talked so much of crisis about oil in the last 18 months that it is difficult to understand why its various nations continue to behave economically as though there were no crisis at all, in spite of rampant inflation and the five-fold increase in the price of oil. More and more government attempts—in most cases halfhearted anyway—to cope with the impact of the energy crisis have been hampered by a growing attitude that says there is no crisis at all. . . . In consequence the West can be expected both to absorb the five-fold price increases and to be forced to pay even more.[24]

If IEA at one time possessed deterrent value regarding higher prices, that deterrent effect in the OPEC view has long since worn off. It appears that if market transformation does occur, the IEA attempt at broad, multilateral consumer solidarity will not be responsible.

APPENDIX I: INDICATORS OF ENERGY AND STATE CHARACTERISTICS FOR IEA MEMBERS[1]

1. Index of membership in international cooperative organizations[2]
   GATT = 2, NATO = 1, EEC = 3, Euratom = 2
   EFTA = 3, ECSC = 3, OECD = 2, IEA = 4
2. Total imports of country, 1972[3]
3. Total exports of country[3]
4. Population in millions, estimated for 1972[4]
5. Coal production, 1972[4]
6. Coal reserves, 1970[4]
7. Lignite production, 1972[4]
8. Lignite reserves, 1970[4]
9. Crude oil reserves, 1970[4]
10. Natural gas reserves, 1970[4]
11. Total energy production, 1972[4]

[1] Selection and interpretation of indicators was based on the answer to this question: Does the indicator affect the foreign energy dependence of the consumer nations? If the answer is affirmative, we included the indicator. But the impact could be either (a) to increase or (b) to decrease energy dependence. If (a) is true, a higher value on an indicator will record greater energy dependence. If (b) is true, the opposite is the case; hence, to retain consistency of theoretical meaning, the index had to be inverted. The following indexes fell into category (b): 2, 4, 12, 13, 16, 17, 18, 19, 20, 24, 25, 26, 31, 33, 34, 35, 36, 37, 38, 39.

[2] GATT, General Agreement on Tariffs and Trade; NATO, North Atlantic Treaty Organization; EEC, European Economic Community; EURATOM, European Atomic Energy Community; EFTA, European Free Trade Area; ECSC, European Coal and Steel Community; OECD, Organization for Economic Co-Operation and Development; and IEA, International Energy Agency.

[3] United Nations, *Yearbook of International Trade Statistics, 1972–1973* (New York: United Nations Department of Economic and Social Affairs, Statistical Office, 1974).

[4] United Nations, *Statistical Yearbook, 1973* (New York: United Nations Department of Economic and Social Affairs, Statistical Office, 1974).

12. Total energy consumption, 1972[4]
13. Energy consumption per capita, 1970[4]
14. Total energy from nuclear sources, 1972[4]
15. Total land area[4]
16. Crude birthrate per thousand population, 1972[4]
17. Number of unemployed persons, 1972[4]
18. Percentage of work force unemployed,[4] 1972
19. Number of passenger cars in use[4]
20. Percentage of economically active population in agriculture, 1972[5]
21. Net capital flow, 1972[6]
22. Capital reserves[6]
23. Production of domestic crude oil, 1972[4]
24. Oil imports as a percentage of total imports, 1970[7]
25. Change in consumer price index from 1971 to 1972, $\dfrac{B-A}{A}$[4]
26. Percentage crude oil, feedstocks, and components coming from the Middle East, 1970[7]
27. GNP, 1972[8]
28. Growth in GNP, 1971 to 1972[8]
29. Dollar value of total imports from other consumer nations, 1972[9]
30. Dollar value of total exports to other consumer nations, 1972[9]
31. Imports by consumer nations from OPEC nations, 1972[9]
32. Exports from consumer nations to OPEC nations, 1972[9]
33. Imports of consumer nations from Israel, 1972[9]
34. Exports from consumer nations to Israel, 1972[9]
35. Oil consumption as a percentage of total energy consumption, 1970[7]
36. Net imports of crude petroleum, 1972[3]
37. Net imports of petroleum products, 1972[3]
38. Net imports of natural and manufactured gas, 1972[3]
39. Net imports of coal and coke briquets, 1972[3]

[5] United Nations, Food and Agriculture Organization, *Production Yearbook*, Vol. 26 (Rome: United Nations, Food and Agriculture Organization, 1974).

[6] International Monetary Fund, Balance of Payments Division, *Balance of Payments Yearbook, 1969–1973*, Vol. 26 (Washington, D.C.: International Monetary Fund, 1974–1975).

[7] Organization for Economic Co-Operation and Development, *Oil: The Present Situation* (Paris: Organization for Economic Co-Operation and Development, 1973).

[8] *The World Almanac and Book of Facts, 1975* (New York: Doubleday and Co., 1975).

[9] International Monetary Fund, Statistics Bureau, *Direction of Trade, Annual 1969–1973* (Washington, D.C.: International Monetary Fund, and the International Bank for Reconstruction and Development, 1974).

APPENDIX II: Coalitions within the International Energy Agency: Factor Score Results

Index	Principal Coalition	Residual Coalition
1	−.898	−1.372
2	1.003	−.819
3	−.987	−.094
4	1.032	−.946
5	−1.058	.540
6	−1.066	.542
7	−.914	−1.347
8	−1.066	.526
9	−1.056	.483
10	−1.055	.470
11	−1.065	.554
12	1.059	−1.234
13	1.005	−.720
14	−1.048	.519
15	−1.019	−.019
16	.906	1.270
17	1.056	−1.226
18	.960	.291
19	1.056	−1.223
20	.893	1.460
21	−.852	−2.338
22	−1.043	.326
23	−1.066	.534
24	.878	.936
25	.871	1.649
26	.849	1.700
27	−1.053	.487
28	−.951	−1.182
29	−1.003	.056
30	−.978	−.221
31	.941	−.043
32	−1.013	.184
33	1.065	−1.222
34	1.022	−1.015
35	.869	1.144
36	.933	.060
37	1.014	−.562
38	.969	−.083
39	.808	1.936

VI

OPEC Cohesion:
The Myth of Perpetual Unity

Perhaps no other myth in the great petroleum polemic is currently as compelling as that of OPEC cohesion. We must explore the grounds for the faith in this myth expressed both inside OPEC and among the consumer nations. We must also consider the changing structure of OPEC as it relates to cohesion and to the nature of coalition formation within OPEC. Whether OPEC oil revenue can legitimately be treated as a collective good or whether various obstacles to cohesion are likely to drive OPEC governments increasingly toward autonomous policies is reserved for the final section.

Origins of Cohesion

Two questions dominate the discussion of the origins of OPEC cohesion.[1] The first concerns the timing of collusion in the fall of 1973 and the winter of 1974. Why should such an enormous change in market pricing have occurred so abruptly? If we can understand the basis of this change, perhaps we can find the key to the success of OPEC collusion.

The second question involves the future maintenance of cartel cohesion. By exhuming the arguments supporting future cartel cohesion, perhaps we can ascertain the likelihood that OPEC will be able to retain control of the market, push prices for oil still higher, and transfer a significant share of the national product of the advanced industrial countries to the producer world. Strongly held, the arguments are thought by proponents to be sufficient to justify faith in unified cartel policies.

The Timing of Cohesion

At least four sets of interrelated forces seem to underlie the surprising capture of the oil market by OPEC within a five-month period: runaway world energy demand, lagging non-OPEC petroleum supply, an indispensable lesson in price psychology and manipulation, and coercion of the majors by the OPEC governments. Let us consider briefly how each of these forces enabled OPEC to conquer the petroleum export market.[2]

For years energy consumption had been climbing in the advanced industrial countries. Moderate projections of a U.N. study completed in 1972 anticipated oil consumption to increase through 1980 at an annual percentage rate of 12.7 for Japan, 7.4 for Western Europe, and 3.9 for North America.[3] Third World countries began to use large amounts of petroleum as development programs improved transportation routes and expanded construction of electric utilities. Reacting to the environmental alarm of the Stockholm conference, electric utilities throughout the advanced industrial countries attempted to clean up emissions not by purchase of expensive stack cleaners and other costly abatement technology but by switching to relatively sulfur-free petroleum. Set against a recent history of unusual growth, world demand for oil shot upward in 1973 because of an abnormally cold winter and the crash response to environmental legislation.

A common assumption of a number of the oil companies in the early 1970s was that for the balance of the decade petroleum production would expand to meet the dictates of energy demand. Nothing could have been more illusory. Not only was U.S. petroleum production actually falling by 1972, but extraction of new, North Slope oil in Alaska had been delayed. When the Saudi government began to realize in the spring of 1973 that Aramco had plans to expand Saudi production to 20 million barrels a day within a decade, the government's planning minister and his staff began to warn King Faisal of the negative consequences for the nation of depletion of Saudi Arabia's enormous petroleum reserves. Surely the worldwide specter of limits to growth and resource scarcity ideas unveiled at approximately the same time had an additional intellectual impact.[4] Venezuela, Kuwait, and Canada all began talking about conservation for conservation's sake rather than simply for economic reasons. The result for world petroleum production was contraction in growth at a time when distortions in distribution were already forcing supply in some areas to lag behind the demand that otherwise would have occurred at prevailing prices.

Collusion was always theoretically possible. That was what OPEC had been about since its birth in 1960. But a political shock was required to show how the simple idea of price increases and production cuts could simultaneously be implemented across the complex OPEC market. That shock was the decision of OAPEC, the Arab producer organization, to interrupt supplies to the West for political reasons. Unlike the production increase reaction to the Arab oil embargo after 1967, the Iranian response in 1973 was to increase prices rather than production, yielding the same effect of vastly increased revenue. Collective decisionmaking requirements to coordinate price increases and production cutbacks were minimal at a time when world oil demand had outstripped supply. Price simply found its upper bound in sales of petroleum to firms that tended to compete in an auctionlike atmosphere, pushed in some cases by frightened governments like France and Japan in search of advantageous bilateral deals. Only because production cuts were real in 1973 was it possible for the OPEC governments to raise petroleum prices and make them stick. This was the genius of the new price psychology.

An uncooperative oil industry might have quashed the collusion effort. But a happenstance of international politics ensured industrial cooperation with the OPEC governments. Incremental nationalization was taking away the upstream assets and privileges and chipping away at the profits of the multinationals. The weakness of the corporate bargaining positions was made clear when governments in Libya, Iraq, and elsewhere demonstrated that they could wrest control of oil operations from the multinational companies. By refusing to compensate the companies fully or push nationalization to completion immediately, the producer governments held open the possibility of better treatment and satisfactory agreements in the post-nationalization phase of relations in exchange for the companies' cooperation with OPEC policy. Having thus lost control of oil operations and lacking political support from the industrial governments as well, the multinationals capitulated to OPEC, enforcing its price policies, collecting its taxes, and selling its refined petroleum worldwide.

Only a combination of these forces of runaway demand, lagging supply, a new price awareness, and industrial coercion could have had such unexpected consequences for OPEC in so short a time. Conspiracy among the producer governments had less to do with the result than a series of accidents of history. Once concerted, however, the powers of collusion would not easily be defused nor offset politically.

The Maintenance of Cohesion

Forces responsible for the initial success of a cartel may not be the same forces carrying the burden of long-term cohesion. Maintenance of cohesion entails a capacity to deal with a changing set of market conditions, new entrants to the market, and the possible emergence of internal tensions and disputes. In the case of OPEC a number of arguments have been advanced in defense of the cartel's capacity to meet these challenges. A brief statement of this position will reveal the grounds for the optimism of the cartel leadership.

Collective Interest in Price Moderation. According to one industry source, the members of OPEC would be "fools" if they failed to recognize the common interest they have in unity. More compelling than economic incentives alone, this awareness that unity is basic to individual benefits is a new consciousness fixed deeply in the energy policy of each member government. Regardless of apparent differences over price strategy or the distribution of revenue, moderation of actual commercial behavior is likely to prevail in this view for evident reasons of collective self-interest.

Scope of Saudi Leverage.   Saudi Arabia, as the price leader within the cartel, has the capacity to enforce a degree of cohesion that complements collective incentives for unity. Saudi leverage stems from a number of origins. Most fundamental is the enormous petroleum reserve of the country, which will keep its pumps busy into the second quarter of the twenty-first century. Its reserves exceed anything available to other OPEC members by a factor of three or better. Since Saudi Arabia has a small population, its need for revenue (capital absorption capability) is minimal. Consequently, with the largest daily production of oil of any OPEC member, Saudi Arabia possesses huge financial reserves, which place the country among the top three producing nations worldwide. Huge financial reserves enable Saudi Arabia to ride out attempted consumer boycotts of Saudi oil. Financial reserves also provide direct leverage within OPEC through grants to poorer states or states disadvantaged by allocation schemes or pricing. Outside OPEC, financial assistance influences vote patterns in the United Nations and dampens criticism of OPEC policies.

The combination of huge financial and petroleum reserves gives Saudi Arabia considerable production flexibility, from a few million barrels a day to over 11 million, allowing the Saudi government to affect price unilaterally over short periods and thereby maintain discipline and satisfaction within OPEC. Should a member attempt to bolt the cartel to obtain a preferential commercial deal, Saudi Arabia could suddenly expand production and thereby undercut the price offered by the delinquent cartel member, thus discouraging pursuit of unilateral deals. By reducing production gradually, Saudi Arabia can allow other OPEC members in greater need of revenue to produce at a higher rate. Either way, Saudi Arabia retains control over the OPEC export market.

With huge petroleum reserves and a small population, Saudi Arabia is not likely to lose its leadership role quickly. Awareness that Saudi Arabia has a long-term commitment to cartel leadership generates a type of legitimacy for this role that further strengthens the Saudi voice in OPEC affairs.

Alignment of the Oil Industry.   Having gained control of all oil production and pricing decisions, OPEC still must rely on multinational corporations for marketing. Cooperation of the major oil companies, albeit initially coerced, remains important if the producers are to get large quantities of oil to retail outlets efficiently. Vertical integration of the industry works as satisfactorily with OPEC calling the signals as if the majors were still in control of short-term market decisions. The OPEC leadership is confident that the major oil corporations will recognize their mutual interest in retaining some discipline in marketing operations.

A second contribution the largest corporations provide is information. Saudi Arabia needs information regarding potential cheaters trying to market oil by shaving the price. Analysis of integrated markets available to the largest corporations provides virtually a daily account of trade flows and thus an invaluable monitor to the price leader in the cartel. According to this argument, so long as the major corporations recognize that cheating is not in their own interest, the stability of the OPEC-industrial relationship is likely to remain intact.

Demand Resurgence.   From one perspective the OPEC governments believe they have achieved collusion at a less than propitious moment and, accordingly, that success under these circumstances indicates the true strength of the cartel. The circumstances are the conditions of recession and industrial slowdown, which have concurrently reduced the demand for petroleum and thus, notwithstanding the price increases, placed a revenue strain on certain OPEC members. With recovery, the leadership reasons, demand for petroleum will return to a somewhat more normal growth rate despite the higher petroleum prices. If collusion can succeed in a period of recession, it should surely prosper, based on the promise of rising demand, in a period of economic expansion.

High Cost of Energy Substitution.   A final source of considerable confidence among the oil producers stems from their awareness of obstacles to the exploitation of new sources of energy by the consumers. Their first observation is that all new energy sources—coal liquification and gasification, shale oil, breeder reactors, solar energy, or simply new discoveries of petroleum—are high-cost propositions. Implicitly this fact builds a price floor under the posted price for OPEC crude. But OPEC is aware also that insofar as the private sector must undertake development projects, ample incentives and investment security must be provided. OPEC is somewhat skeptical that the consumer governments are prepared to offer either the incentives or the security. Since seven to ten years is required for most prospects to yield results, a considerable interval is available in which to maximize OPEC gains without significantly hastening substitution. Insofar as an enlarged effort to discover new deposits of oil or to develop new sources of energy is postponed, OPEC faces even less danger of substitution.

Environmental concerns are associated with a number of the plans for energy independence in the consumer countries. The producers count on the environmental trade-off to hinder the development of offshore oil and to discourage construction of much refinery capacity in the advanced industrial countries. Shale oil, with a ratio of one barrel of oil per nearly three tons of high-grade shale rock, is virtually prohibitive in environmental terms to develop on a large scale. Besides an initial cost of about

$20 a barrel (1975 prices), shale oil will cause secondary pollution and a drain on scarce water resources, making it even less attractive. Energy substitution in the OPEC viewpoint is for these reasons not a very urgent threat to cartel cohesion.

ECONOMIC THEORY OF CARTELS

Since the work of Augustin Cournot (1838), the question of the stability of markets dominated by a few sellers has been of continuing interest to economists.[5] Emerging from the theoretical debate regarding cartel stability in the writings of Bertrand, Edgeworth, Hotelling, Sweezy, Hitch, Chamberlain, and others is the view that conclusions about stability are in part dependent upon the assumptions one makes concerning the complexity of the market and the degree of knowledge shared by the cartel members.[6] Demonstrating the *incentives to cheat* for the member of a cartel is rather an easy matter; demonstrating its *capacity to cheat* successfully, as we shall see in a moment, is much more problematic.

We now apply to OPEC the same graphical representation of oligopolistic behavior depicted in Chapter IV (Figure IV-1). We add a second demand curve *dd* and corresponding marginal revenue curve *mr* representing the market situation facing an individual member of the cartel that attempts to cheat (Figure VI-1). The chief difference between these curves and those for the cartel as a whole (*DD* and *MR*) is that the curves for the individual member are much less steep, that is, more elastic. Demand for the individual members is assumed to be much more subject to price than is true for the cartel as a whole. The individual cartel member can increase or decrease price and obtain a much greater change in the quantity of oil sold than the cartel acting as a whole in the market (this is equivalent to the argument of the significance of insignificance for the individual producer).

If OPEC elects to set a collusive price *P'* at the point at which marginal revenue *MR* and marginal cost *MC* for the cartel as a whole meet, the cartel sells *OQ* quantity of oil at price *P*, the collusive price. If an individual producer decides to cheat, however, and the other members adhere to the pricing agreement, allowing the cheater to succeed, the individual producer would lower its price to P', increase its quantity of oil sold to Q', and thus enjoy a revenue bonus of P'C'QQ', an ample reward. Thus, incentives to cheat seem so great that one may wonder why cartel stability prevails at all.

But when we turn to Figure VI-2 (p. 140) the phenomenon of *administered price* (or of "kinked demand," as it is called in textbook economics) helps explain why price is so sticky and stability not so easily upset. The point C is the critical price for the cartel and it occurs at the kink in the demand curve, where other members of the cartel reduce price as well

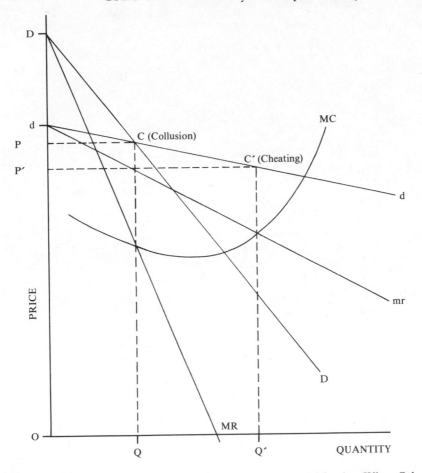

Figure VI-1. Incentive to Surreptitious Cheating by Cartel Member When Other Members Hold Price Constant

(that is, the point at which *DD* and *dd'* meet). Above C the individual producer raises price and moves along *dd* at its own peril because the remaining members of the cartel refuse to go along and simply expand their market share at its expense. Below C the individual producer may attempt to cheat by lowering the price, but here the other members of the cartel join and demand moves along *DD*, the demand curve for the state under conditions of joint price movement. The other members of the cartel refuse to allow any single member by itself to lower price and thus earn a revenue bonus. In consequence, price tends to rest at C—the "posted," or agreed, sale price for oil.

Because of the kinked demand curve at C the effect on the marginal revenue curve is to introduce a vertical segment *FH* between the marginal revenue curve *mr* for the individual producer and the marginal revenue curve *MR* for the cartel as a whole. Again, if the individual producer

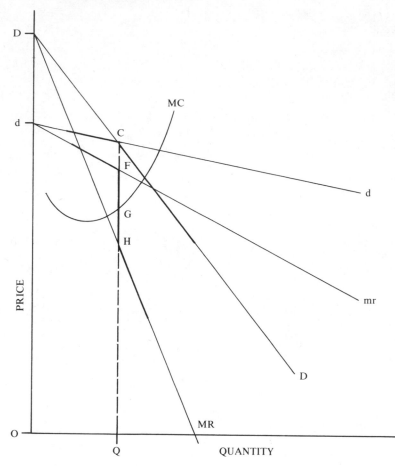

Figure VI-2. Administrated Prices Achieved by Cartel Leadership

should attempt to raise price alone, marginal revenue increases slowly along *dF*; if the state tries to cheat by lowering price, marginal revenue drops from *F* to *H* and from there along *MR* for the cartel as a whole. Thus, by attempting to cheat, the individual state suffers an immediate and precipitous decline in marginal revenue, a sufficient deterrent to delinquency, perhaps, for most cartel members.

One feature of this representation that is of some interest is the range *FH* over which the marginal cost curve *MC* could vary and still provide a maximum return to the cartel. Thus, room for cost variation is another reason why analysts credit administered prices with strengthening cartel cohesion.

We draw two conclusions from this analysis regarding cartel stability. First, cartel cohesion ought to remain quite high even over a range of cost differentials for cartel members. This range widens as demand inelasticity increases. Stated in opposite terms, however, as demand becomes more elastic over time because new oil enters the market and alternative energy sources come on line, widely varying marginal costs within the cartel could become a problem for price administration. Second, the phenomenon of administered prices shows a tendency toward stability even without separate and explicit action by the price leader. But when one combines this tendency for price to hover around a single point and the leverage available to a price leader like Saudi Arabia, the potential stability of OPEC appears enhanced. Saudi Arabia, for example, could absorb a disproportionate portion of the reduction in market share necessary to keep price on DD rather than allow it to follow dd, which the cheater would prefer. Indeed, by cutting production rapidly and sufficiently the Saudi government could perhaps even raise price in spite of cheating behavior on the part of one or more small cartel members. While a Saudi production cut would stabilize price, it would also erode the Saudi market share and scarcely penalize the cheater. But the critical observation is that price leadership and price administration mutually reinforce cartel stability.

Before exploring cohesion in the context of conflict analysis and surveying the general contribution of the economic theory of cartels to our understanding of cartel theory, we note several analytic concerns. First, the theory of administered prices does not explain how or where the price or market share distribution is actually determined by the cartel. We speculate that historical conditions prior to the formation of the cartel and market inertia thereafter are extremely important in making this determination. Second, both conservation cutbacks in petroleum use and substitution effects of new energy supply must, according to this analysis, be rather large to upset the price behavior we have just evaluated. *Inelastic energy supply and demand surely favor cartel cohesion.* Third, probably only low-cost producers can even conceive of substantial price reduction as a way of increasing their own revenue in the period in which the cartel is first formed. Where there are widely different production costs, maximization of return in a way that satisfies all of the producers, however, is very difficult. In time, inequities and inefficiencies may arise. Hence, as substitution increases and demand and supply become more elastic, a low-cost producer like Iraq having great need of revenue may ultimately discover great dissatisfaction with the manner of cartel revenue maximization; such a state may increasingly find incentives to gain more revenue by undercutting its partners.

HANG-UPS AND HINDRANCES TO COHESION

Despite the confidence of the OPEC leadership that unity is eternal, other analysts have raised doubts concerning the longevity of the cartel.

There can be little doubt about OPEC's strength through the first five years of market control, that is, through 1978, and possibly through the next five years as well. Beyond this period cohesion is far more problematic for a variety of reasons.

Conflicts of Intra-OPEC Market Interest

OPEC is marked by a fundamental schism of opinion regarding optimal pricing. Two camps, the high-price preference and the low-price preference states, differ vigorously over strategy and goals. Led by Iran, the high-price preference states are characterized by large populations, massive development programs, major plans for military buildup, and hence demand for huge amounts of revenue, provided in part by high export prices for crude. Most of these states also possess relatively small petroleum reserves whose impact is to drive prices higher. For one thing, these states do not have to worry about the threat of much future energy substitution because the bulk of their reserves will be used up shortly. For another, higher prices tend to reduce the quantity of petroleum produced to obtain a given amount of revenue, and hence higher prices conserve limited petroleum stocks. Given both the revenue and conservation aspects of higher prices, it is not hard to see why states like Iran and Nigeria favor strong upward price movement.

In contrast, the low-price preference states led by Saudi Arabia are characterized by small populations, limited capital absorption capability, large and vulnerable financial reserves, and huge untapped reserves of petroleum. High prices for petroleum would serve only to increase the financial reserves already subject to exchange controls and devaluation and to hasten the threat of energy substitution. Since these countries have a production horizon that stretches into the twenty-first century, they are not as attracted by the conservation effects of high prices as are states like Iran, and conversely they are much more worried about the depressing effect of substitution on the future price of crude. Saudi Arabia is also concerned about the impact of high energy prices on the economic stability of the West, the source of its technology and guardian of its own increasingly anachronistic political regime (measured by contemporary Middle East political standards). Low-price preference countries have strong incentives, and capacity, to defend their own interests within the cartel.

But the split in price preferences does not end with commercial and economic questions. Rivalries exist among the OPEC states. Saudi Arabia is distrustful of Iranian military ambitions in the Gulf region, particularly in looking forward to a time when Iranian petroleum reserves will have run out but Saudi reserves will offer a potential aggressor an inviting prize. Since high current prices for crude add to the Iranian military budget, Saudi Arabia has a persuasive reason for opposing marginal increments in already high oil prices.

Other political conflicts between Iran and Iraq, Oman and the People's Democratic Republic of Yemen, between Kuwait and Iraq, and the Arab world versus Israel all would tend to disrupt commercial linkages inside and outside the region. While for the time being the trend of events within OPEC seems to be moving toward conciliation and internal development, students of Middle East politics are not altogether convinced by such appearances of calm.[7] Certainly it is in the interest of both OPEC and the noncommunist consumer nations to see peace prevail in the Middle East. Indeed, another major war in the Middle East would probably hurt the cohesiveness of the producer cartel without providing any net long-term benefits to the consumer nations. But the inevitability of such political calm in a period in which tensions may be higher inside and outside the cartel is another matter.

Inability to Agree on Market Shares

A mature cartel ultimately decides explicitly or implicitly on a division of market shares. This division must be efficient from the viewpoint of meeting but not exceeding market demand. It must also be perceived as equitable by the members of the cartel so that they are willing to live within its constraints. So far, however, OPEC has not been able to achieve an agreement on market shares.

The impact of failure to establish a market share arrangement opens possibilities for fragmentation. In the first years of OPEC, the members were more concerned with spending their huge surpluses than with defending their market shares. But as the reserves disappear and upward price movement becomes more difficult, the size of each nation's market share becomes more important in the eyes of domestic decision elites responsible for government policy.

Only when the market behavior of each member becomes sufficiently sensitized to coordinate production and price decisions with virtual automaticity is the cartel free of commercial tensions and threats of rebellion. When a tacit market share arrangement becomes institutionalized in the nature of a formal agreement, the cartel leadership is in a position to act more vigorously relative to new entrants and to damaging consumer strategies. Without such an agreement Saudi Arabia must proceed cautiously in dealing with the consumers for fear of losing the support of one or more of the cartel members. Without a market share agreement, OPEC is something of an untested phenomenon, formidable in appearance but lacking in the obvious resilience that deters challengers.

Saudi Reluctance to Assume Full Burden of Production Constraint

In the three years following the OPEC capture of the market, Saudi Arabia absorbed the bulk of the production cutbacks. When measured against its total production potential, the size of the production cuts is even more striking. The problem for the cartel is whether Saudi Arabia will be content to absorb the same proportion of the cuts in the future as it has since 1973. Insofar as a reduced Saudi market share becomes accepted within the cartel and legitimized as fair, other governments such as Iran, Iraq, Kuwait, and Venezuela will obtain more influence over OPEC decisionmaking since the differential between the size of their shares and that of Saudi Arabia will have declined.

Mere capacity for *future* production (size of petroleum resources) is not the sole criterion for influence within the cartel. Indeed, past production levels are as important as any other variable in determining current production quotas. Hence, Saudi Arabia faces the dilemma of *retaining* its market share (and hence its leadership edge) and at the same time *reducing* its market share to placate other cartel members. Neither the Saudi government nor the other cartel members can burn the oil candle at both ends. Saudi Arabia could at some point decide to stiffen its current position regarding concessions to other members in order to strengthen its future leadership position based on the size of its OPEC market share. Such a decision to sacrifice current harmony for future leverage could shake the cartel to its foundation if other member governments become obdurate.

Growing Appetite in OPEC for Revenue

Expenditure of large sums of money becomes habit-forming for governments as much as for individuals. Within two years after the fourfold price increase, Iraq, Iran, and Nigeria all had begun to borrow in the international money market; Iran had revised downward the expenditures in its fifth five-year plan; and Indonesia and Venezuela began to feel the financial strains of the production cutbacks. The bulge in revenues caused by the price increases served to raise expectations of the elite and middle classes regarding government programs and employment. A kind of rachet effect easily increased investments but only reluctantly yielded to constraint when budgets were overspent.

Some of the governments like Iran and Nigeria (post-1975 coup) with high centralization and a marked degree of military discipline adapted to the new conditions rather rapidly. Others seemed hesitant to make the appropriate sacrifices. The explanation is not hard to find. A government attempting to wrench sacrifices out of an elite recently convinced of rapidly expanding wealth is a government ripe for overthrow. Much easier for the government decisionmaker is the application of pressure on fellow cartel members to allow an expansion of the government's market share. Internal political pressure on the government is thus diverted into external pressure within the cartel, first to redefine the distribution of OPEC market shares and second to raise the price of OPEC crude even at the cost of a loss in the overall OPEC share of the world energy market. Such pressures when widespread within a cartel are difficult for even patient leadership to offset.

Of the thirteen OPEC members, it is estimated that only three—Saudi

Arabia, Kuwait, and the United Arab Emirates—will have sizable excess financial reserves by 1977. A factor that enhances large spending is the increased capacity for imports created by improved infrastructure—ports, roads, communications systems—and higher standards of living. Thus, the capital absorption capability of the deficit countries will be expanding most rapidly at the precise time when oil revenues are beginning to decline.

Insofar as an internal banking arrangement is set up within the cartel whereby the surplus countries lend to the deficit countries, cohesion could vastly be strengthened. Everyone would theoretically gain. The surplus countries would earn a good profit on their excess financial reserves and would thus be more willing to add to them through support for the campaign within OPEC to raise prices. The high-price preference countries like Iran and Algeria with deficits would not need to press so hard for price increases, nor would they have to disappoint powerful sectors of their elites by curtailing development programs, since ample money could be borrowed from within OPEC. But what appears so appealing economically may not be so attractive politically.

In order to make such a financial program work, high trust and tolerance is essential across the cartel. Very conservative financially as in other ways, the surplus countries are likely to be skeptical about the quality of the investments made by some of the OPEC countries. Moreover, there are political differences between such countries as Iran and Saudi Arabia or Iraq and Kuwait that discourage long-term lending. Surely some of these banking arrangements will evolve, but whether they will be sizable enough to satiate the appetites of revenue-hungry governments is questionable. Hence, should the governments fail to curb their expenditures, pressures will build up within OPEC for higher prices and market share revisions that the leadership will not easily contain.

Slowing of World Energy Demand

While it is true that the recovery from world recession has given the cartel an extended life, the converse long-term development—reduction in world energy demand—is likely to have a negative effect. Before the OPEC takeover, energy demand was increasing at 4 percent a year. A reduction of perhaps one-quarter of this growth to 3 percent per year is a possible consequence of price increases, energy conservation, and innovation of more energy-saving technology. Such a reduction in energy demand will mean that the total pie is not increasing as rapidly as it had been, thus leaving OPEC with a possible smaller slice than would have been true at 1973 price levels. Under these conditions the current seller's market could more quickly become a buyer's market once again.

In considering the arguments on behalf of continued cohesion and the potential obstacles that OPEC will have to overcome in sustaining cohesion, it becomes clear that one of the central factors in the cohesion debate is the issue of market share distribution among the OPEC partners. Since this issue will become more, not less, pressing over time, it is critical to review how market share distribution is currently being resolved.

THE OPEC STRUGGLE FOR MARKET SHARE

In the first years after OPEC's capture of the market, market share distribution was easy because everyone had more money than he could properly invest, and quarrels over future distributions seemed contentious. But the relevance of large market shares became increasingly apparent for two reasons. First, countries with growing capital absorption capability and political expectations are likely to seek a larger market share as a source of additional revenue. The need for a larger market share is accentuated since price tends to follow an equilibrium around the level of inflation, setting an upper bound on returns. Second, a large market share also provides greater political leverage over price and production decisions announced and implemented collectively. The size of a nation's market share tacitly figures in the extent to which that nation's preferences are incorporated in ultimate OPEC policy, the price leader having predominant decision authority. On the basis of what criteria, then, has OPEC reached market share decisions, and to what extent do these decisions reveal information concerning the nature of subcoalitions and changing structure within the cartel?

Criteria for Market Share Distribution

Specifically, two questions about OPEC market behavior relate to cartel stability and lend themselves to empirical test. First, have the criteria for market share distribution changed since the OPEC takeover? Second, is there a difference in the way the cartel led by Saudi Arabia as a whole views market share distribution compared to the way a hypothetical coalition of ten members (minus Saudi Arabia, Kuwait, and the United Arab Emirates) led by Iran views distribution?

The cartel is already on the road to greater harmony and cohesion with or without formal production share agreements *if* the answer to the first question is affirmative, with market share distribution under OPEC decision leadership undergoing the following changes:

1. a shift toward allocating production in direct proportion to the reserve-to-production ratio, a decision that rationalizes the flow of oil in technical terms;
2. a trend toward recognizing the importance of capital absorption capability, allowing those to earn revenue that have a greater ability to use revenue;
3. recognition that political and economic power should be restrained

and production levels made somewhat inverse to GNP, allowing smaller states to become free riders; and

4. a shift toward more equitable distribution by allocating production shares inversely to per capita wealth, allowing the poor states a larger fraction of current oil revenue.

In addition, the cartel will also be strengthened if the answer to the second question is negative and the subcoalition of ten states led by Iran enjoys the same distributive pattern as the whole (or at least a pattern not more detrimental to either their own interests or that of the whole).

On the other hand, if the answer to either of these questions is reversed, cartel cohesion may be harmed. In other words, if there is no evidence since 1973 of greater technical rationality in the flow of oil, of awareness of capital needs, of a collective goods mentality, or of equity, then OPEC will likely have to contend with internal dissatisfaction over the manner of share distribution.

Summarizing in essentially a nonquantitative manner the evidence of correlation, regression, and path coefficient analysis for 1973 and 1975, one observation becomes very clear.[8] There is a great deal of inertia in the patterns of oil distribution. Changes come slowly. The strongest correlate of this year's oil production is last year's production, but this correlation drops off sharply as one continues backward in time. Hence, change occurs, but it occurs smoothly as historically established patterns gradually erode.

What evidence do we have regarding the first question, the distribution of OPEC production shares after 1973? While the absolute size of a nation's oil reserves continues to influence production, production for the cartel as a whole seems to be coming more in line with the reserve-to-production ratio. The reserve-to-production ratio showed a striking increase in importance between 1973 and 1975, from negative association to the more technically feasible positive association. Once decisionmaking was in the hands of the OPEC states, the reserve-to-production ratio appears to have become a very important variable sustaining the reserves of the low-reserve states by reduced production levels. Although it is clear that OPEC has adopted petroleum reserve size as a guideline to desired production share distribution, as of 1975 there was little evidence for OPEC as a whole of greater attention to capital absorption capability or of equity as a basis for dividing production shares. Nor was economic size a very important factor in making production share decisions. Average *change* in market shares did favor the efficiency and equity variables, but change has occurred only very gradually.

In sum, only on the critical issue of rationalizing the flow of oil to petroleum reserve size has there been major progress toward efficient distribution. If our evidence is correct that OPEC has not addressed successfully the question of capital absorption criteria, that OPEC is not following a collective goods philosophy, which would allow states with small GNPs to become free riders by advancing their production levels, and that poverty is not yet a sufficient justification for a larger production share, then on any one if not all of these grounds OPEC may experience internal strains and tensions.

Concerning the second question, whether the criteria of distribution are different for the ten states than for the thirteen led by Saudi Arabia, the evidence again is ambiguous. Last year's production and the size of reserves are equally significant for both groups of states. Equity is similarly unimportant (or unaccomplished) for both groupings. The direction in the change of correlation for reserve-to-production size (from inverse to direct correlation) is the same for both groups, too, although not as marked for the ten states. But economic size is a much more important variable for the ten states, with the larger states obtaining the greater production—the opposite of the collective goods thesis. If free riders are to be tolerated within OPEC, they will be tolerated because of concessions made by Saudi Arabia, Kuwait, and the United Arab Emirates, not because of the wishes of the economically most powerful states in the subcoalition. Equally revealing of difference is the capital absorption variable. Ability to absorb capital is much more important as a guideline to distribution of shares among the ten than among the thirteen, but the cartel as a whole has not been able to reorder production along capital absorption lines.

We thus see both congruence and difference for the ten states led by Iran and for the cartel as a whole. The larger economic states like Iran, Venezuela, Nigeria, and Indonesia seem to be able to exploit their size to obtain better production shares. The ten states have not as successfully rationalized their production along the lines of reserve-to-production criteria. Capital absorption considerations could likewise become an important grievance for members of the Iranian coalition: despite the importance of revenue needs as a predictor of change in market shares, market share distribution as of 1975 has been altered very little by this variable.

OPEC may well adopt new criteria for production share distribution. As of 1975 pressures have not been great to resolve differences because, as we noted earlier, everyone was concerned with investing windfall gains rather than with obtaining a larger slice of total OPEC revenue. But as price increases become more difficult because price is already bumping against the substitution threshold, debates over market share distribution are likely to become more rancorous. These results suggest that change since 1973 has improved the production share situation, especially on the technical side, but has far from eliminated all snarls over bargaining or differences in perspective between subcoalitions.

Instability after 1977 is a growing possibility for internal reasons when only three states—Saudi Arabia, the United Arab Emirates, and Kuwait—will have large financial surpluses and several of the states will have growing foreign debts. Barring far-reaching internal production share reforms, a number of states may display grievances; in the event of growing external pressures, these states are likely to remain within OPEC only if Saudi Arabia is able through leadership skill and leverage to hold the cartel together.

A Theory of Cartel Conflict

So far we have probed arguments for and against continued cohesion. We have seen potential weaknesses due to factors as diverse as the differences in such state attributes as population and oil reserve size, bargaining and structural issues affected by the relative desire for revenue such as the allocation of market shares, and external market conditions as varied as conservation effects and the threat of energy substitution. The question that immediately arises is how these multiple factors interact. Are some factors reinforcing while others are offsetting? How is OPEC likely to cope with these potential strains and stresses?

In this section we present a framework within which the analyst might begin to assess the possible interplay of forces.[9] Identification of primary political relationships is essential to analysis and facilitates judgments concerning the potential impact of future OPEC and consumer alternatives.

For purposes of analysis we identify two sources of potential OPEC conflict, type A and type B. The two types of conflict are interrelated and cannot meaningfully occur in isolation. The probable relationship between type A and type B conflict is multiplicative; that is, at very low levels of conflict the product is minimal but at higher levels the product is much greater than the sum of the parts. What appears on the surface to be effective amelioration of conflict within the cartel may at a slightly higher level of discord lead to an explosive political mix of forces. We believe the relationship between the types of instability is multiplicative because the presence of both types is essential to a significant impact for either. But the combined effect of moderate levels of turbulence is much more grave for the cartel leadership than is perhaps currently envisioned.

Type A conflict is the tension between the members of the cartel arising over an equitable and efficient distribution of market shares. It is conflict internal to the cartel. It is also likely to increase in periods of excess petroleum supply and between countries with high capital absorption capability, substantial surplus production capacity, and rather weak ideological affiliations with other members of the cartel. Internal conflict over market share is always a potential threat to cartel unity but can be tempered in a number of ways that we shall explore momentarily.

Type B conflict is the tension generated by external pressure on the cartel from policies of the consumer nations and from other entrants into the market (through large new discoveries). Hence type B conflict operates on the cartel, while type A conflict operates from *within* the cartel. Type B conflict results from pressures that reduce the total size of the OPEC share of the world energy market. If the price of oil goes too high or the activity of rival producers and the consumer nations becomes too aggressive, the OPEC slice of the world energy pie will diminish beyond a point acceptable to the cartel. Type A conflict, on the other hand, stems from pressures within the cartel over the proper distribution of rewards and benefits whatever the size of the collective OPEC slice.

Here is where the interaction of the two types of conflict, however, becomes critical. Without some external pressure on the cartel, internal disagreement is likely to be minimal since the price can always be raised to create revenue, which in turn dissipates tensions. Without the impact of type B conflict, price always acts as a safety valve rescuing the cartel from the effects of type A (intra-OPEC) conflict. Conversely, without type A conflict among the cartel members regarding the proper distribution of rewards, type B (external) pressures have comparatively minimal impact. In a perfectly coordinated cartel, in which infighting is virtually absent because of an authoritative market share agreement or some other compelling arrangement, a cartel is likely to be able to survive. In the face of hostile external pressure, the cartel members simply band together more closely. Military alliances, for example, often display this kind of behavior. Cooperation emerges not for positive reasons but for the negative external reason of a common enemy. Without the imminence of external hostility the alliance would disappear, a condition plaguing Western alliance systems today. So with a cartel—unless there is internal disagreement over market share arrangements, then external consumer pressure or the pressure of new entrants like China into the market is unlikely significantly to affect cartel cohesion. In short, type A or type B conflict alone is virtually no threat to the cartel's existence.

But when one considers the two sources of conflict together, the potential impact on cartel cohesion is more plausible. As consumption is whittled back by conservation measures and more efficient energy use, as new discoveries add to petroleum supply, and as substitutes for petroleum begin to come on line, the OPEC slice of the world energy market must shrink. The effect of this shrinkage is gradually to render the price safety valve useless as a constraint on intra-OPEC turmoil. For to raise price in the face of a diminishing OPEC share of the world market is to commit revenue suicide. What then happens to OPEC unity in the presence of type A conflict?

If it cannot raise prices further (indeed, if type B pressures build, the cartel will have to *reduce* price in order to maintain OPEC leverage as the swing producer), the cartel must resolve internal disputes. Such internal disputes are likely to multiply and worsen in time for at least two reasons. First, countries like Iraq, Iran, Nigeria, and Algeria that have not been able to import as heavily as they would like because of problems of infra-structure (e.g., crowded port facilities and inadequate railroad networks) will have overcome these problems in a few years, boosting their appetites for petroleum revenue. Second, not only Saudi Arabia but also countries like Iraq, Libya, Kuwait, and Nigeria are likely to develop significant excess productive capacity in a period of stagnating demand. The existence of this surplus capacity will place further strains on the cartel leadership to allow this capacity to be utilized. An internal struggle, monitored but scarcely supervised by the multinationals, which are now the virtual hostages of the cartel leadership, is likely to shake the cartel, leading to competitive price-cutting and deals with national oil companies and undisciplined independent companies able to offer the retail advantages of vertical integration.

Type A and type B conflict are thus fully interactive and reinforcing. As type A internal conflict increases, the OPEC armor is likely to develop chinks, inviting external penetration of the type B variety. Disagreement over market shares, for example, could lead a dissatisfied state to seek a bilateral deal with a national oil company. As type B conflict worsens externally, the pressure increases on the cartel members to get a larger share of whatever oil OPEC exports. Gradually, types A and B conflict begin to co-vary, escalating as the two sets of forces undermine cohesion. Type A conflict creates pressure within the cartel for dissolution. Type B conflict stimulates external pressure on the cartel either to lower price in order to maintain its production level or to cut back production in order to sustain price; either way the strength of the cartel is eroded, thus making it more vulnerable to type A tensions.

We mentioned earlier, however, that from the OPEC perspective this gloomy outlook may be altered by a series of actions that the cartel itself may initiate. First, the cartel may create an atmosphere of fair treatment in which each member believes that no other member is any better off than it is in relative terms and that it would do much worse alone if it bolted the cartel. A production share agreement would add legitimacy to the prevailing sense of equity. Second, the cartel leadership could rely on the coercive ability of the price leader, Saudi Arabia, to drop the price by raising output if any member sought a bilateral deal outside the cartel. If both the proportion of the shares held by the price leader and its surplus production capacity are increased, the commercial muscle of the price leader is increased in two ways. It can drop the price by utilizing some of its surplus capacity, or it can lower its own production and thereby allow another member a larger chunk of OPEC revenue. Either way the price leader gains leverage. Third, the cartel leadership can discourage excessive exploration activity by the industry, particularly outside OPEC, by keeping profits down, thus reducing type B pressures. Fourth, the leadership can establish an internal credit system whereby the countries that need additional revenue can borrow from countries that are capable of making loans. Fifth, the cartel can seek to preserve unity within its marketing operations so as not to damage market discipline. All of these polices would tend to strengthen OPEC internally and hence, since cartel conflict is interactive and multiplicative, to lessen the threat of impact of external pressures.

ALTERNATIVE FORMS OF OPEC STRUCTURE

In order to clarify further the effects of alternative options for OPEC and consumers, we will examine more systematically three basic models of OPEC structure addressing the problem of conflict.

1. Axis model. Saudi Arabia is at the center of this model, the other producers, on the periphery. Saudi Arabia has substantial discretion in terms of increasing its production in order to put downward pressure on price or in terms of decreasing production in order to allow another cartel member to advance its production share. But what distinguishes this model is that as demand for petroleum increases through recovery and growth, the bulk of this demand is met from Saudi fields. This expansion of Saudi production strengthens the coercive potential of Saudi leadership since it gives Saudi Arabia more leverage over other members of the cartel (should they attempt to undermine collective policy). This leverage equals the difference between the level of current production and the level of production that would just cover Saudi revenue needs. If new demand is diverted toward Saudi Arabia, this difference, or margin, can be increased, adding leverage to the leadership and potential cohesion to the cartel.

In some sense this model could be described as a core state model with the members in a dependency relationship with Saudi Arabia. It is a strong configuration and the one perhaps most internally resistant to disruptive political and commercial conflict. While U.S. policymakers may think this OPEC configuration headed by Saudi Arabia would also be the most conservative pricewise, this remains to be seen. A resilient OPEC is understandably not one that necessarily will place American interests high on its list of objectives.

2. Fair share model. In this model one significant change occurs relative to the axis configuration. As demand increases, it is allocated in such a way among the cartel members that Saudi Arabia receives only a small proportion, while the other members get increases that they may argue constitute their fair share. The effect is to create more equality among the production levels of the larger producers, namely, Saudi Arabia, Iraq, Iran, Kuwait, and Venezuela. Decisionmaking power is thus more diffused, the conservative policies of Saudi Arabia are less likely to prevail, and the future stability of the cartel is more in jeopardy.

This tendency is further enhanced if other producers like Iraq and Nigeria begin to acquire excess annual productive capacity that approaches (but of course is not likely to equal) that of Saudi Arabia. In any short-term policy confrontation with Saudi Arabia, the other states with excess capacity can by expanding production place much more pressure on the cartel leadership than the previous model permits. Since the margin Saudi Arabia enjoys beyond its minimally acceptable production level (estimated by some to be as low as 3 million barrels per day) is not as great in this model as in the previous one, the cohesion of the cartel is more easily threatened by instability. While this configuration of commercial power is in no sense inherently unstable, the increased threat of cartel instability is in direct proportion to the size of the leadership edge lost by Saudi Arabia.

This model can also be called the collective goods model: the leadership absorbs a disproportionate percentage of the burdens (in this case, the large petroleum reserve states assume relatively greater production constraints) because the association would decline without such a policy.[10] Free riders emerge because they have no real impact on policy regardless of the sacrifices they make. The leadership tolerates the free riders because it cannot eliminate them and still achieve its own long-term interests. So long as the free riders do not press their parasitic advantage too hard, or the leadership does not expect more of them than tacit allegiance, the association remains cohesive. But the vigor of such an alliance does not match that of the prior model.

3. Team model. Unlike the previous models, in which the states compete as individual actors, the team model posits that members compete and bargain within the cartel as groups. The effect is twofold. First, it establishes a deep cleavage between states holding substantially different perspectives on price, production preferences, and negotiation tactics with the consumer countries. The depth of the cleavage worsens acrimony within the cartel and hinders conflict resolution. Second, the effect is to bolster the bargaining power of the weaker states (not necessarily the states with the smaller GNPs but those with the lower reserve-to-production ratios) against the strength of the primary coalition. Hence this model is the weakest of the three with respect to long-term cohesion.

A plausible cleavage is between Saudi Arabia, Kuwait, and the United Arab Emirates and a second group composed of the remaining states and led perhaps by Iran. Crossovers might occur and some states might refuse to join either cluster, but the outlines of these two groupings are quite defined. Why would intracartel politics break down into such teams of opposed states? What interests underlie such fragmentation? The logic for these developments is clear if one recalls our prior discussion of the differences in market interests between OPEC members and our subsequent empirical demonstration that effects of this cleavage are already being felt somewhat in OPEC decisionmaking. In brief, one group led by Saudi Arabia is a low-price coalition, the other led by Iran is a high-price coalition. Low-price preference countries, we recall, are characterized by low capital absorption capability (essentially because of small population size) and large petroleum reserves ensuring a long production horizon. They prefer lower crude prices for essentially three reasons: first, they do not have good alternative investments and would rather leave the oil in the ground for the present than subject the revenue to the risks of devaluation or exchange control; second, they fear the effects of future oil discoveries, energy substitution, and conservation measures on the future price of petroleum, each of which may be vigorously pursued by the consumer nations if the current price is pushed too high; and third, they are unhappy with the uses to which certain governments, particularly Iran, might put extra revenue, thus possibly shifting the military balance against themselves in the Gulf region. These attitudes are well defined and based rather firmly on commercial and state interests.

In contrast, the group led by Iran, although more diverse, is united in the preferences for high immediate prices. They do not have such large reserves and thus do not worry about substitution. They have huge appetites for revenue (high capital absorption capacity) and ambitious military programs, thus necessitating large amounts of funding. For these states confrontation with the consumers is less frightening, and their own comparative intra-OPEC weakness encourages them to oppose the Saudi coalition with vigor and in concert.

This coalition model is less stable than the others because the lines of conflict are more precisely drawn. Existence of coalitions by no means indicates that the cartel will inevitably tear itself apart. Indeed, coalitions could become a new, more institutionalized and sophisticated form of OPEC decisionmaking. On the other hand, the dominance of Saudi Arabia is less assured in this model, quarrels are more likely to escalate, and governments are less likely to feel impotent in the face of unfavorable judgments by the leadership.

Regardless of structural model, the rules governing the interaction between type A and type B conflict apply. As long as the two sources of instability remain isolated, cartel cohesion will remain high. But moderate levels of internal tension and external pressure could create explosive prospects for OPEC, an organization that has no historical equivalent either in terms of structure and function or in terms of comparative success.

Conclusion: Critical Decisions for the Swing Consumer

Having explored the arguments favoring unity within OPEC and those that predict demise, and having probed both the nature of political conflict affecting the cartel and the alternative structural forms that the cartel may assume, we are in a good position to consider the validity of the cohe-

sion myth. What should be strikingly apparent to the reader is that there
is no hard evidence at this time to predict breakdown, just as there is no
evidence to suppose that cohesion is permanent. Rather, we have weighed
the factors that are likely either to reinforce or to weaken the cartel politically and commercially. The myth of cohesion rests precariously not
only on internal OPEC factors over which the importing countries have
little control but also on the *external reaction* of the consumer countries,
especially the United States. In other words, the importing governments
by their own actions will provide much of the proof regarding whether the
myth of cohesion is right or wrong. What they believe will have some presumed effect on their actions, and by their actions the consumer governments will provide the ultimate test of OPEC cohesion.

As the swing consumer—the largest importer and consumer of petroleum—the United States can reduce its foreign oil dependency in at least
four ways:

- through incentives to non-OPEC oil exploration and discovery
- through guarantees for research and development into new energy
  sources, especially coal in this century and possibly fusion or other
  high-risk, large payoff technologies thereafter
- through serious, planned conservation efforts to reduce waste without
  curtailing growth or development
- through concerted energy policies with the two other high-technology countries in the noncommunist world that have peculiar defense
  relations with the United States and that therefore are more than
  slightly affected by U.S. resolution of its own energy problems—
  namely, West Germany and Japan.

These four policies are more than options for the United States, they are
imperatives.[11] OPEC governments have demonstrated a wisdom concerning international politics that advanced industrialism has so far clearly not
been able to match. To the extent that the consumer governments fail to
solve their own energy problems, the producers ought to be praised for the
sagacity and skill that have enabled them to upset and divide their opposition and to rewrite the rules of international discourse. Surely, the historian
looking at this period of statecraft ought to have little sympathy for governments that either did not see their own interests clearly or refused to
make use of the human resources, science, technology, and material wealth
that would make the pursuit of those interests feasible.

An objection to greater energy self-sufficiency is cost. But energy is at
the hub of industrial civilization.[12] Its centrality justifies substantial investment with the prospect of high returns. But are the costs out of step with
other massive projects of twentieth-century endeavor? Most estimates of
the cost of the Vietnam war are placed above $400 billion spread over a
ten-year period. A 100 billion program of public and private investment in
energy substitution, properly insured against downside price risk, could

probably yield a return to national security and welfare far exceeding that obtained by a corresponding expenditure on military arms. By establishing a set of intermediate goals and a schedule of preplanned inputs into the energy program, the nation could reduce its foreign dependence on oil and preserve a measure of price stability in energy matters.

OPEC deserves the respect its accomplishments to date warrant. Whether the myth of OPEC cohesion is flawed or accurate depends less, however, upon these accomplishments than on the political will of the United States and the ethos of postindustrialism.[13]

VII

Energy Strategies for the United States: Ideal and Real

PART OF THE REASON that myth is so prevalent in the energy area is that a disparity exists between *ideal* energy strategies and *real* or feasible strategies. Such a disparity runs to some extent through all of political decisionmaking but is especially marked in decisionmaking of high uncertainty. Crisis intervals providing too little opportunity for sound research and reflection, and highly polarized and politicized decision settings, also tend to generate disparities between real and ideal solutions. Since all of these conditions prevail regarding energy matters, proposed U.S. energy strategies not surprisingly have displayed a gap between idealism and realism, a gap that some of the myths discussed in prior chapters attempt to fill.

We intend to examine two so-called ideal energy strategies for the United States, a free trade strategy and a national security strategy. Obstacles to the successful implementation of these strategies become apparent, however, as the analysis proceeds. We then turn to the general outline of a more realistic energy strategy for the United States, focusing upon four rather specific aspects of energy policy that hold implications for the U.S. economic and politico-military position over the next decade.[1]

SOME IDEAL ENERGY STRATEGIES

A Free Trade Strategy

From the perspective of dominant economic theory in Europe and the United States, free trade, promoted through the General Agreement on

157

Tariffs and Trade (GATT), is a method of expanding commercial exchanges and, through this process, expanding the total volume of goods and services available to the world community. Tariffs, subsidies, artificial controls on prices—all tend to inhibit the free flow of trade and thus limit the productive potential of the system as a whole. It perhaps follows that free trade notions ought to apply equally well to the important energy area. Rather than responding to the energy price rise in a fashion calculated to undermine the unity of the OPEC cartel, for example, the free trade approach emphasizes other paths to equilibrium.

Since each country trades on the basis of a comparative advantage in those goods and services that it produces, it follows that the U.S. comparative advantage has been shifting away from the production of oil toward the production of manufactured goods, particularly those in high-technology areas and those in heavy equipment needed by the OPEC nations. OPEC, in turn, is exploiting its comparative advantage in that factor of production that it has in large quantities, importing the services and manufactured goods that its new oil revenue enables it to purchase. According to trade theory, a country like Saudi Arabia should not expect to manufacture at home all the diversity and sophistication of equipment and materials that a high-technology country like the United States produces; similarly, the United States should not expect to become self-sufficient in petroleum production (despite some prospect of finding high-cost offshore oil reserves if sufficient investment funds are forthcoming). Indeed, for either nation to try to produce greater quantities of that which it does poorly would hurt not only that nation's economy but the global economy as well. Thus, the argument runs, through external trade in petroleum and manufactured goods, both the United States and Saudi Arabia can benefit. Indirectly other nations in the system trading with each of these countries may also benefit, and ultimately the total production of both oil and manufactured goods as well as other commodities such as food will have increased.

Of course no proviso exists in this argument that all trading partners will benefit *equally* (or indeed benefit at all). Speculation regarding who is likely to benefit most from free trade thus presumably becomes a critical element of one's acceptance or rejection of the free trade argument. If, in the abstract, free trade benefits the system as a whole or one's trading partner but not oneself, one would be reluctant to accept arguments of the utility of free trade put forth by academicians and poets and the more favored trading partner. But if free trade has some prospect of benefiting *all polities* fairly, then the theory has considerable merit as a guide to the formulation of a practical energy strategy.

Since the free trade strategy involves acceptance of the current high price for oil rather than a concerted effort to force the price lower, the question of who in fact will benefit most from this price scenario is of more than casual interest. Conventional analysis holds either of two main theses regarding who has benefited most from the oil crisis. The more popular view is explicated in Chapter III and rejected; namely, that the oil industry has been the greatest beneficiary of the price rise. An alternate view is embodied in the first and sixth myths of price inequity and OPEC cohesion, respectively; namely, that since the oil exporting countries are earning the increased revenues they therefore are the ones that logically have enjoyed the most benefits from the price increases.

A minor and more complicated argument sometimes is heard that the Soviet Union, with its large, untapped oil reserves and its interest in weakening the Western economies, has gained political and economic advantages from the oil crisis. But if the Soviet Union obtained such advantages in the short run, they have been overshadowed by its inability to extract, transport, and sell large amounts of oil abroad and by the decision of Egypt, Iraq, Saudi Arabia, and Iran to turn their backs on the Soviets by obtaining military equipment and training from the West.[2] The commercial bubble of 1973 burst, leaving the Soviets adrift in Middle East politics.

An Outrageous Oil Hypothesis. In partial rejection of all of the above arguments of benefit, and as an extension of the free trade viewpoint, we offer an alternative hypothesis, outrageous in particular because of the climate of opinion in the United States today, which has vacillated between the hyperactivity of proposed military intervention and the despair of inevitable dependence on foreign energy supplies. We ask whether the United States, not the other seemingly more plausible actors, will ultimately be viewed as the largest beneficiary of the energy crisis in relative terms. A historian reflecting on the last quarter of the twentieth century is perhaps likely to ascribe to the energy crisis not the beginning of decline for the United States as a world power but an indication of the relative strength of the United States in its ability to sustain its leadership role.

While the United States, like the other consumer countries, did absorb an initial economic shock as the cost of energy abruptly rose, the impact on inflation was a once through process. Already in recession, the United States experienced slower recovery. But at the time of the initial 1973 crisis, the United States was providing more than half its petroleum needs from domestic sources—unlike Japan, West Germany, and France, America's nearest noncommunist competitors, which suffered far more directly. In addition to these relative advantages over commercial rivals in the advanced industrial world, the reason the United States stands possibly to benefit from what has appeared to some as catastrophe is twofold.

First, the enormous amounts of foreign exchange generated by the oil price increases are of absolutely no value to the producer nations unless they are translated into goods and services. Because of the size of its economy, the quality and diversity of its products, and the competitiveness of its prices, the United States is likely to be the principal supplier of those products and skills needed by OPEC. Such is the dynamism of the private sector that the sometime fear of an inability to recycle petro-dollars has given way to a scramble by businessmen throughout the capitalist countries for the vestige of these monies.[3]

Three countries, Saudi Arabia, Kuwait, and Abu Dhabi, hold the largest financial surpluses, which cannot be translated into immediate imports of goods and services because of the limited capital absorption capability of their economies and must instead be invested, largely abroad. Restrictions on Arab money coming into the United States are not only ill-advised but also impractical. The United States is the safest economy in the world in which to invest, both politically and commercially. Seeking security more than a high-risk, high return, the Arabs are likely to choose the United States as the logical recipient of these funds. Transmitted through a hundred brokerage houses and banks in Europe and elsewhere, the actual ownership of these investments is impossible to trace and essentially unimportant.

What is very important is that OPEC is providing the United States, in particular, with cheap, long-term loans, which employed intelligently can earn a much higher return than that which the original lender receives. By increasing the size of the money supply, this influx of investments and foreign exchange will keep inflation at a significant (perhaps even uncomfortable) level, creating new opportunities for aggressive entrepreneurship in an economy that has long demonstrated adaptability and risk-taking propensity. The multiplier and accelerator effects of these loans and investments should propel the U.S. economy forward at a pace somewhat above (not below, as several recent studies have suggested) the historical average.

Second, the energy crisis has given technological change in the United States, a nation with a comparative advantage in technological innovation, an important potential nudge. In the aftermath of the first space age and the era of computer automation, the economy requires a new stimulus to create a technology with far-reaching impact for society. New developments in semiconductors used to transmit energy more easily and efficiently, in storage cells employed to cut down the loss of energy and to increase the utility of less conventional energy sources, in breeder reactors and fusion itself all are likely over the next two decades to provide large, additional capacity for energy conservation and production in as yet unforeseen ways. It would be rather naive to anticipate a sudden decline in human ingenuity at precisely the time when society had substantial need for it, especially on the heels of three and one-half centuries of rather continuous scientific and technological advancement. Even if the discoveries are not made in the United States originally, they will be applied in this country because of the size and flexibility of its economy.

In one sense the energy crisis is demanding more of modern technology than the inaccessibility of British coal demanded of the Newcomen engine, for example, or than the decline of wood in the United States as a fuel required of the new gasoline. To some extent the present energy shortage necessitates the creation of an *artificial* energy source (e.g., fusion) to replace diminishing stocks of *conventional* energy materials. But such an energy source is not needed in the twentieth century. For example, while environmental and processing costs may prevent coal from being competitive with foreign imports of petroleum for several decades, thus keeping U.S. industry harnessed costwise to foreign energy supplies, appropriate technical innovations could reduce these costs in two ways. First, such innovations could enable industry to capture huge economies of scale by constructing installations of the appropriate size. Second, such innnovations are likely to reduce costs over time as the learning curve effect in new technical areas leads to ideas that suggest impressive cost savings. Overall, these two cost tendencies are likely to make coal and other conventional energy sources, previously unattractive, quite competitive with foreign reserves of increasingly expensive petroleum.

Thus, both in terms of the thrust of technological innovation and in terms of value added through accelerated economic development, the United States according to this hypothesis may gain *relative to its competitors* from the stimulus of the energy crisis. This does not mean that the United States can ever be said in an absolute sense to have been better off with $12 a barrel oil than $2 a barrel oil (unless fusion, for instance, should produce energy at less than the $2 equivalent). But the transfer of $10 per oil barrel from the United States to OPEC in the form of a quasi-excise tax may or may not be invested fruitfully by the producer countries; moreover, the loss of this revenue to the United States may or may not stimulate it to adopt policies that ultimately enhance the competitive position of the United States commercially. Perhaps historical analogies, not precisely similar in all details but instructive, can shed further light on what in a curious way must be considered an unusual opportunity of political economy.

From the sixteenth to the eighteenth century Spanish bullion and booty acquired in the New World and transferred to Europe provided a great stimulus to economic growth and development in Britain, the Low Countries, and France. Since precious metals and jewels are not productive capital, however, they did little to spur the growth of Spain, which did not seem to be able to combine these capital resources in such a way as to build an industrial base. Instead, the financial resources contributed to the ultimate wealth of the countries that received them secondarily as loans on investments or as the result of an expanded money supply. Far from hurting the rest of Europe relative to Spain, the new riches hurt Spain (by diverting creative resources into the wrong pursuits) relative to other parts of Europe.

According to the economic historian David Landes, "the silver of

America did little for Spain, which re-exported most of it to pay for military operations in other parts of Europe and for imports of food and manufactures from 'less fortunate' countries."[4] Yet for countries like Britain, which were able to grasp the opportunity, the great colonial windfall of Spain strengthened these states and fed the industrial revolution. "While the inflationary expansion lasted," notes Landes, "it promoted abiding changes in the structure of the European economy: new scope for commercial enterprise, greater specialization in agriculture and manufacture, larger concentrations of capital, an increased scale of production in certain branches."[5] The first recipient of wealth is not always the greatest or the final beneficiary.

Similarly, following the Franco-Prussian War of 1871, the Germans demanded and received substantial reparations payments from France as a condition of the peace agreement. But ironically, while the Germans anticipated a large absolute gain from the transfer payments, the influx of capital into German markets caused excessive inflation, thus depressing the German export capacity; conversely, prosperity returned to France more rapidly despite the reparations payments because French goods became more competitive in world markets and French external trade boomed.

Likewise, after World War II who would have guessed that even with Marshall Plan aid and other bilateral assistance, the defeated corpses of Germany and Japan would have come alive again to rank third and fourth, respectively, in GNP and world trade. War and military defeat did not benefit these societies directly; indeed, each government paid a very high cost in human and financial terms for its aggression. But by destroying most of its industrial plant and machine tools, for example, war forced Germany to update its entire capital base; once this goal was achieved, Germany was in a very strong competitive position relative to the "winners" of World War II, Britain and France. History plays strange tricks upon windfall "losses" and "gains."

So with petroleum today, as long as the oil producing nations fail to transform rentier economies into advanced industrialism, the bulk of their earnings may pass into the hands of the Japanese, the Europeans, or the Americans, especially the last. The United States may obtain not only oil from OPEC but a bonus as well. A society that is commercially nimble and aggressive may obtain an economic stimulus from the new capital available for reinvestment or used to pay for imports of goods and services. Insofar as the producer countries are foolish or unfortunate enough to expand large fractions of their oil revenue on nonproductive investment such as military weaponry, the best of which comes from the United States, the analogy with eighteenth-century Spain is even closer. Spain acquired a huge, costly navy to protect its trade routes and access to mineral wealth while neglecting the construction and development of home industry. Insofar as Iran, for example, diverts a large fraction of its oil receipts into military capability, this investment detracts from the Persian ability to modernize all facets of its industrial base within the few short years allowed it by the magnitude of its oil reserves.

The United States, like its seventeenth-century British forebears, may also be able to improve its technology while getting someone else to foot the bill. A number of Middle East countries have shown an interest in acquiring exotic technologies such as nuclear energy before the technology has been perfected in the advanced industrial world and at a time when it is not needed within the OPEC country (assuming that the real purpose of the technology is not a military one). Insofar as the presence of a nuclear reactor trains Iranian scientists how to employ nuclear isotopes for agricultural, medical, or military purposes, for example, the cost may be sensible although the training might better and more effectively be done abroad. In reality, the impact of the purchases is to help finance American or French research and development costs on a partially mature technology. Moreover, by the time the reactors are in place and in operation, this particular generation of technology is likely to be obsolete.

Not unaware of these problems, OPEC countries are attempting to transfer technological production capability and not just technology or foreign technologists. What they really need is indigenous capacity to invent, develop, and produce their own technology. Capital absorption capability (essentially the size and sophistication of a nation's population) and time are the two factors that will determine whether they succeed or instead follow the pattern of colonial Spain.

The United States meanwhile is certainly in a position to take advantage of the historical opportunity created by the energy crisis. On the one hand, the size of its economy can enable the United States to expand its exports rapidly and with cost savings through internal and external effects of scale. U.S. technology is generally thought of as the most sophisticated of any available today and thus is greatly in demand by governments capable of paying for first quality equipment for their modernizing programs; the conservative orientation of many of the OPEC governments with the largest financial surpluses makes purchase of military technology from the United States attractive as well. On the other hand, the United States still has enough indigenous energy production to offset a large share of its energy costs. Past waste of energy in the United States means that substantial conservation is perhaps possible (West Germany uses half the per capita energy consumption of the United States) without major constraints on growth rates. All of these conditions together suggest that the hypothesis of relative U.S. benefit from the energy crisis may not be so outrageous as it first seemed, provided the United States adopts an energy policy that facilitates large-scale substitution and new oil discoveries.

Free trade notions suggest that the United States may be able to capture its share of the benefits from the oil crisis albeit indirectly and belatedly. Attention to the logic of comparative advantage and to the merits of unimpeded global commercial exchange should, in this view, shape long-term U.S. energy policy.

A National Security Strategy

A second ideal energy strategy might be described as a *national security strategy*. The logic of this strategy is that other things being equal it is better to use somebody else's oil than one's own. By using foreign instead of domestic oil, one draws down foreign reserves first. Should access to foreign reserves be denied for whatever reason, including political ones, then the domestic petroleum reserves would be available for use.

An additional assumption makes this strategy more plausible. In order to assure the nation adequate supplies of petroleum in time of a potential supply disruption, the wells ought to be drilled in advance and capped. Immediate access to the oil would then be guaranteed. Meanwhile, the nation could continue to buy oil abroad at the world price, trading its manufactured goods for imported petroleum. Should unforeseen innovations in petrochemical applications radically increase the future demand for petroleum, and hence the future petroleum price, the government retaining large domestic oil reserves might additionally gain.

Assessing the Idealist Strategies

The free trade strategy and the national security strategy each have in common reliance on the world petroleum market for oil. They differ in that the free trade strategy makes no effort to distinguish domestic and foreign petroleum reserves, while the national security strategy does, placing a high priority on conservation of the former. The free trade approach emphasizes the comparative advantage to a capital-rich country of trading manufactured goods for a primary commodity like oil. It assumes that the value added in the manufacturing process and the rate of scientific innovation in the industrial country more than offset the rate of inflation in the price of foreign oil. In contrast, the national security strategy consciously hedges against the possibility that markets do not perfectly reflect the impact of future innovations, and the strategy makes the uncommon assumption that these innovations will be more important in the industrial and chemical use of petroleum than in non-petroleum-based areas of the economy.

Flaws in each of these two ideal strategies, however, negate them for practical reasons as effective energy policy. Free trade notions of energy face a continuing obstacle. Oil markets are far from perfect. Where great rigidities exist in the market and lags in investment behavior complicate decisionmaking, domination of the pricing mechanism is possible for some time by the OPEC producers. Should OPEC decide to raise prices by limiting production, the consumer government practicing a free trade policy could remain dependent politically and economically on foreign oil for a long period. Even though the value added in manufactured goods may be quite high, the ability of the oil producer to push oil prices even higher makes the free trade idea one-sided and unattractive.

While there may be desirable and undersirable ways of achieving a release from energy dependence according to efficiency criteria, as long as producers have the capacity to concert their pricing and production strategies, then consumers pursuing free trade notions will remain divided and subservient pricewise. Little advantage accrues to a state through trade if the trading partner has all the leverage over prices. The oil producing countries learned this lesson well in the pre-1973 era and are now teaching Japan and the advanced industrial states in the West as OPEC reverses control.

Specialization in the manufacture of high-technology goods is fine for the consumer nations if they face a cartel willing to accept an increase in oil prices that follows the rate of world inflation. But if the cartel chooses to raise prices more rapidly, the benefits of comparative advantage are likely to escape the consumers unless they are able to exercise some control over petroleum pricing directly. The principal way to obtain such control is to produce oil at home or to generate cost-competitive energy from alternative sources. To continue to rely on comparative advantage in industrial production alone as an offset to OPEC price manipulation is to transfer substantial revenue from the consumer countries to the producer nations, the richest of which already enjoy an equity edge.

Perhaps if industrial production occurred solely within a cartel, such an organization could offset OPEC effectively and the industrial nations could leave energy production to OPEC while relying on trade to equalize benefits. But of course no such industrial goods cartel exists, nor is any such future cartel likely. Hence, the consumers must find an offset to OPEC in the energy field itself unless disproportionate costs in the production of energy prohibit such a venture. As the price of oil continues to rise, even high-cost new energy becomes more attractive.

Likewise, the national security strategy contains flaws. It is unsatisfactory first because the cost in interest terms of drilling wells and capping them is very high. They must begin producing immediately if they are to pay back properly. The higher the exploration costs, the more difficult the petroleum is to extract, and the higher the interest rate on borrowed money, the more significant this criticism regarding the attempt to save one's own resources while using someone else's.

Second, unless domestic energy sources of some type are made available, the same problem facing the free trade strategy confronts the ideal national security strategy. Consumer governments will obtain no leverage in oil pricing. If a consumer government attempts to rely solely on foreign oil, OPEC will probably supply that oil but at a premium price.

Third, whether domestic oil is worth keeping in the ground for future generations is a function of many variables, not the least of which is the rate of return on alternative investments. Oil will increase in value over the very long term at the rate of inflation or over the shorter term at the "rent," or rate of return, OPEC can exact for it. But wise investment of oil revenue in industrial development, for example, should yield a return in income terms to future generations far in excess of the value of the unexploited oil per se.

The argument that unforeseen innovations making use of petroleum in the drug industry or in artificial fabrics, for example, are likely to raise the future demand for petroleum disproportionately is a difficult argument to counter. But if there is no scientific *evidence* today that *future* demand for petroleum and petroleum products will increase more rapidly than the demand for other industrial goods, then perhaps we can do no better than accept the hypothesis that demand for oil, and derivatively oil prices, will increase about as they have in the past, an ineluctable, albeit a speculative, conclusion. Such a conclusion reinforces the wisdom of *using* rather than *saving* domestic petroleum stocks while investing the proceeds wisely in industrialization known to earn a higher return.

Neither the national security nor the free trade strategy in its ideal form is a practical strategy for the United States to follow. Elements of each strategy, however, suggest the basis for a more comprehensive energy strategy that the nation might embrace.

REALISM AND THE U.S. ENERGY PROBLEM

A general strategy that the United States could realistically pursue in energy terms would reduce, but not entirely eliminate, the fraction of petroleum imported from abroad. From the U.S. perspective there is nothing inherently wrong with the importation of foreign energy or other raw materials (indeed, as was seen earlier, in trade terms it is desirable) provided that either of two conditions do *not* obtain: that supply interruption threatens the welfare and the security of the nation or that foreign suppliers exact a high and arbitrary rent for their commodity. Unfortunately for the consumer, both of these conditions are currently present in the energy field and hence the need for an improved and realistic consumer energy strategy.

We attempt to sketch such a general strategic outline, part of which has already been implemented, part of which is unformulated or still pending.[6] Following this very brief outline of the general energy strategy, we shall focus on four additional and related substrategies that involve greater detail, find their origins uniquely within the prior analysis of this book, and are supportive of the objectives of the more general strategic outline.

First, any U.S. energy strategy ought to recognize that proved petroleum reserves are highly stocastic and lumpy as major new discoveries of oil and natural gas come on line. The definition of "new discovery" is itself debated. Successful *exploratory* wells, for example, are much more significant for purposes of supply estimation than the drilling of new producing wells in existing fields. Political decisionmakers must recognize an important statistical fact regarding discoveries. Since 1950 world *estimated proven reserves of petroleum have increased by 500 percent*. Five times as much oil and gas was available in 1970 as was estimated to exist twenty years earlier. Conservative methods of estimation may account for this artifact, but the uncertainty of geologic and economic factors also contributes to the error in projections. Significantly, however, the error was systematic; that is, it occurred in the same cumulative direction each year. The error was also shared in ten of eleven major fuel and nonfuel minerals, thus making it a statistical phenomenon with relevance beyond petroleum. Given these characteristics of reserve estimation, one might expect substantial amounts of undiscovered oil and gas in non-OPEC regions heretofore not adequately explored.

Since large new petroleum reserves undoubtedly exist and since the development of these reserves would put downward pressure on the world price, U.S. energy strategy must make available proper incentives to find and develop these reserves. Decontrol of oil and gas prices domestically so that the domestic and world price of petroleum are one is a valid incentive. Another stronger incentive is the establishment of a price floor for domestically produced petroleum in certain new higher cost areas. Five to seven years will be required to see the positive effects of either of these incentives regarding new non-OPEC discoveries.

Second, energy from alternative energy sources such as coal, nuclear breeder reactors, fusion, and solar receptors is needed to supplant foreign and domestic petroleum. Research into techniques that will make these energy sources economically competitive with petroleum must receive governmental support. But the principal policy question is to determine the correct mode of support as well as the relative research priority between the long-term, high-cost, high-risk, high-payoff option such as fusion and the short-term, low-risk, lower payoff option such as coal. In general, the private sector using the storehouse of applied technology currently available can probably develop large amounts of competitively priced energy from such a source as coal—if entrepreneurship is protected through some sort of price floor scheme whereby energy produced by high-cost techniques will earn not less than a preestablished threshold income regardless of how low the world price for petroleum falls. Similarly, long-range, more speculative research into such techniques as fusion can more adequately be carried out in the universities and with directly funded research. Mode of support and location of research activity are probably as critical in the alternative energy field as a decision regarding relative amounts of funding.

Third, the United States, because of the unattractiveness of aspects of its foreign policy to some of the oil producing countries, is in a particularly vulnerable supply position. Deterrents to oil embargo in the form of adequate domestic storage of petroleum, cooperation among consumer governments in the event of financial disturbances or selective embargoes, and the development of alternative channels of influence that could supplement petroleum safeguards per se—all are of importance in maintaining stable ties with the oil producing nations. In most of these areas, the mechanics of a deterrent policy have at least been articulated.

Fourth, the United States must attempt to achieve cooperation among the consumers beyond that of a deterrence policy. Cooperation regarding a price floor plan, joint research in alternative energy sources, and possibly some joint marketing arrangements would strengthen the consumer bargaining position.

Fifth, the United States as the largest energy consumer and the consumer with the highest per capita consumption of energy must take energy conservation seriously. Other things being equal, if the United States can maintain approximately the same rate of economic growth while employing less energy, the energy saving could have a very positive effect on price in a period in which energy supply is rapidly increasing. Inasmuch as the United States alone consumes almost 8 million barrels a day of petroleum to fuel automobiles, a doubling of the gas mileage per car could produce a net saving of 4 million barrels a day, an objective that is technically feasible and practicable through the use of a sizable excise tax on gasoline. Conservation of a similar type is feasible in a number of other areas of the economy in which some change in life-styles, perhaps, but no fundamental change in growth or productivity would result.

Given these five broad, and quite familiar although but no means universally accepted, elements of energy strategy, we now turn to four additional recommendations that emerge out of our prior analysis.

Creation of a Trilateral International Research Commission: Japan, West Germany, and the United States

Rationale for a Trilateral Energy Research Commission (TERC) is severalfold. First, the cost of a major attack on the development of new energy sources will be high in financial terms and will require a significant fraction of the total scientific and engineering talent of several countries. Only the richest and most technologically advanced nations, however, are likely to be able to mount such an effort.

Second, the ultimate benefits of energy research ought to be distributed widely among many societies capable of employing the research findings. Conversely, since the research findings will be distributed rather broadly and since the financial and manpower costs of the research are so great, no single society alone should be asked to bear them. Surely the United States should not undertake this research by itself.

Third, if energy research is coordinated, then the costs of duplication (which already are high because antitrust concerns and natural competitive instincts of the oil industry have led to research fragmentation) will be kept to a minimum. While repetition and replication of experiments can be extremely valuable in an atmosphere of free exchange of ideas and data, such an atmosphere has not existed in the rather secretive energy field and will not exist in the absence of specially administered research programs.

Fourth, as the foregoing analysis on the International Energy Agency revealed, coordination of research among all of the IEA members will be difficult and may not be especially desirable. Britain, for example, has a far different set of energy research and development priorities from those of the other IEA members. It is emphasizing a crash program of North Sea oil development at high financial cost. Much of this oil is calculated to earn foreign exchange on world markets. Hence Britain has little interest in expensive energy research that when applied will have the effect of driving the world price of petroleum downward.

Like Britain a number of other consumer governments in Europe will have little interest in supporting an aggressive program of energy research at the moment—because their research priorities differ from those of the United States, or because the financial cost of the research is too great for them to bear, or because they do not have the research facilities and scientific manpower to make a major contribution at this time. In these circumstances a realistic evaluation of harmonized energy research suggests that the IEA as an organizational sponsor is too broad and too disparate to carry out the specialized goals of technical and scientific development. Our analysis of the IEA coalition structure, however, provides insights into an alternate cluster of states that could implement a successful research program and that may have a sufficient identity of energy interest to make a substantial policy commitment.

By focusing upon the potential for energy research as well as the comparative dependence of the respective economies upon Middle East oil, the United States, Japan, and West Germany may *increase* their communality of energy interest, a point relevant to the empirical findings on IEA cohesion in Chapter V. Each of these states has great technical and scientific research capability, a desire for lower energy prices through supply increase, and a preference for avoiding threats to trade links with the oil producing countries. Research on alternative energy sources offers this type of potential. By uniting the three largest industrial democracies in a concordant investigation of the energy problem, the consumer governments will create the best opportunity for reduction of their mutual energy dependence by 1990.

Finally, the originality of this experiment in international research col-

laboration, and the positive impact of the undertaking on alliance relationships, should not be underestimated. An international "Manhattan Project"
addressing the global energy problem is unprecedented in terms of size and
ambitiousness of goals. But the enterprise could indeed become a prece-
dent in related fields in which the cost and the diversity of research talent
exceed the economic and technological capacity of a single nation. By
sharing the social risk associated with the project, the respective partners
are able to pursue simultaneously other individual scientific and technical
projects such as space exploration and major medical research, thus dis-
placing the fear of overconcentration within a single field.

At a time when alliance relations are strained and when the United
States is seeking new ways of injecting spirit and purpose into aging institutions and linkages, a mutual research and development effort of this
magnitude could genuinely enhance the basis for interdependence.[7] Regardless of specific outcome, the prospects are positive for an international
research accord, for improved world order, and for increased energy supply.
In short, a Trilateral Energy Research Commission among Japan, West
Germany, and the United States appears to maximize the chances of political and economic benefit from energy research in a number of ways.

Conservation, Energy and Economic Growth

Designed to cut the annual increase in the rate of U.S. energy consumption in half, the Carter energy program ought to move the nation a long
way toward greater energy efficiency. The excise tax on petroleum, gasoline
taxes, the "gas guzzler" tax on cars that get below standard mileage, the incentives for installation of energy-saving insulation, restructuring of utility
rates to reflect cost of service, and accelerated implementation of more
efficient building standards are measures that are needed to constrain petroleum consumption. However, all of these interventions into the market
may in time create distortions, some of which will be economically per-
verse.

For example, the proposal to force utility conversion from oil to coal
has precisely the opposite intent of the 1971–72 environmental legislation
which has the effect of encouraging utilities to quit coal and to burn larger
amounts of low-sulfur crude. Likewise, the Carter energy proposals would
force Texas and Louisiana to charge the same controlled rate for natural
gas inside these states as is charged in the interstate market. But the oil
producing states have long known that to charge less than the world market price for gas or oil (as is common practice in interstate markets) in-
duces shortages, precisely the shortages experienced at various times on the
East Coast in the winter of 1976–77. Thus the law would force the oil producing states to charge less than they are prepared to charge residential
consumers with the prospect that shortages will emerge for the first time in
those states where the gas itself is produced—a consequence that seems

illogical to the citizens of these states who would prefer security to artificial cost savings. All of these problems have emerged because the country has in the past attempted to sell a depleting resource to itself at less than the true world price for that resource.

In spite of the current need for many of the tough energy measures advocated by the Carter administration, the United States may be committing some of the same mistakes in public policy terms regarding energy that it committed earlier regarding the environment. Too little research precedes crash implementation of increasingly coercive government controls. For instance, little was known what the impact on transportation would be prior to the decision to append various new excise taxes to the cost of petroleum. To what extent will energy conservation attempts reduce the physical mobility within American society, and what effect in turn will constraints on mobility have on the life-style and earning capacity of the citizen? To what extent will increased energy costs and energy conservation efforts make some forms of transportation and physical mobility perhaps virtually obsolete, while creating a substantial spur to *communications*, particularly the electronic media, enabling people to see and hear one another if not to congregate as often for business and social purposes?

Ironically, the call to "limits to growth" heard earlier in the decade may in fact become a call to prevent economic stagnation brought about by necessary but precipitous energy and environmental controls that were dictated by years of imprudent social policy.

Conservation policies in the energy area are realistic only after careful research has been done on questions of this type. Insofar as price rises induce greater efficiency, that is, actual innovations that allow us to consume less energy,[8] these breakthroughs may enable other countries approaching the GNP and wealth of the United States to avoid investments in costly infrastructure such as highway systems that have virtually condemned the United States to continued policies of energy waste. It is these massive social commitments to currently unwise projects and endeavors requiring years and even decades for completion—often presupposing the availability of cheap energy—that demand continuing analysis and rethought.

Formulating an Oil Strategy in the Middle East

Politics and economics are intertwined for the United States regardless of what oil policy the government adopts. But politics and economics also are separate tools with which to shape energy policy. The margin of decision choice among foreign policy options may not be great, but it is genuine and exists whether consciously employed. In particular, the United States has three quite different politico-commercial strategies from which to choose.

We shall identify each strategy and then discuss it in detail later. First, the United States could pursue a strategy of commercial *fragmentation* on the OPEC fringe. Second, the United States could follow a strategy in the Middle East of *division and balance*. Third, the United States could attempt to forge a strategy with respect to Saudi Arabia, the largest oil producer and the OPEC price leader, of *tacit alliance*. Implications of each of these three politico-commercial strategies are quite different for U.S. foreign policy.

By *commercial fragmentation on the OPEC fringe* is meant a strategy whereby oil is purchased from the smaller producers at negotiated prices in such a manner that they are encouraged to bid against one another to get access to the American market and thus to obtain for themselves a larger market share and more revenue. This strategy has as its principal purpose *price reduction*. It allegedly will work best under two conditions: one, when surplus petroleum production puts pressure on OPEC to establish production constraints, a politically difficult exercise; two, when internal demands for revenue escalate beyond what the OPEC-allocated market share of petroleum sales provides. Let us look further at each of these conditions.

The question of surplus petroleum production is complex. On the one hand, because of the initial cutbacks in petroleum production during the embargo and because of the recession, excess production still exists in most countries as of 1976–1977. But increasing nationalization of oil properties in the host countries has disrupted some exploration efforts. As petroleum demand increases, surplus crude production will disappear and with it some of the opportunity to make the policy of commercial fragmentation work.

On the other hand, as new non-OPEC discoveries and oil from alternative sources (stimulated by the price rise) begin to come on line, the trend toward declining production surpluses could reverse itself. But the effect of the new oil production is likely to be quite delayed. In addition, Saudi Arabia has by far the greatest production flexibility because of its enormous financial reserves and low capital absorption capability. Thus, Saudi Arabia could subvert the U.S. strategy of OPEC commercial fragmentation by allowing the smaller producers more of its own market share. Since Saudi Arabia does not need the revenue currently anyway, loss of market share is relatively unimportant to it in revenue terms. In terms of power or internal OPEC leverage, the loss of market share could figure significantly, however, particularly at a time of critical decisions regarding price. Saudi Arabia might lose control over price decisionmaking if its market share dipped substantially and the high-price preference countries like Algeria, Libya, Iran, and Iraq obtained larger influence within OPEC. Ironically, by pushing price higher the OPEC governments will increase revenue but continue to reduce their collective market share in the face of larger and larger amounts of high-cost energy from the North Sea, Alaska, and elsewhere. Combined effects of reduced Saudi influence in OPEC and a declining OPEC market share of world energy production would together abet this strategy of fragmentation.

Concerning revenue needs the projections are somewhat simpler. Greater amounts of revenue will be needed as the development programs in Nigeria, Iran, Indonesia, and Venezuela rapidly expand. A number of these governments also are spending heavily on military training and arms procurement, programs that grow in cost over time. Thus, for those regimes without financial problems today (because of the combination of comparatively high oil revenues and bottlenecks in the economy that prevent the spending of all of the oil proceeds), revenue demands are likely to escalate rapidly in the future. But government budgets after all are determined by the regime and not solely by exogenous forces. When the needs for revenue increase, the government can always attempt to place brakes on various kinds of expenditures. Despite the social and political opposition this may create both within the decision elite and outside it, strongly centrist regimes can perhaps sustain themselves, while placing a ceiling on the rising aspirations of their peoples.

Where does this assessment leave us with respect to the general plausibility of a strategy of OPEC fragmentation on the fringe? To some extent the production surplus and the revenue need sides of the argument are opposed. Revenue needs currently are being met for most OPEC governments, thus making them less vulnerable to the fragmentation strategy than they will be when revenue needs increase beyond 1978. Current production surpluses, on the other hand, reinforce fragmentation, but these surpluses may decline in the medium term as the demand for oil climbs until major new fields are discovered or new energy from alternative sources comes on line beyond 1985. A host of further variables such as the fate of Saudi leadership within OPEC makes the analysis even more complicated.[9] Only one conclusion appears rather certain assuming vigorous consumer energy policies, namely, that both OPEC revenue needs and world production surpluses are likely to favor the strategy of fragmentation in the period *beyond* 1985.

Second is the strategy labeled "division and balance." It is a strategy that concedes that OPEC commercial cohesion is likely to remain quite high during the period in which the strategy is being implemented regardless of consumer efforts. It attempts therefore to obtain reasonable price policies from OPEC by reducing power concentrations within the cartel and by keeping the producers divided on *political* grounds. It borrows influence from the more purely political sphere and attempts to apply this influence within the commercial realm. How is such a strategy implemented?

Recognizing the centrality of Saudi Arabia for oil policy, the strategy identifies other major decision centers in the Middle East over which the United States may have some influence. Insofar as these other governments pursue policies that contradict Saudi objectives, Saudi Arabia needs support from the United States. Insofar as these other governments feel the pressure of Saudi commercial and political policies, the governments need help from the United States to balance relations with the principal oil producer. Hence, the United States is needed by both sides, and in contributing to a policy of balance within the Middle East the United States attempts to promote its own objectives, one of which is commercial gain, the other of which is stability and peace. The two rivals to Saudi influence of which we speak are, of course, Iran and Israel.

Iran facilitates a strategy of balance because it has very ambitious plans of economic development that the United States can further and because it has a substantial security problem along the Soviet and Iraqi borders and in the Gulf, which the United States can alleviate through military assistance. But in pursuing these two objectives, Iran also presents a security problem for Saudi Arabia, its smaller, weaker, albeit richer, neighbor. Since both of these regimes are politically conservative monarchies both tend to rely upon the United States, whose political ideology does not challenge them. Out of this reliance emerges the political leverage that the United States may attempt to convert into oil price stability.

Israel creates a different kind of problem for Saudi Arabia and correspondingly has received a different kind of support from the United States. Traditionally, Israel alone has been the preeminent military power in the Middle East matched only by the collective efforts of Egypt, Syria, and Jordan with backup support from the second tier of Arab countries. While Riyadh knows that Washington will never sacrifice the territorial security of Israel in a Middle East conflict and will not allow the military balance in the Middle East in terms of either quality or quantity to shift seriously against Israel, a considerable margin of maneuver, posturing, and strategy is still left the respective powers in negotiation. The fate of the West Bank of the Jordan, the Golan heights, the Moslem Holy Places in Jerusalem, and the Palestinian claims all are theoretically negotiable provided that the sovereignty and security of the Israeli state can be and is guaranteed. Saudi Arabia, moreover, for reasons of its own would like to see progress in the Middle East peace talks: the absence of progress creates problems for the oil-rich kingdom.

In periods of no war–no peace (1967 to 1973, for example) the political tension within the Arab world becomes virtually unbearable. Saudi Arabia, because of its conservative political regime and its wealth, becomes the target of attacks and vituperation by the "moderate," "radical," or "progressive" regimes within the Middle East as they are variously labeled. Hence, tension regarding Israel can very easily become tension regarding the identity and political survival of the Saudi monarchy. It is the seriousness and intensity of this latter issue that worries the Saudi leadership as much as the central question itself of Arab-Israeli relations.

The difficulty with the divide and balance strategy for the United States, then, is not that the strategy has no effect on Saudi Arabian foreign affairs but rather that the effect is often *too* large and *too* unpredictable. It is very hard, for example, to translate influence in the political sphere between Iran and Saudi Arabia smoothly and confidently into an implicit agreement on pricing between OPEC and the United States. For one thing, the former relations are direct and involve three polities, while the latter are indirect and involve a host of countries some of which have little interest in the resolution of Middle East political squabbles. For another thing, shifts in the Middle East power balance, particularly when Israel is involved, run risks concerning war. Hence, the balance of power cannot easily serve two masters, both peace and commercial issues; pursuit of the latter necessarily creates some *risk* of sacrificing the former, and the *cost* of war is so great that no responsible statesman can tolerate even small increases in this kind of risk.

What, then, is the utility of the divide and balance strategy in terms of international energy politics? At a maximum, from the consumer viewpoint, this is a second-best strategy to be pursued largely in the pious hope that it will avert a war by power-conscious nations. But its import for commercial policy and the price of oil must be greatly discounted. It may be used in conjunction with other strategies or as an interim strategy until another, better one is found. So many variables, however, cloud decision-making regarding the divide and balance notion that its timing and substance are not likely to extract much commercial benefit.

Arms sales to Iran at the wrong time, for example, are likely to strengthen the Iranian hand in OPEC vis-à-vis prices rather than weaken that hand by putting pressure on Saudi Arabia to stiffen its own opposition to a price increase. The subtleties of commercial negotiation are multiple and the weight of balance of power politics is so great that temporary energy gains are likely to be swept aside by the very process that insists upon them. Divide and balance ideas may play an auxiliary commercial role but never the central one they assume per se in international politics.

This analysis thus leaves the final Middle East energy strategy on the table for discussion, namely, that of tacit alliance with Saudi Arabia on grounds that are mutually acceptable to each state. For some both in the United States and Saudi Arabia, consideration of such a strategy is itself alarming. For others establishment of such an alliance is moot because of obligations and associations shared by both governments that would preclude closer ties. For others, however, such a tacit alliance has been impending ever since the effects of the first major price rises dissipated, the Saudi leadership position in OPEC solidified, and the merits of price stability and a stable political association with the United States became apparent. For such analysts a tacit Saudi-American alliance epitomizes the new era of interdependence.

What would the basis for such a tight association be and what would be its alleged benefits? According to the logic of such an association, Saudi Arabia would obtain two principal benefits. First, it would have access to advanced military technology and training that would transform its relatively small army and air force into a first-rate fighting unit capable of providing its own territorial security. Second, it would obtain from the United States the best educational assistance, equipment, and technology necessary to develop the country industrially. In return, the United States could expect guaranteed access to Saudi petroleum at prices that would increase at no more than the rate of world inflation. Such an alliance of interests might also include security guarantees to Saudi Arabia in the event of external military aggression and should include a provision which would reduce the risk to the United States of a renewed oil embargo. But the alliance would necessarily be tacit and covert because Saudi Arabia could not afford to alarm its OPEC partners on the one hand, nor could the United States afford to disturb its relationship with other consumer nations or its alliance with Israel on the other.

Despite a foundation in mutual state interests, the precondition of any successful alliance, this Saudi-American rapprochement would face stern tests on both sides. For Saudi Arabia would be strongly tempted to hold out as a future possibility the tempting prospect of an alliance along these lines, while causing a delay in the American ability to follow this strategy or any other practical alternative energy strategy—the longer the delay, the slower any meaningful energy response to joint OPEC initiatives.

Conversely, the United States might be tempted to offer an agreement along the proposed lines while in fact gearing up for the first strategy of fragmentation on the OPEC fringe or the second strategy of division and balance. Each of these latter strategies could be interpreted as injurious to Saudi state interests and hence any movement in their direction would undermine the idea of tacit alliance.

Tacit alliance, moreover, would cause each government to give up something, perhaps something more than each is prepared to yield. On the Saudi side the government would virtually have to forego use of the oil embargo as an instrument of diplomacy. Furthermore, the United States would probably have to give up its vision of a decisive decline in oil prices and an eventual collapse of OPEC. Neither objective is compatible with the aims of tacit alliance. Indeed, Saudi-American relations could stumble on a renewed Arab-Israeli war or on the Saudi decision to capitulate to demands for major price increases by the bulk of its OPEC partners. Plenty of room exists throughout such an agreed association for failure, default, or diversion from the original aims of the relationship. Nonetheless, a tacit commercial alliance between the world's largest oil exporter and the world's largest oil consumer contains elements worthy of extended reflection.

Which Middle East oil strategy the United States adopts is a function of many things, including the success of its own energy programs, the responsiveness of Saudi Arabia to initiatives, the general international political setting, and the particular period in which one envisions implementation of the strategy. While each strategy—fragmentation on the OPEC margin, division and balance, and tacit commercial alliance with Saudi Arabia—is self-contained, the United States may in fact vacillate among the strategies or attempt to straddle all of them. Yet the assumptions that underlie each strategy, as well as the probable effects, are quite different and not readily subsumed. Formulating an oil strategy for the Middle East is only one component of a larger set of long-range energy strategies. It is by no means the easiest component to devise, the least controversial, or the least important.

A Strategy for the Non-Oil, Non-Arab, Non-Moslem, Non-African, Poor Countries

Among the strategies that the United States ought to consider in the wake of the oil price hikes is a new program of foreign assistance to the group of countries most disadvantaged by the oil price increases. Since this group consists neither of Arab nor Moslem countries nor of black African nations eligible for Arab aid, they are much worse off than either the advanced industrial consumer nations or the favorites of OPEC in the Third World.[10] Many of these countries also must import food, a commodity that in price has paralleled the rise in the cost of petroleum. But U.S. aid is especially appropriate because of two further factors.

First, in relative terms, U.S. foreign economic assistance has declined to about a quarter of one percent of the U.S. GNP, thus placing the United States well down in rank among the world's aid donors. The United States is providing disproportionately less foreign aid than many of its leading allies. A place to increase this aid would be among those states jointly disadvantaged by high food prices and large petroleum import bills.

Second, although one underlying purpose of foreign aid is to redistribute wealth to the poor, U.S. aid has rarely been distributed among the poor countries on equity grounds. In Latin America, for example, there is no evidence that the poorer a country is, the more likely it is to receive large amounts of aid. Instead, aid has been distributed on the ground of capital absorption capability, that is, on the ability of the nation to employ aid in its economy successfully. Surely this latter criterion is a critical one and one that must take priority where large volumes of aid are concerned. It also seems to incorporate a system of self-reward since the larger a nation's capital absorption capability, the more aid for which it becomes eligible. Yet, when we realize that the most important single indicator of capital absorption capability is population size, the dynamic properties of this aid justification may appear less appealing.

But on both equity and capital absorption grounds, the poor countries having to pay more for imported oil today than they did in the past are justifiably anxious. While the actual dollar figure of their oil deficits may not be large, the impact of petro-inflation and balance of payments deficits make their cumulative economic burden quite grave. In dealing with these poor countries having petroleum import problems, the United States might consider a combination of two programs.

First, a calculation ought to be made regarding the size of their net oil deficits and a fund ought then to be devised from which the poor non-oil consumers could draw. They could use allocations from the fund to obtain petroleum directly from the producer governments or via normal transnational oil channels wherever the oil can be obtained most cheaply.

Second, many of these presently non-oil countries may have some prospects of oil production capability. This capability may have been unexplored or unexploited for a variety of reasons, including high political risk to private industry responsible for the investments. Should these non-oil countries find the arrangement satisfactory, they might be encouraged to pursue joint ventures with private oil firms to develop whatever reserves they possess, both as a means of meeting their own domestic needs (thus saving foreign exchange) and as a means of obtaining foreign earnings at a time when the world price of petroleum is very attractive.

In any case, the poorest countries of the world ought to receive attention from the United States in a period in which a major transformation of the world petroleum market has moved against them. Not only is this strategy in the interest of the countries receiving the offset to added petroleum costs plus the opportunity to discover new oil deposits. It is a strategy that combines the best characteristics of altruism and consumer self-interest as well.

A Strategic Overview

We began this chapter by noting the gap between the ideal and the real in the formulation of U.S. energy strategies. Despite the theoretical appeal of a pure free trade strategy, benefits are not likely to flow equally from it to all trading partners; in this period of arbitrary controls the consumers are likely to remain disadvantaged. A variant of the free trade notion is phrased in terms of an outrageous hypothesis, namely, that *in the long run* the nation with the greatest industrial base and technological dynamism may be the greatest beneficiary of the energy crisis. But for such a set of circumstances to occur, the United States would have to respond to the shock of the energy crisis with a spurt of inventiveness and industrial vigor created by both the stimulus of the relative shortage of cheap energy and the sudden availability of new capital. In comparative terms the United States may indeed develop more rapidly and more fully in the aftermath of the oil price increase than the producers themselves, which are being forced to modernize their economies in a fraction of the time the great industrial states of the present were allowed by history. A second prerequisite for this rapid U.S. advance to occur is the choice of a reasonable energy strategy for the more immediate present and future. Surely, neither the free trade strategy nor the national security strategy in its pure form, as we have argued, is a valid strategic option.

Realism suggests that only two conditions will lead to an improvement in the U.S. bargaining position, and both conditions will require time for fulfillment: first, plausible constraints, some of which may be in addition to price itself, on the increase in demand for energy in the United States and elsewhere among consumers; second, enormous increases in the supply of non-OPEC energy from a variety of sources. We then outlined the elements of a general consumer energy strategy that the United States rather clearly must follow if it expects to achieve a new equilibrium of energy supply and demand at substantially more favorable prices.

But the special contribution of this chapter was the formulation, based on prior analysis contained in this volume, of four sets of ancillary energy strategies focusing on specific problem areas. First, in the area of research into alternative energy sources, we recommended the creation of a Trilateral Energy Research Commission composed of the three nations most likely to share a capacity for this research and to have compatible energy goals, that is, West Germany, Japan, and the United States. Second, we observed that energy conservation is too serious a question to be left to the market alone to decide. Fundamental research into the economic, social, and political factors that facilitate prudent use of energy must precede realistic policy in the energy conservation area. In particular, the nation needs to take a hard look at its enormous long-term investments in such energy-intensive efforts as the highway program to determine how the forward and backward linkages stemming from such a program limit the ability of the market to determine efficient price outcomes. In other words, to what extent does prior broad-based social investment become deterministic and compelling for those decisionmakers in a *subsequent* generation who must make energy choices under entirely different price assumptions?

Third, strategy in the narrower sense of Middle East oil politics requires careful assessment and action. Three quite different politico-commercial strategies were posited, ranging from an effort to detach the marginal producers from the remainder of the cartel, to a policy of division and balance, to a policy of tacit commercial alliance between the largest oil producer, Saudi Arabia, and the largest oil consumer, the United States. The task here was to delineate differences among these strategies and to identify their strengths and weaknesses from the U.S. perspective. Some fairly firm conclusions resulted.

Fourth, the United States has an obligation to help those countries in the Third World most disadvantaged by the oil price rises that for reasons of religion, ethnic composition, or geographic location are not likely to receive aid from the principal donors in OPEC. In the process of providing assistance to offset the incremental oil deficits among the poorest of the Third World countries, the United States may also find ways of solving the global energy problem.

In sum, U.S. energy strategy is not a monolith but a complex of pragmatic policies that blend to achieve the dual objective of restraints upon demand and stimulus to supply. Energy strategies must avoid the Odyssean dilemma of unfounded optimism in short-term solutions and the evident fear of hopelessness and lack of real progress associated with long-range solutions. By adopting the correct complex of energy strategies, the United States already possesses the right combination of resources and manpower to escape both the Scylla and the Charybdis of energy politics.

VIII

Desanctifying Oil Myth: New Structures, New Political Relations?

Co-dependence: Emerging Political Reality

Properly used the term "interdependence" has its largest meaning when applied to pairs of states of roughly equal economic size, level of development, and modernization.[1] Interdependence is possible where a substantial volume of trade passes between countries and where the importance of this trade transcends fissiparous issues of politics for both partners. Cooperation marks interdependence. One speaks of the interdependence of the Japanese and American economies, for example, in a way that would scarcely be appropriate regarding the Soviet Union and the United States (for reasons of political incongruity and trade volume) or Japan and Syria (for reasons of comparative size and development). Interdependence entails at least nascent erosion of power politics.

Emerging between the United States and OPEC—particularly the Arab coalition—is a new political and commercial relationship characterized by respect plus a certain wariness. But the relationship cannot fairly be described as interdependent. It is rather *co-dependent*. Co-dependence involves *reciprocal, nonidentical forms of coercive capability*. Each partner needs the other and hence is dependent upon the other, but each also has an imminent capacity to restrain the other from acts damaging to its welfare or security. This capacity is coercive and mutually present but the nature of the coercive instrument differs for each partner.

Needs
As of 1973 the United States was importing 35 percent of its petroleum largely from OPEC, and the margin of this foreign dependence was rapidly

181

growing. The United States seeks from OPEC nations not only an adequate supply of oil at reasonable prices but also understanding regarding American security obligations to Israel. Conscientious OPEC behavior would also acknowledge responsibility toward international financial stability, economic assistance to the Third World, and the political viability of noncommunist regimes inside the Middle East and outside.

OPEC in turn needs the United States for several reasons. First, the United States as consumer of half of the industrialized world's total oil intake is OPEC's largest petroleum market, a fact that becomes especially important in periods of slack demand. Second, OPEC seeks from the United States the high technology that is often available in insufficient quantity or at unacceptable prices elsewhere—or not available elsewhere at all. Third, the conservative members of OPEC, which contribute the bulk of current oil exports, recognize that no major power is more tolerant of their internal political preferences or more sanguine concerning capitalist enterprise than the United States. Fourth, despite occasional irritations with American political leadership, all of the OPEC members, including Algeria, count on the United States to balance Soviet military ambitions. Fifth, the OPEC leadership seeks evenhandedness from the United States regarding the Arab-Israeli dispute and the settlement of Palestinian claims, acknowledging that only the United States has the political leverage to make these claims reality.

Both trading partners are thus dependent. Mutual dependence, however, is accompanied by important reciprocal capabilities for restrictive action.

Capabilities

OAPEC demonstrated in 1973 that the oil weapon was a powerful diplomatic instrument capable of bringing the advanced industrial economies of the West to the brink of strangulation. If they once did, no policymakers in Europe, Japan, or the United States today underestimate the potency of this weapon. Despite efforts by the consumers jointly to protect themselves with a year's supply of petroleum, two considerations make the oil weapon more formidable than ever.

First, the companies that once acted as an interface between the quarreling consumers and producers—exacting a sizable profit for their trouble —are no longer in a position to make future embargoes leak. Following nationalization of upstream production, the OPEC governments are now capable of controlling decisionmaking. Iran and Venezuela are also relatively less significant producers within the cartel today and are thus less likely to be able to supply all outside demand should they choose not to support a future embargo.

Second, OAPEC is rapidly investing in downstream production, particularly in tanker trade and petroleum refineries, thus creating much greater leverage over distribution than was the case in 1973. Since the ability to switch destinations and manipulate refinery stocks was the key in 1973 to a reduction of pressure on the two isolated states, Holland and the United States, loss of this flexibility will mean that country-specific embargoes will become much more feasible. By focusing a potential embargo on specific countries (a task that will never meet complete success because of IEA countermeasures regarding sharing), the utility of the oil weapon is greatly increased because recalcitrant consumer nations can to some degree be conquered by division.

If the producer countries have strengthened their capacity for embargo, the United States has strengthened its hand with respect to other forms of coercive capability. First, as Egypt discovered with Soviet military aid in mid-March 1976, failure to supply spare parts, ammunition, and training can virtually immobilize a modern air force. So worried about this capability, the shah of Iran immediately warned the United States that he would cut off supplies of oil if the United States attempted a policy of spare parts blackmail. Curiously, this was a revelation of producer weakness as well as consumer strength. All of the major oil exporting countries have increased their military dependence upon the United States since 1973, for reasons previously discussed, instead of reducing dependence. If an aid cutoff occurred at a time when Iranian security, for example, was in some jeopardy, or when supplies of oil had been guaranteed from other quarters, the cutoff could have a devastating short-term impact upon the security of isolated nations.

Second, and seldom articulated, the principal oil exporting countries are vulnerable to intraelite power struggles encouraged from outside the country. While the consumers benefit from regime stability so long as the oil flows between countries, the situation would be quite different in a period of prolonged embargo, a consideration that is tacitly admitted by most informed observers of oil matters.

Third, if (and only if) the consumer countries were made sufficiently desperate by the interruption of oil supplies, the U.S. government might feel compelled by the insistence of allies and the pressures of domestic opinion to employ interventionary force. This last resort strategy might be opposed by the increasingly powerful Russian attack navy deployed in the Mediterranean Sea and the Indian Ocean. But the capacity of the U.S. military to strike quickly with a large occupation force focused on a critical target can hardly be ignored. Much has been made of the willingness of certain governments to destroy their own facilities rather than submit to occupation. Yet the time required to rebuild those same facilities for a government with the industrial capability has been estimated by knowledgeable sources to be not more than a year.

The upshot of this analysis is that the coercive capability that certain OPEC countries and the United States hold regarding each other is in some ways as disagreeable for the wielder as for the target. Moreover, most of this capability is of the low-probability-use, high-cost variety in both political and economic terms. Neither side wants to see a situation in which it would be forced to play its last cards.

Given the mutual dependence of the United States on OPEC and vice versa, and given the reluctance of each to employ coercive capabilities, a kind of strategic stalemate emerges, which we have described as co-dependence. Periodic admonitions issue from Teheran and Washington, but even these warnings are so discounted by the intended audience that the commercial actors take virtually no notice. In the absence of an outside event such as a renewal of the Arab-Israeli war or a large-scale conflagration within the Gulf region, the relationship of co-dependence between the United States and OPEC would have to be described as stable. Co-dependence may not be as tension-free as interdependence, but its outcome for stable association amounts to approximately the same thing.

IMPACT OF OIL ON THE STRUCTURE OF THE INTERNATIONAL SYSTEM

Stripped of mythology, oil politics has nonetheless a significance for change in the structure of the international system that is easy to misinterpret. In a period in which the tight bipolarity of the system is disappearing and some but not all of the cold war tensions have relaxed, the ideological cleavage between the advanced industrial countries and the Third World can be exaggerated. Likewise, the trend toward greater equality of power in the system and hence toward greater autonomy of foreign policy—while unmistakably present—is subject to exaggeration in terms of rapidity if not direction. Oil politics has by no means simplified the interpretation of these structural trends.

The real structural weight of oil politics falls on the nations in the middle of the power hierarchy. We may think of this impact as *structural turbulence* at the middle level. Venezuela, Nigeria, Indonesia, Iran, and a number of the Arab countries are enjoying sudden upward mobility. Inside their respective regions they have obtained prominence and growing commercial influence. Provided that indigenous Saudi financial skills can quickly be developed to match the size of the Saudi financial reserves, Saudi Arabia may replace some of the older powers, for example, as a leader in international monetary affairs.

But the *extent* of the upward mobility and the *scope* of the newly acquired influence of the oil producers are subject to definite limits. Within the Middle East, for example, *none* of the oil producing nations has *all* of the characteristics that would enable it to achieve the status of a great power and thus a global international political role. Saudi Arabia, Kuwait, and the United Arab Emirates have the financial capability (because of the immensity of their petroleum reserves) but not the population size, the industrial base, or the military strength to exert balanced global influence. Egypt has the population and territorial size, the potential for industrial development, and the military capability but, even with current discoveries, insufficient petroleum reserves. Iran has ambitious development plans, adequate population size, a large army, but petroleum reserves the bulk of which will be exhausted before the end of the century; this is adequate time to lift the nation out of poverty but not sufficient time to develop a lasting political role as a global actor.

In terms of per capita wealth the several OPEC countries already match the richest nations in the system, but unless the generation of wealth is made independent of petroleum production, the oil exporting nations will have difficulty sustaining current high living standards, let alone building an invulnerable power base. A rapid rise for several of the OPEC states from the bottom third of the status and power hierarchy to the top third is a predictable outcome of the oil bonanza. But none of the OPEC nations is likely to penetrate the elite 10 percent of the system accustomed to broader political leadership.

At the same time, the oil price increases will contribute to the further downward mobility of some states on the middle echelon. Governments like Denmark, Belgium, Greece, Spain, and Italy, considered to be among the upper tier of contemporary nation-states, are likely to slip on the scale of status and political power. Unable to produce the kind of high-technology items that many of the OPEC countries want and unable to match the rate of economic growth and military spending of these new middle powers, the older states are likely to enter a phase of relative decline.

Within the Middle East itself the states with oil for export are likely to play a much more vigorous role politically than they have in the past relative to the non-oil governments Lebanon, Syria, and Jordan. Since the states with the largest oil reserves also possess some of the most conservative regimes, one might anticipate a moderation of Middle East international politics. But the cleavage between radical and conservative ideologies, plus the continued support of Israeli confrontation by the Arab governments in each group, scarcely guarantees that moderation will climax the rise of the new middle class of nations to regional power.

Underscoring the greater complexity of Middle East international relations today is the fact that the political center of gravity has shifted geographically or rather it has splintered into two separate focuses. From 1948 to 1973 Middle East politics centered on the Suez Canal region involving principally Egypt and Israel. Since 1973 the Suez region continues in political importance but the Gulf region has achieved ascendance involving principally Saudi Arabia and Iran. Confrontations in the Gulf region acquire as much global significance today, because of oil, as the Arab-Israeli dispute alone could claim a decade ago.

While each of these sets of subregional rivalries is autonomous, the rivalries are not without potential impact for one another. In particular, the ambiguous role that Iran is likely to play in any future Arab-Israeli dispute is a new variable in an always uncertain calculation. What is certain is that Iran has both the capacity and the apparent intention of extending its influence, by diplomatic if not military means, as far as the Mediterranean shoreline. Neither side could count on the neutrality of Iran in a future confrontation. Although Iran leaned toward the Arab states in the October war, neither the weight nor the direction of that posture can be assured today. Indeed, political stability in the Gulf region is sufficiently important to Iran such that the shah or his successor is likely to find stability in the Suez to his advantage as well. One can easily envision Iran attempting to play the role of holder of the balance in the Middle East between the conservative and radical states, on the one hand, and between the Arabs and Israel, on the other. But unlike an island state, Iran is at the center of the "continental" powers and consequently may have concealed territorial ambitions of its own, ambitions that may make prudent stewardship of the balance of power unacceptedly tedious.

During the early 1980s another deep-laid transformation is likely to pass slowly over the Gulf region. Iraq is likely to replace Iran as the second leading Middle East oil producer. Not only will this change create new opportunities for an Iraqi imprint on OPEC policies, but also it will place Iran at a disadvantage relative to the phalanx of rich Arab oil states beginning at the Soviet border with Iraq and stretching through Kuwait, Saudi Arabia, and the United Arab Emirates to the Indian Ocean. Such a change could elicit a crisis in Persian foreign relations that in the midst of its massive development program will not easily disappear. But since unity within OPEC is prefaced upon political cooperation among neighbors and rivals, all parties have ample incentive to settle disputes without violence. The question for analysts to ponder is whether in the face of possible regime instability and international instability, commercial incentives for peace are sufficient.

In addressing this question one must ask a further question, too. Has the revolution of "progressive" politics halted in the Middle East? Has Arab socialism permanently lost ground? Certainly, the Lebanese civil war must be interpreted in the light of this battle between the forces of radical socialism, on the one hand, and capitalism and political conservatism, on the other. While the roles of Egypt's Sadat and Syria's Assad seem curiously inverted in terms of ideological proclivities and the Lebanese war, the historically more diverse roles of the Palestinians and Saudi Arabia are sufficiently transparent.

One suspects that for the interim, Arab socialism has been blunted by the new wave of capitalism sweeping across the Middle East oil economies. Even in Libya, Algeria, and Iraq socialism for the time being seems to have made its peace with government-controlled free enterprise. While Saudi Arabia, Iran, Jordan, the United Arab Emirates, and Kuwait have found capitalism and the oil price rise to be a great boon to their monarchic style of political leadership, it is too early in the day to argue that the pendulum of political change has stopped permanently right of the clock's nadir.

Turning to a related impact, how will the new concentration of wealth in the hands of OPEC statesmen affect the Soviet-American military balance? Despite the desires of some OPEC governments not to tamper with this balance, the spiraling cost of energy carries a potential for shifts in power at least in relative terms during the next twenty-year interval. Should the United States find the previously discussed, so-called outrageous hypothesis a persuasive stimulus, the effects on the United States may be marginal to moderately positive relative to the Soviet Union. A boost to its foreign trade sector combined with a new thrust of technological and scientific change fostered by the effort to make alternative energy sources competitive could enhance the vitality of the U.S. economy. Hence, depending upon its response the United States may be able to convert the energy crisis into a horn of Amalthea.

On the other hand, if the United States fails to meet the challenge of its dwindling internal energy supplies, the consequences for its international political position relative to the Soviet Union will be negative and measurable. With almost three times the declining American 5 percent of the world's petroleum reserves, the Soviet Union has been a large potential beneficiary of the price rise in resource terms. A lower rate of past consumption promises a comparatively larger future stock of this precious natural resource, increasing the capacity for future Soviet economic development. Talk of constraints on economic growth is likely to alter Soviet development patterns less than the American for reasons of greater Soviet nationalist commitment. While Americans may share a greater ideological predisposition to limit growth elicited by problems of pollution and overcrowding, greater resource constraints (in the form of higher relative prices) could also of necessity induce declining American economic growth rates. Parity of Soviet and American power may be one of the first casualties of the price revolution of 1973 (although we discount the earnestness of such a prediction).

Regardless, however, of relative power shifts between the United States and the Soviet Union or among the old and new industrial states catalyzed by the energy shortage, the nakedness of the six energy myths explored in these pages remains evident.

The consumer nations may berate the OPEC cartel for price inequity and exploitative commercial practice. Elements of the world community may blame Israel for the transformation of commercial relationships, and Israel may continue to misread the shifting currents of world politics. Multinational oil companies may retain the profit label "obscene," just as their power collapses and migrates toward a genuine cartel. Members of the U.S. Congress may flail away at the corpse of multinational oil power, thinking thereby that the case of OPEC has been sabotaged. Efforts within the eighteen-nation International Energy Agency may create the atmosphere of unity, without the similarity of interest to translate that unity into concerted price policies. OPEC may convince the consumer nations of its unity and impregnability, thus undermining the determination of the advanced industrial countries to help themselves. But all of these myths distort serious analysis and decisionmaking. Governments will find a much sounder basis of policy in a delineation of interests, an effort to distinguish fact, and a formation of objective strategy. Desanctified, political myth becomes as harmless and irrelevant as the purpose to which it was first called. Oil myth should find no firmer advocacy.

Epilogue

IN ENERGY MATTERS myth is ever present. In terms of their assumptions about the causes of the energy crisis and in terms of the manner in which they attempt to justify their policies, governmental decisionmakers exploit myth that they think others are likely to believe and in turn are manipulated by a reality that often they only partially perceive.

Contrasts between the Ford and Carter energy programs are enlightening in this regard. Although not excessively partisan, one program was typically Republican, the other typically Democratic. One emphasized the supply side while rejecting energy conservation measures as insufficient to constrain world oil price increases; the other stressed the demand side, while denying that U.S. energy production could be substantially accelerated through governmental policy in the next decade. By dissociating the program from production and exploration, President Carter also obtained the confidence of constituents who might reject any proposal appearing to favor the oil industry. Hence, in orientation, each program is a seeming repudiation of the other, a fact that neither the architects of the policies nor the press have noted.

Just prior to announcement of Carter's energy program, a number of studies including a propitious CIA analysis of declining Soviet oil production were released, which bolstered demand constraint and conversely justified ignoring the supply side. The view that supplies cannot be substantially increased also supported continued control of oil and gas prices. The extreme assumption that there is no petroleum left to be discovered inside the United States and offshore may indeed be necessary to make Americans accept energy conservation. However, even the less exaggerated view that any existing petroleum, if discovered, would not temper world oil prices contradicts evidence that most areas have yet to be explored and that incentives to accelerated development of reserves are feasible. Such views create few policy options and rely primarily upon OPEC prudence regarding future price advances since demand constraints alone cannot guarantee price stability. From the OPEC viewpoint, the absence of additional exploration incentive makes current U.S. energy policy look like a conspiracy by the world's largest oil consumer "to drain them first." The producers fear that despite constraints on demand the United States will have to press for much more OPEC oil than OPEC is prepared to supply.

There are numerous forks on the road to a sensible energy policy, some of which end in blind alleys. Although oil myth makes selection of the correct route confusing and somewhat fortuitous, a number of the blind alleys can be identified in advance.

As Chapter IV argued at length, divestiture of the large oil companies is one such mistaken path.[1] Divestiture is superficially attractive as an economic means to lower energy prices. Psychologically pleasing to individuals with a populist impulse, divestiture is attractive in an economic sense because it promises greater competition among a series of smaller companies. Greater competition supposedly yields leaner profit margins and therefore a better deal for the consumer. But what such a calculus neglects is that large corporate size may generate major economies of scale. In particular, these economies of scale may stem from vertical integration, namely, the ownership of all operations from wellhead to gas pump within a single organization. Transaction costs between levels of integration may be minimized, thus making the overall operation more efficient. Efficiency, according to some analysts of capitalist enterprise, is what the capitalist process has most to offer the consumer.

Somewhat skeptical of both of these sets of arguments regarding the comparative merits of divestiture (that is, the advantages of market competition among smaller corporate units versus the advantages of efficiency through vertical integration), we labeled the problem of weighing these advantages to the consumer the paradox of uncapturable efficiencies. We do not deny that vertical integration creates the possibility of greater economic efficiency. We are merely skeptical that the benefits from these efficiencies are ever fully transferred to the consumer in the modern oligopolistic setting. Conversely, however, neither would divestiture ensure the transference of advantages to the consumer because although the *market* might be considered more efficient after divestiture (i.e., more competitive), each individual firm would be less so. Indeed, the breakup of the large oil companies would guarantee that for the resulting entities many economies of scale would disappear. Divestiture thus would destroy precisely that which it seeks to create—transferable benefits to the consumer through enhanced corporate efficiency.

We concluded from our analysis that if the proponents of divestiture have a case, the case must be made elsewhere. The logical place for this case concerns the industrial relationship with OPEC. If it were possible to demonstrate that OPEC would be weakened by divesting the large oil companies of some of their assets, then divestiture perhaps could be regarded as an instrument to further consumer energy policy. While the arguments are too many and too complex to recap here, we observe that this area is where the debate over divestiture centers. We further maintain that divestiture is incapable of achieving anything like the proposed fragmentation of OPEC, however, and may in the long-run assist in the opposite: OPEC control over the oil market may be *enhanced* by ill-considered efforts at divestiture. Other arguments that we examined carefully, moreover, revealed that regardless of the impact on OPEC, divestiture may have a very negative effect on the U.S. competitive position in the world oil market by enabling firms based outside the United States to achieve a dominant position in the industry now primarily occupied by corporations displaying a still essentially American composition and perspective.

An additional oil myth that appears to reinforce the logic underlying divestiture and surely the emotion surrounding it is the obscene profit assertion. Despite many ways corporations have of hiding profits and despite admittedly large cash flows, the oil companies in recent years have on the average revealed no astonishing profit levels. In Chapter III we considered the postwar profit experience of the oil industry. The ill-timed profit bubble of 1974, which burst a year later following predictable governmental fiscal moves in both the consumer and producer countries, left the oil industry with a strong cash position, a very negative public image, and a completely altered long-term asset posture. In reviewing the profit picture of the oil industry relative to that of the other major industries in the United States, we also examined the relationship between the profit issue and the divestiture movement. Without the myth of corporate exploitation of the consumer via excessive profits, the divestiture movement would probably have found little backing within the Congress or the electorate.

In the absence of an ability to make the oil industry a scapegoat for the nation's energy problem, a small but intense effort has been mounted to apportion Israel and Arab-Israeli politics in general that responsibility. Prima facie grounds for this identification stem from the simultaneous occurrence of the October war of 1973 and the initial fourfold oil price increase. In Chapter II we looked at the origins of the price increase and the respective motivations of statesmen inside and outside OAPEC to find an adequate justification for the oil price hikes. We noted the varying behavior of governments in 1973 and in 1967, when an oil embargo likewise was instituted but with very differing results. Our conclusion regarding oil price policy in 1973 and thereafter was that it has been far more a matter of *sound economic policy* on the part of the members of the cartel aided by fortunate external events than a matter of Arab-Israeli relations or American foreign policy toward Israel. A significant measure of this contention is that those non-Arab states and even non-OPEC states that have oil to sell but no particular conflict with Israel over foreign relations nonetheless have sought to maintain high oil prices with at least as much vigor as the central oil power in the Middle East and the architect of the oil embargo,

Saudi Arabia. But having shown that neither Israel nor Israeli politics is a genuine cause of the consumer energy dilemma, we also attempted to show that the obverse relationship, namely, the influence of oil politics on Israel, is very real. We assessed the dimensions of this influence and the reasons for its understatement. The burden of high energy prices, however, can scarcely be placed upon Israel; yet this myth is in some quarters still stoutly maintained.

Hence, attacks upon the credibility of the oil industry and upon Israel are less than helpful in finding a solution to the world energy crisis. An alternate shortcut to cheaper energy that is sometimes recommended is *consumer solidarity* in the form of large, multilateral association via the International Energy Agency. The purpose of consumer solidarity is to coordinate the energy policies of the major consumer nations so as to encourage energy conservation, to protect the industrialized countries against supply interruption, and to prevent competitive upward bidding of oil prices. Whether or not IEA is an organization dedicated to confrontation, as some OPEC leaders assert, its objective is probably to create at least as much unity among, and confrontation by, consumers as the oil producers themselves have achieved through OPEC. The problem, as some observers see it, is that IEA has generated less confrontation, or unity, or mutual impact on consumer energy policy than the myth of consumer solidarity contends.

IEA efforts may be divided into two groups. First are its efforts to protect members against the sudden, short-term impact of another oil embargo, particularly a selective embargo aimed at one or two countries. While the capacity for implementing such a future embargo has grown apace since 1973, especially since the United States is now much more dependent upon imported oil and since the tanker trade is much more directly under the control of the exporting countries, the IEA effort to build reserve stocks of petroleum, to share oil during crisis, and to establish decision procedures is in the main quite impressive.

But whereas IEA displays success regarding potential emergency measures, it lags behind badly in the second area of coping with long-term energy needs. Energy conservation programs are missing or poorly implemented where most needed, and only a modicum of actual production coordination or price policy exists among the members. Why is there such a dearth of collective long-term energy policy among the consumer governments?

The analysis reported in Chapter V indicated that the lack of coordinated long-term energy initiatives is not hard to explain. A fundamental cleavage in energy characteristics and preferences exists between the United States, the largest and politically most significant energy importer, and the remaining members of the agency. This cleavage is so wide that the United States is isolated inside a coalition of one. Britain and Norway, for example, will become energy exporters of some importance in the next few years, which will remove them from the group of states seriously wishing to place downside pressure on energy prices. Other governments do not have the large coal deposits of the United States or the capacity for research into alternative energy sources. Others like Italy are even more vulnerable to the economic and financial consequences of any future tensions between consumers and producers and are thus not prone to support any form of collective political action. Thus, the United States faces a situation within the IEA in which it and it alone can lead. But because of its isolation, the United States finds consumer solidarity to be an inopportune myth. Not able to conjoin a collective energy policy with IEA via consensus, the United States is reduced to leadership via domination or hegemony, an option that Washington prudently has rejected. Formally attractive, consumer solidarity among a large group of industrial states appears doomed for reasons much more fundamental than leadership style or administrative skill. The separate interests of the consumer nations in energy matters prevent them as a bloc from responding to the OPEC challenge.

Where, then, does this analysis leave the policymaker and the observer of oil politics? Is some sort of possibly violent frontal attack on the members of the Organization of Petroleum Exporting Countries justified by an assumed moral superiority of the consumer cause and by the material extremity toward which the consumers find themselves driven? The realm of politics necessarily encompasses that of law, and that of law surely must encompass concepts of justice, no matter how multifold. Every time a political decision is made to distribute economic resources, a concept of justice is invoked whether implicitly or explicitly. Should we find that a just price for petroleum can be ascertained, and should we be able to demonstrate that this price has been exceeded by current OPEC cartel policy, then the consumer nations led by the United States might be on firm ethical ground to demand a price reduction. Moreover, insofar as OPEC refused to acknowledge the validity of the consumers' moral claim to fair commercial treatment, the consumer governments might feel impelled toward stronger action in order to obtain observance of this claim. But the validity of these ethical arguments in the international commercial realm must surely rest on the degree to which a just price for oil can be determined and the degree to which this price has been exceeded, with subsequent material harm, social unrest, and spiritual duress among the affected populations.

Exploring the grounds for the determination of a just petroleum price both in practical terms and in the theoretical context of utility (Chapter I), we found that very little evidence exists in support of a particular price as just or in support of a method to determine such a price. Unable to defend any given petroleum price as just, we find ourselves in the awkward ethical position of not knowing whether a given oil price level is unjust.

Thus, according to this analysis, the issue of a fair, or equitable, price for petroleum is incapable of present resolution, and the political debate regarding preferred governmental action in energy matters must be carried on rather blindly in some other arena, perhaps that of state interests.

A consequence of this inability to determine analytically a just price for oil is that the analysis cannot resort to stereotyped heroes and villains. The great petroleum polemic is not easily broken into moral absolutes or simple imperatives. Rather, it is composed of actors pursuing their own short-run and long-run interests, interests that tend to conflict or to be reinforcing depending upon circumstance and actor preference. As de Gaulle was fond of saying with respect to international politics, there are no lasting friends or enemies only state interests. So it is with oil politics. In order to perceive these interests accurately, we might add, we must free them from the myth that tends to obscure them.

Where does this conclusion regarding the indeterminacy of a just price for petroleum leave the consumer nations? Are they forever condemned to accept the dictates of a manipulated cartel price for petroleum? More narrowly, is OPEC itself likely to become the permanent successor to the Texas Railroad Commission, calculating and adopting production quotas and price levels suitable to the preferences of the OPEC membership? In attempting to answer these questions, we examined the final petroleum myth—the myth of perpetual OPEC unity (Chapter VI).

An important property of this final myth is illustrative of most political myths. Each political actor can passively accept an externally established set of events, thus translating myth into real situations. Or the actor can contest this set of events defined by some other actor or force and create an alternate reality in defiance of that which may have seemed predestined. Not all of oil politics is subject to the free will of the consumer governments, certainly, but neither is all of the commercial context in which they presently find themselves predetermined. In other words, it is quite largely up to the consumer governments themselves to decide whether the myth of perpetual OPEC unity is valid or flawed.

The analysis of OPEC demonstrated that coalition formation within the organization is far advanced. At least two coalitions and possibly as many as four coexist and bargain for advantage regarding overall OPEC policy. Perhaps the most powerful coalition, headed by Saudi Arabia, is the low-price preference coalition. Saudi Arabia favors comparatively lower prices than some of the other OPEC states because it has a very small population and huge annual petroleum revenue. This combination of factors has created enormous financial reserves that are vulnerable to foreign exchange risks. At the same time, the huge petroleum reserves of the low-price preference countries are vulnerable to a future price dip if alternative energy sources developed because of fear of high energy prices should come on line before the end of this century. Thus, Saudi Arabia would prefer to settle for slightly lower prices today and thereby reduce the chance of stimulating the production of cheaper energy in the future.

In contrast, the high-price coalition of states led by governments like Iran and Algeria need as much revenue as they can quickly obtain. They have comparatively large populations and ambitious economic development programs. They also in some cases are investing large sums in military purchases. Most important, despite seemingly large annual oil production levels, their overall petroleum reserves are not large and they have no large financial surpluses. Hence, they have a triple incentive to raise oil prices rapidly. First, countries like Iran do not have to worry about foreign exchange risks in the way Saudi Arabia does because Iran has no highly vulnerable financial reserves. Second, Iran has every reason to raise prices quickly *as a conservation measure* in order to make its petroleum last as long as possible. Third, Iran has no fear of energy substitution in the future by the consumer nations because regardless of upward pressure on oil prices, Iran's oil will be virtually exhausted before cheaper energy comes on line.

Thus, the high-price coalition and the low-price coalition are quite opposed regarding the best price strategy for OPEC to follow. Global economic factors also affect the judgments of the decisionmakers, encouraging price increases in good times and price restraint in bad.

A consequence of the dichotomy between price strategies, sharpened in some instances by cultural and political factors, is that conflict within OPEC results from two sets of forces. Conflict stems first from the natural tensions arising *internal* to the cartel over the optimal price strategy. Conflict stems secondly from the policies adopted by the consumer governments *external* to the cartel regarding constraints on energy demand and regarding increases in energy production.

It is important to recognize that the cartel is likely to remain stable in the absence of one or other set of forces, the internal or the external. But modest levels of internal tension and external pressure are likely to place cartel unity under great strain. Indeed, in social scientific terminology, the relationship between internal tensions and external pressures is multiplicative. Above a certain threshold the impact of these joint forces upon cartel unity is likely to be explosive. Unless the consumer governments are able to restrain their energy consumption and to increase the production of oil, gas, coal, solar, and atomic energy substantially, the threshold of fragmentation may, however, not be reached. Thus, the myth of perpetual OPEC unity is at least as much a product of consumer choice as it is of producer resolve.

In dynamic terms the evolution of cartel behavior follows three stages. In the first stage, huge price increases generate vast revenues that the cartel members have difficulty spending and that for the most part eliminate the need for debate over the question of appropriate market shares. In the second stage, the battle over cartel leadership and optimal price strategy pre-occupies the members. Saudi Arabia is obliged to demonstrate its power over production levels and cartel decisionmaking by attempting to keep oil price increases at a modest level, much to the dismay of other cartel members. In the third stage, the issue of fair market share for oil production is earnestly debated since prices are no longer rising rapidly and the revenue needs of the high-price preference states are growing more burdensome by the month. Since Saudi Arabia has the power within the cartel to veto rapid price increases, the only way the smaller producers can obtain sufficient revenue is to expand their own market shares surreptitiously by cheating on the posted price of oil. Large-scale cheating spells the de facto end of the cartel as a functioning organization.

But what must be emphasized is that fragmentation of the cartel means precisely *loss of ability to raise prices at will* in the fashion experienced since 1973. It does not *necessarily* mean that prices will precipitously drop following fragmentation. Too many rigidities on the downside prevent such an occurrence, including the increasing commitment to high-cost energy produced by countries like Britain, Norway, and Canada, entrepreneurs involved in high-cost exploration and production, investors in alternative energy sources, and the oil industry itself—to say nothing of the OPEC membership. Undiminished world energy demand also helps establish a price floor for energy. Moreover, the swing producer, Saudi Arabia, because of its huge annual production capability with or without OPEC at its side, will continue significantly to influence price levels by sharply varying its output. Finally, even a leveling out of oil prices may not occur unless and until *the consumer nations themselves pursue aggressive energy programs*.

With this assessment of OPEC unity our survey of oil myth and the political economy of petroleum is complete. Specific proposals regarding U.S. energy policy were made in Chapter VII. No political shortcuts can solve a problem caused by decades of lagging petroleum production in the United States, however. Stripped of the myths that surround them, most such shortcuts appear to be rationalizations for the absence of comprehensive energy policy not the foundation for such a policy. Wiser, more efficient use of energy and increased production of energy by those countries that consume the bulk of it are inescapable guidelines to sound energy policy. Illumination of the bases for oil myth will perhaps underscore the plausibility of these imperatives.

Notes

INTRODUCTION

1. Bronislaw Malinowski, *Magic, Science, and Religion* (Garden City, N.Y.: Anchor, 1948), pp. 93–148.

2. Karl Mannheim, *Ideology and Utopia* (New York: Harcourt, 1936); see also Robert Lane, *Political Ideology: Why the American Common Man Believes What He Does* (New York: Free Press, 1962).

3. For an extensive discussion of the role of myth in aggression and the projection of hostility see Erich Fromm, *The Anatomy of Human Destructiveness* (New York: Holt, Rinehart & Winston, 1973); George F. Solomon, "Psychodynamic Aspects of Aggression, Hostility, and Violence," in *Violence and the Struggle for Existence*, ed. David N. Daniels, Marshall F. Gilula, and Frank M. Ochberg (Boston: Little, Brown, 1970), pp. 53–78; and Franco Fornari, *The Psycho-Analysis of War* (Garden City, N.Y.: Anchor, 1974). For an introduction to the behavioral literature evaluating political conflict see Ted Robert Gurr, *Why Men Rebel* (Princeton: Princeton University Press, 1970); and Morton Deutsch, *The Resolution of Conflict: Constructive and Destructive Processes* (New Haven: Yale University Press, 1973). For an application to Middle East politics consider Charles F. Doran, "Leading Indicators of the June War: A Micro Analysis of the Conflict Cycle," *International Journal of Middle East Studies* (Cambridge: Cambridge University Press, in press).

4. One short but extremely detailed participant's account of the company-producer country negotiations, for example, is G. Henry M. Schuler, "The International Oil Negotiations," in *The 50% Solution*, ed. I. William Zartman (Garden City, N.Y.: Anchor, 1976), pp. 124–207. Interviews with OPEC government representatives and oil company executives, plus careful analysis of trade journals such as *Platt's Oilgram* and the *Middle East Economic Survey*, provide important additional data and material.

5. An excellent treatment of the role of ideology in governmental-corporate transactions is Bruce M. Russett and Elizabeth C. Hanson, *Interest and Ideology: The Foreign Policy Beliefs of American Businessmen* (San Francisco: Freeman, 1975).

CHAPTER I

1. John Litchblau, director of the Petroleum Industry Research Foundation, for example, has demonstrated that OPEC oil prices have kept pace with increases in export prices of industrial products between 1955 and 1970. While oil increased in price in 1974 by 343 percent, the index of industrial export prices rose by about 25 percent only (*UPI*, 2 September 1975). Several private U.S. government studies reached the same conclusion. For an introductory discussion of the terms of trade consult Armen A. Alchian and William R. Allen, *University Economics*, 3d ed. (Belmont, Calif.: Wadsworth, 1972), pp. 767–769; a more advanced account is Richard E. Caves, *Trade and Economic Structure: Models and Methods* (Cambridge: Harvard University Press, 1963).

2. A vigorous defense of these arguments is found in Edward Friedland, Paul Seabury, and Aaron Wildavsky, "Oil and the Decline of Western Power," *Political Science Quarterly*, 90, no. 3 (Fall 1975): 437–450; for an alternative economic viewpoint stressing trade relations read Douglas R. Bohi and Milton Russell, *U.S. Energy Policy: Alternatives for Security* (Baltimore: Johns Hopkins Press, 1975).

3. In particular, consider the use of the notion of free competition price in William D. Nordhaus, "The Allocation of Energy Resources," *Brookings Papers on Economic Activity*, 4, no. 3 (1973): 529–576; Michael Kennedy, "An Economic Model of the World Oil Market," *Bell Journal of Economics and Management Science*, 5, no. 2 (Autumn 1974): 540–577; and Basil A. Kalyman, "Economic Incentives in OPEC Oil Pricing," mimeographed (Toronto: University of Toronto, 1975). A useful summary and comparison of these models and others is Dietrich Fischer, Dermot Gately, and John F. Kyle, "The Prospects for OPEC: A Critical Survey of Models of the World Oil Market" (Paper presented at the National Science Foundation Conference for Applications of Game Theory to Energy Problems, Rice University, 5 August 1975).

4. Three classic papers on this topic are Paul A. Samuelson, "The Evaluation of Real National Income," *Oxford Economic Papers* (January 1950): 1–29; Kenneth J. Arrow, "Values and Collective Decision-Making," in *Philosophy, Politics, and Society*, ed. Peter Laslett and W. G. Runciman (Oxford: Blackwell, 1967), 3: 215–232; and J. Rawls, "Distributive Justice," in ibid., pp. 58–82. All of these essays, plus a number of other good analyses, are available in E. S. Phelps, ed, *Economic Justice* (Middlesex: Penguin, 1973).

5. William S. Vickrey, "The Goals of Economic Life," in *Goals of Economic Life*, ed. A. Dudley Ward (New York: Harper, 1953), pp. 148–177, reprinted in Phelps, op. cit., p. 57.

6. Paul A. Samuelson, *Foundations of Economic Analysis* (Cambridge: Harvard University Press, 1947); Vilfredo Pareto, *Manuel d'économie politique*

(Paris: Marcel Giard, 1909); A. P. Lerner, *The Economics of Control* (London: Macmillan, 1944); Abram Bergson, "A Reformulation of Certain Aspects of Welfare Economics," *Quarterly Journal of Economics*, 52 (February 1938): 310–314; Nicholas Kaldor, "Welfare Propositions in Economics and Interpersonal Comparisons of Utility," *Economic Journal*, 69 (September 1939): 549–552; John R. Hicks, "The Foundations of Welfare Economics," ibid. (December 1939): 696–712; and T. Scitovsky, "A Note on Welfare Propositions in Economics," *Review of Economics and Statistics*, 9 (1941–1942): 78–79.

7. Kenneth J. Arrow, *Social Choice and Individual Values* (New York: Wiley, 1951); and James E. Meade, *The Theory of International Economic Policy*, Vol. 2, *Trade and Welfare* (Oxford: Oxford University Press, 1955).

8. Francis M. Bator, "The Simple Analytics of Welfare Maximization," *American Economic Review*, 47 (March 1957): 22–59.

9. Marwan Iskandar, *The Arab Oil Question*, 2d ed. (Beirut: 1974), p. 73.

10. John C. Fisher, *Energy Crises in Perspective* (New York: Wiley, 1974), pp. 41–50; see also John E. Tilton, *U.S. Energy R and D Policy: The Role of Economics* (Washington, D.C.: Resources for the Future, September 1974); Harold J. Barnett and Chandler Morse, *Scarcity and Growth: The Economics of Natural Resource Availability* (Baltimore: Johns Hopkins Press, 1967), pp. 235–251; and *Energy: Future Alternatives and Risks*, ed. Academy Forum, National Academy of Sciences (Cambridge: Ballinger, 1974).

11. The official Exxon viewpoint expressed in *Energy Outlook: 1975–1990* (Houston: Exxon Company, U.S.A., 1975), projects the world price of oil to increase at the U.S. inflation rate. A now standard theoretical justification of approximately this position is Harold Hotelling, "The Economics of Exhaustible Resources," *Journal of Political Economy*, 39 (April 1931): 137–175.

12. Amory B. Lovins, *World Energy Strategies: Facts, Issues, and Options* (New York: Friends of the Earth, 1975); Robert E. Hunter, *The Energy "Crisis" and U.S. Foreign Policy*, U.S. Overseas Development Council Development Paper no. 14 (Washington, D.C.: U.S. Overseas Development Council, 1973); and Lester R. Brown, *The Global Politics of Resource Scarcity*, U.S. Overseas Development Council Development Paper no. 17 (Washington, D.C.: U.S. Overseas Development Council, 1974).

13. Iskandar, op. cit.; Yusif A. Sayigh, "Oil in Arab Developmental and Political Strategy: An Arab View," in *The Middle East: Oil, Politics, and Development*, ed. John Duke Anthony (Washington, D.C.: American Enterprise Institute for Public Policy Research, 1975), pp. 37–44; Charles Issawi, "Economic Development in the Middle East," *International Journal*, 28, no. 3, (1973): 729–740; and Robert Mabro and Elizabeth Monroe, "Arab Wealth from Oil: Problems of Its Investment," *International Affairs*, 50, no. 1 (1974): 15–27.

CHAPTER II

1. Prince 'Abd Allah ibn "abd al-"Aziz, interview with *al-Hawadith* (Beirut), 17 August 1973, reprinted in full in *Middle East Economic Survey*, 16, no. 43

(17 August 1973): 7–10, quotation from p. 8; Prince Saud al-Faisal, interview with *al-Hawadith*, 31 August 1973, reprinted ibid., 16, no. 45 (31 August 1973); King Faisal, interview with *Newsweek's* Beirut bureau chief Nicholas C. Proffit, published in the 10 September issue of *Newsweek* and in *Middle East Economic Survey*, 16, no. 46 (7 September 1973); King Faisal, talk on NBC television, 31 August 1973.

2. Among the best discussions of the oil weapon per se are Hans Maull, "Oil and Influence: The Oil Weapon Examined," *Adelphi Papers*, no. 117 (1975): 1–37; and Fuad Itayim, "Strengths and Weaknesses of the Oil Weapon," ibid., no. 115 (1975): 1–7.

3. Interview with Sadoon Hammadi, *al-Anwar* (Beirut), 18 December 1973, translated and reported in full in *Middle East Economic Survey*, 17, no. 9, 21 December 1973 (supp.): 1–9.

4. A measure of the distance between Israel and her neighbors is the Arab lack of political recognition for Israel as a state and the corresponding denial by Israel of the existence of a Palestinian people. The struggle to interpret the new political meaning of oil is revealed in governmental literature. See Y. Carmon, *The Significance of Egyptian Development* (Jerusalem: Israel Universities Study Group for Middle Eastern Affairs, 1975); and Aryeh Oded, "Slaves and Oil: The Arab Image in Black Africa," *Wiener Library Bulletin*, n.s., 27, no. 32 (1974): 34–47.

5. John C. Campbell, "The Energy Crisis and U.S. Policy in the Middle East," in *The Energy Crisis and U.S. Foreign Policy*, ed. Joseph S. Szyliowicz and Bard E. O'Neill (New York: Praeger, 1975), pp. 110–124; George Lenczowski, "The Oil-Producing Countries," in *The Oil Crisis*, ed. Raymond Vernon (New York: Norton, 1976); and Geoffrey Kemp, "The Military Buildup: Arms Control or Arms Trade?" *Adelphi Papers*, no. 114 (1975): 31–37.

6. Note the exchange on Mideast guarantees among Shlomo Avineri, Zbigniew Brzezinski, François Duchene, Amos Perlmutter, and Richard Ullman in *Foreign Policy*, no. 21 (Winter 1975–1976): 212–223. For problems of extending the deterrence umbrella over allies in a world of many nuclear powers see Richard Rosecrance, "Deterrence in Dyadic and Multipolar Environments," in *The Future of the International Strategic System*, ed. Richard Rosecrance (San Francisco: Chandler, 1972), pp. 125–140; and Charles F. Doran, "A Theory of Bounded Deterrence," *Journal of Conflict Resolution*, 17, no. 2 (June 1973): 342–369. The standard source on Middle East power for the earlier period is J. C. Hurewitz, *Middle East Politics: The Military Dimension* (New York: Praeger, 1969).

7. Fouad Ajami, "Between Cairo and Damascus," *Foreign Affairs*, 54, no. 3 (1976): 444–461; Udo Steinback, "The Arab World: Where Is It Going," *Aussenpolitik* [English ed.], 27, no. 1 (1976): 54–65; Nadav Safran, *From War to War* (New York: Pegasus, 1969); and Charles F. Doran, "Leading Indicators of the June War: A Micro Analysis of the Conflict Cycle," *International Journal of Middle East Studies*, in press.

8. Despite hostility toward Palestinian claims in some parts of the Arab world and in Israel and indifference outside the Middle East, and despite major in-

ternal disagreements regarding leadership, the Palestinians have retained a unity as a refugee people that makes any permanent solution in the Middle East impossible without consideration of their interests. For a self-estimate of their own organizational development see Lelia S. Kadi, *Basic Political Documents of the Armed Palestinian Resistance Movement*, Palestine Books, 27 (Beirut: Palestine Liberation Organization Research Center, 1969).

9. The Zionism-as-racial-discrimination vote deepened cleavages between governments that would have preferred to resolve differences outside the emotionally charged atmosphere of the General Assembly. Certainly, Egypt and the United States felt this way. On November 10, 1975, the final resolution was adopted by a vote of seventy-two in favor, thirty-five against. There were thirty-five abstentions plus three absences. Pressures of oil politics are seen especially among those countries that abstained or were absent from voting. UPI press release, 10 November 1975.

Chapter III

1. Literature on the multinational corporation and its relation to government is large and diverse. Contrast Richard Barnet and Ronald Mueller, *Global Reach* (New York: Simon & Schuster, 1975); Anthony Sampson, *The Sovereign State of ITT* (Greenwich: Fawcett, 1974); and Abdul A. Said and Luiz R. Simmons, *The New Sovereigns* (Englewood Cliffs: Prentice-Hall, 1975), with studies of a considerably different orientation: C. P. Kindleberger, *American Business Abroad* (New Haven: Yale University Press, 1969); John Fayerweather, *International Business-Government Affairs: Toward an Era of Accommodation* (Cambridge: Ballinger, 1973); and Raymond Vernon, *Sovereignty at Bay* (New York: Basic Books, 1971). A major problem with some studies is their failure to recognize the reversibility of dependence.

2. For a general discussion of the economic aspect of antitrust procedure and rationale see Fritz Machlup, *The Political Economy of Monopoly: Business, Labor, and Government Policies* (Baltimore: Johns Hopkins Press, 1967); and Lee Loevinger, "Antitrust Law in the Modern World" (Paper presented at the Antitrust Law Symposium of the New York State Bar Association, New York, 25 January 1962). The theory of imperfect competition is argued in the classic work, Joan Robinson, *The Economics of Imperfect Competition*, 2d ed. (London: Macmillan, 1969). Recent pleas for divestiture of the oil industry are Robert B. Krueger, *The United States and International Oil* (New York: Praeger, 1975); and Norman Medvin, *The Energy Cartel: Who Runs the American Oil Industry* (New York: Random House, Vintage, 1974).

3. Ch. F. Doran, M. Hinz, and P. C. Mayer-Tasch, *Umweltscultz-Politik des peripheren Eingriffs* (Darmstadt and Neuwied: Luchterhand, 1974).

4. Each of the following studies independently reinforces the findings of the others. Ted Bartell, "The Effects of the Energy Crisis on Attitudes and Life Styles of Los Angeles Residents," mimeographed (Los Angeles: University of California, Los Angeles, Survey Research Center, July 1974); Opinion Research

Corporation, "How the Public Sees the Energy Crisis," results reported in *Business Week*, 16 March 1974, p. 24; and Rene D. Zentner, "Communication: The Real Energy Gap" (Paper presented at the New World of Energy III Conference, Columbia University, 28 February 1976).

5. Data in this section are drawn from Neil H. Jacoby, *Multinational Oil: A Study of Industrial Dynamics* (New York: Macmillan, 1974), pp. 248–250; *President's Economic Report, 1973–76* (Washington, D.C.: Government Printing Office, 1974); U.S., Congress, Senate, Committee on Finance, *Oil Company Profitability*, 93rd Cong., 2d sess., 12 February 1974; and idem, *1974 Profitability of Selected Major Oil Company Operations*, 94th Cong., 2d sess., 25 June 1975.

6. Careful analyses of the implications of this orientation for corporate-producer government relations are Theodore H. Moran, *Multinational Corporations and the Politics of Dependence* (Princeton: Princeton University Press, 1974); and Robert Gilpin, *U.S. Power and the Multinational Corporation: The Political Economy of Foreign Direct Investment* (New York: Basic Books, 1975). See also Charles F. Doran, review of *U.S. Power and the Multinational Corporation* by Robert Gilpin, *Journal of Politics*, 38, no. 4 (November 1976): 1052–1053.

7. Edith Penrose, "The Development of Crisis" in *The Oil Crisis*, ed. Raymond Vernon (New York: Norton, 1976), pp. 39–58; Richard B. Mancke, "The Genesis of the U.S. Oil Crisis," in *The Energy Crisis and U.S. Foreign Policy*, ed. Joseph S. Szyliowicz and Bard E. O'Neill (New York: Praeger, 1975), pp. 52–72; William D. Smith, "Shortage Amid Plenty," in *The National Energy Problem*, ed. Robert H. Connery and Robert S. Gilmour (New York: Academy of Political Science, 1973), pp. 41–52; and Peter R. Odell, *Oil and World Power* (Middlesex: Penguin, 1970).

8. Concern has been expressed in the U.S. Congress and in the press (e.g., in a special series of articles during the spring of 1976 in the *Christian Science Monitor*) about corporate ethics abroad. See also James W. McKie, ed., *Social Responsibility and the Business Predicament* (Washington, D.C.: Brookings Institution, 1974).

9. Karl Mannheim, *Ideology and Utopia* (New York: Harcourt, Brace and World, 1955). Kenneth N. Waltz establishes the basis for the debate in *Foreign Policy and Democratic Politics* (Boston: Little, Brown, 1967); he attacks the elitist thought of Walter Lippmann, *The Public Philosophy* (New York: New American Library, Mentor, 1955).

CHAPTER IV

1. Exponents of the market structure approach are Carl Kaysen and Donald F. Turner, *Antitrust Policy* (Cambridge: Harvard University Press, 1959).

2. See in this regard Robert H. Bork, "The Role of Reason and the Per Se Concept: Price Fixing and Market Division," *Yale Law Journal*, 75 (1966): 430–438; and Harlan M. Blake and William K. Jones, "Toward a Three Dimensional Antitrust Policy," *Columbia Law Review*, 65 (1965): 430–454.

3. Any standard textbook on introductory economics can provide insight into the graphical representation of monopolistic pricing. See, for example, Paul A. Samuelson, *Economics*, 9th ed. (New York: McGraw-Hill, 1973), pp. 506–532. Consider also F. M. Scherer, *Industrial Market Structure and Economic Performance* (Chicago: Rand McNally, 1970); and Oliver Williamson, *Markets and Hierarchies: Analysis and Antitrust Implications* (New York: Free Press, 1975).

4. Neil H. Jacoby, *Multinational Oil: A Study of Industrial Dynamics* (New York: Macmillan, 1974); and Edward Mitchell, "Capital Cost Savings of Vertical Integration," in *Vertical Integration in the Oil Industry*, ed. Edward Mitchell (Washington, D.C.: American Enterprise Institute for Public Policy Research, 1976), pp. 73–104.

5. Exxon, *Happy Motoring News*, 15 (July 1976): 5; U.S., Congress, Senate, Committee on Finance, *Oil Company Profitability*, 93rd Cong., 2d sess., 12 February 1974; and idem, *Profitability of Selected Major Oil Company Operations*, 94th Cong., 2d sess., 25 June 1975.

6. G. Stigler, *The Organization of Industry* (Homewood, Ill.: Irwin, 1969); and David J. Teece, "Vertical Integration in the U.S. Oil Industy," in Mitchell, op. cit., pp. 105–190.

7. For a survey of antitrust results in broad comparative terms consult Simon N. Whitney, *Antitrust Policies: American Experience in Twenty Industries* (New York: Twentieth Century Fund, 1958). An attempt to treat the international aspects of antitrust but one that remains largely American in orientation is Earl W. Kintner and Mark R. Joelson, *An International Antitrust Primer* (New York: Macmillan, 1974).

8. Brown Show Co. v. United States, 370 U.S. 294 (1962).

9. U.S., Federal Trade Commission, "Preliminary Federal Trade Commission Staff Report on Its Investigation of the Petroleum Industry," in U.S., Congress, Senate, 93rd Cong., 1st sess., Committee on Government Operations, Permanent Subcommittee on Investigations, *Investigation of the Petroleum Industry* 12 July 1973, p. 51; and Melvin de Chazean and Alfred Kahn, *Integration and Competition in the Petroleum Industry* (New Haven: Yale University Press, 1959), pp. 221–229.

10. Mancke has dealt with this issue most specifically in several of his writings. See Richard B. Mancke, *Squeaking By: U.S. Energy Policy since the Embargo* (New York: Columbia University Press, 1976), chap. 7.

11. A somewhat sensational but nonetheless empirically supported attack on this problem is Norman Medvin, *The Energy Cartel: Who Runs the American Oil Industry* (New York: Random House, Vintage, 1974), pp. 96–113.

12. R. A. Smith, "The Incredible Electrical Conspiracy," *Fortune*, May 1961, pp. 161–224; and Armen A. Achian and William R. Allen, *University Economics*, 2d ed. (Belmont, Calif.: Wadsworth, 1972), pp. 354–356.

13. See the exchange between Senators Birch Bayh and Dewey F. Bartlett in U.S., Congress, Senate, Judiciary Committee, Subcommittee on Antitrust and Monopoly, *The Petroleum Industry: Hearings on S. 2387 Vertical Integration*, 94th Cong., 1st sess., September–November 1975, pt. 1:200–208.

14. See the statements of Jesse M. Calhoun, president of the National Engineers' Beneficial Association, and Stanley Ruttenberg, in ibid., January–February 1976, pt. 3:2200–2202.

15. Anthony T. S. Sampson, cited in ibid., pp. 2186–2187; and Anthony Sampson, *The Seven Sisters: The Great Oil Companies and the World They Shaped* (New York: Viking, 1975).

16. Consider Stephen J. Kobrin, "Foreign Direct Investment, Industrialization, and Social Change," *Journal of Conflict Resolution*, 20, no. 3 (September 1976): 497–522.

17. Arthur M. Johnson, *Petroleum Pipelines and Public Policy, 1906–1959* (Cambridge: Harvard University Press, 1967); and John G. McLean and Robert W. Haigh, *The Growth of Integrated Oil Companies* (Boston: Harvard Graduate School of Business Administration, 1954).

18. Gulf Publishing Company, *Hydrocarbon Processing: 1977 Market Reports* (Houston: Gulf Publishing, 1976); see also "The Arab Oil Wealth: Where Is It Going?" *Arab Economist*, 6, no. 65 (June 1974): 20–28; and June 1974 special issue of ibid. entitled "Saudi Arabia."

19. This trend was evident as early as 1972. See Ch. F. Doran, M. Hinz, and P. C. Mayer-Tasch, *Umweltschultz-Politik des peripheren Eingriffs* (Darmstadt and Neuwied: Luchterhand, 1974), pp. 175–177.

20. Joseph P. Mulholland and Douglas W. Webbink, *Concentration Levels and Trends in the Energy Sector of the U.S. Economy*, Staff Report to the U.S. Federal Trade Commission (Washington, D.C.: U.S. Federal Trade Commission, March 1974).

Chapter V

1. Henry Kissinger, "A New National Partnership," *U.S. International Energy Policy October 1973-November 1975*, U.S. State Department Selected Documents, no. 3 (Washington, D.C.: U.S. Department of State, Bureau of Public Affairs, Office of Media Services, 1975), pp. 27–29, p. 28. For a general discussion of IEA from an OECD perspective see Ulf Lantzke, "The OECD and Its International Energy Agency," in *The Oil Crisis*, ed. Raymond Vernon (New York: Norton, 1976), pp. 217–228.

2. "Before we could negotiate effectively, or even gain the necessary respect for serious discussions, we had to undertake unified actions in the energy field that would demonstrate strength and consistency of purpose." See the statement of Charles W. Robinson, undersecretary of state for economic affairs, in U.S., Congress, House, Committee on International Relations, Subcommittee on International Resources, Food, and Energy, 1 May 1975, p. 1.

3. Henry Kissinger, "Energy: The Necessity of Decision," *U.S. International Energy Policy October 1973–November 1975*, U.S. State Department Selected Documents, no. 3 (Washington, D.C.: U.S. Department of State, Bureau of Public Affairs, Office of Media Services, 1975), pp. 29–30.

4. As we shall see in Chapter VI the debate revolves around essentially two issues: timing; and means and methods. That the analysts were wrong regarding the immediacy of cartel dissolution does not guarantee that they will be permanently wrong. But correct identification of the conditions underlying cartel instability does not mean necessarily that policies will evolve to foreshorten consumer dependence either.

5. See, for example, U.S., Executive Office of the President, Council on International Economic Policy, *Special Report: Critical Imported Materials* (Washington, D.C.: Government Printing Office, 1974), pp. 16–17.

6. A strong proponent of this viewpoint has been M. A. Adelman. One of the difficulties with the proposal, however, is that the smaller producers are among the higher cost producers and price-cutting narrows their financial return more than it does the financial returns of other OPEC states. One variant of the proposal is an "auction" of consumer demand. M. A. Adelman, "Oil Import Quota Auctions," *Challenge*, 18, no. 6 (January–February 1976): 17–33.

7. Michael Z. Brooke and H. Lee Remmers, *The Multinational Company in Europe: Some Key Problems* (Ann Arbor: University of Michigan Press, 1972), pp. 152–159; and David Blake and Robert S. Walters, *The Politics of Global Economic Relations* (New York: Prentice-Hall, 1976), pp. 76–125.

8. Actual application of this proportionate cut idea occurs at two levels. At the first level, when the IEA as a whole loses between 7 percent and 12 percent of normal consumption, all members reduce demand by 7 percent and the remaining short fall is shared. At the second level of 12 percent loss of oil consumption or above, each member constrains demand by 10 percent, and any further losses are shared equally in percentage terms. The United States is eligible to consider the East and West regions as separate markets, applying the 7 percent threshold fully to either region.

9. One of the related problems is that much of the money is in three- to six-month securities, which necessitates rapid turnover. In addition, some of the large investors have a tendency to chase the highest current interest rate, thus precipitating large flows in and out of the capital accounts of the major trading nations.

10. Organization for Economic Co-Operation and Development, "Future Investment Requirements and How They Can Be Met," *Oil: The Present Situation and Future Prospects* (Paris: Organization for Economic Co-Operation and Development, 1973), pp. 155–157.

11. *Encouraging Investment in Domestic Energy: Minimum Safeguard Price*, U.S. State Department Special Report, no. 16 (Washington, D.C.: U.S. Department of State, Bureau of Public Affairs, Office of Media Services, April 1975).

12. Historically, prices in most markets have shown great resistance to downward pressure, and this experience has been likewise true for oil. One should not assume that decision latitude regarding cartel pricing is symmetric. Among cartel members unity is likely to be much greater regarding upward price shifts than downward shifts, even for plausible strategic purposes. Domestic constituencies would object strongly to even brief reductions in oil revenue brought about by a price drop.

13. See statement by Henry Kissinger, ministerial meeting of the International Energy Agency, Paris, 27 May 1975.

14. Dorthy K. Newman and Dawn Day, *The American Energy Consumer* (Cambridge: Ballinger, 1975), p. 8; and Eric Hirst, *Energy Intensiveness of Passenger and Freight Transportation Modes: 1950–1970* (Oak Ridge: Oak Ridge National Laboratory, April 1973).

15. An updated version of conservation estimates is to be found in U.S., Energy Research and Development Agency, *A National Plan for Energy Research, Development, and Demonstration: Creating Energy Choices for the Future* (Washington, D.C.: U.S. Energy Research and Development Agency, 1975), 2:53–82; for U.S. government estimates of future energy demand see Hermann Enzer, Walter Dupree, and Stanley Miller, *Energy Perspectives: A Presentation of Major Energy and Energy-Related Data* (Washington, D.C.: U.S. Department of the Interior, February 1975), pp. 52–69.

16. See the U.S. Department of State statement presented by Charles W. Robinson, "International Energy and Economic Policies," in U.S., Congress, House, Committee on International Relations, 19 February 1976, U.S. Department of State News Release. See also Roger D. Hansen, "The Politics of Scarcity," in *The U.S. and the Developing World*, ed. James W. Howe (New York: Praeger, 1974), pp. 51–65; and "What Now: The 1975 Dag Hammarskjöld Report on Development and International Cooperation," *Development Dialogue*, no. 1–2 (1975): 1–123, prepared on the occasion of the Seventh Special Session of the United Nations General Assembly, September 1975.

17. Latin American writers have been among the leaders in developing the dependency thesis. André Gunder Frank, *Capitalism and Underdevelopment in Latin America* (New York: Monthly Review Press, 1967); Celso Furtado, "The Concept of External Dependence in the Study of Underdevelopment," in *The Political Economy of Development and Underdevelopment*, ed. Charles K. Wilber (New York: Random House, 1973); and Fernando Henrique Cardoso, "Dependency and Development in Latin America," *New Left Review*, no. 74 (July–August 1972).

18. For a critical comment regarding the success of such attempts see Raymond F. Mikesell, *Nonfuel Minerals: U.S. Investment Policies Abroad*, Washington Papers, no. 23 (1975).

19. See Appendix I for a listing of the indicators used in this analysis and the criteria by which they were chosen.

20. For a more detailed explanation of factor-analytic technique consult R. J. Rummel, *Applied Factor Analysis* (Evanston: Northwestern University Press, 1970); and H. Harmon, *Modern Factor Analysis* (Chiago: University of Chicago Press, 1967).

21. Organization for Economic Co-Operation and Development, *Statistics of Energy: 1959–1973* (Paris: Organization for Economic Co-Operation and Development, 1964).

22. Organization for Economic Co-Operation and Development, *Oil: The Present Situation* (Paris: Organization for Economic Co-Operation and Development, 1973), pp. 71–82.

23. Newman and Day, op. cit., pp. 33–65; and Eric Hirst and John C. Moyers, "Efficiency of Energy Use in the United States," *Science*, 30 March 1973, pp. 301–307.

24. *Middle East*, no. 9 (June 1975): 38.

Chapter VI

1. One surprisingly durable book remains a standard source on OPEC and OAPEC although reader interest is likely to generate many further treatments. Zuhayr Mikdashi, *The Community of Oil Exporting Countries: A Study in Governmental Cooperation* (Ithaca: Cornell University Press, 1972); see also F. Rouhani, *A History of OPEC* (New York: Praeger, 1969).

2. Aspects of these developments are discussed in a number of sources. U.S., Congress, House, Committee on Foreign Affairs, Subcommittees on Foreign Economic Policy and on the Near East and South Asia, *Oil Negotiations, OPEC, and the Stability of Supply: Hearings*, 93rd Cong., 1st sess., April 10, May 14, 16, July 11, September 6, 18, 1973; Davis B. Bobrow and Robert T. Kudrle, "Theory, Policy, and Resource Cartels: The Case of OPEC," *Journal of Conflict Resolution*, 20, no. 1 (March 1976): 3–56; and Philip Connelly and Robert Perlman, *The Politics of Scarcity: Resource Conflicts in International Relations* (London: Oxford University Press, 1975). A view supportive of the viability of the cartel is C. A. Gebelein, "The Effect of Conservation on Oil Prices: Analysis of Misconceptions," *Journal of Energy and Development*, 1, no. 1 (1975): 70–93.

3. United Nations, *Report of the Ad Hoc Panel of Experts on Projections of Demand and Supply of Crude Petroleum and Products* (ESA/RT meeting 11/14), January 1972.

4. Jay W. Forrester, *World Dynamics* (Cambridge: Wright-Allen, 1971); Donella H. Meadows, Dennis L. Meadows, Jørgen Randers, and William W. Behrens III, *The Limits to Growth: A Report for the Club of Rome's Project on the Predicament of Mankind* (New York: Universe, 1972).

5. Augustin Cournot, *Researches into Mathematical Principles of the Theory of Wealth*, trans. N. T. Bacon, 2d ed. (New York: Macmillan, 1927).

6. Joseph Bertrand, "Theorie mathematique de la richesse sociale," *Journals des Savants* (Paris), September 1883, pp. 499–508; F. L. Edgeworth, "Le teoria pura del monopolio," *Giornale degli Economist*, 15 (1897): 13–31, 307–320; Harold Hotelling, "Stability in Competition," *Economic Journal*, 39 (March 1929): 41–57; Paul M. Sweezy, "Demand under Conditions of Oligopoly," *Journal of Political Economy*, 47, no. 4 (August 1939): 568–573; R. L. Hall and C. J. Hitch, "Price Theory and Business Behavior," *Oxford Economic Papers* (May 1939): 12–45; and E. H. Chamberlin, *The Theory of Monopolistic Competition*, 7th ed. (Cambridge: Harvard University Press, 1958). For more current summaries see William J. Baumol, *Business Behavior Value and Growth*, rev. ed. (New York: Harcourt, 1967); and Peter Asch, *Economic Theory and the Antitrust Dilemma* (New York: Wiley 1970).

7. Mordechar Abir, *Oil, Power, and Politics: Conflict in Arabia, the Red Sea, and the Gulf* (London: Cass, 1974); R. M. Burrell and Alvin J. Cottrell, *Politics, Oil, and the Western Mediterranean*, Washington Papers, no. 7 (1973); and Malcolm H. Kerr, "Soviet Influences in Egypt, 1967–73," in *Soviet and Chinese Influence in the Third World*, ed. Alvin F. Rubenstein (New York: Praeger, 1975), pp. 88–108.

8. Charles F. Doran, "OPEC and Reform of the International Energy Order: Aspects of Cartel Cohesion and Coalition Formation" (Paper presented at the 1977 Annual Meeting of the International Studies Association, St. Louis, 17 March 1977); and Charles F. Doran, "Conflict, Cohesion, and Coalition Formation in OPEC: A Quantitative Assessment" (Paper to be presented at the 1977 Annual Meeting of the American Political Science Association, Washington, D.C., September 1–4, 1977). See also T. W. Park, W. F. Abolfathi, and M. Ward, "Resource Nationalism in the Foreign Policy Behavior of Exporting Countries" (Paper presented at the 1974 Annual Meeting of the American Political Science Association, Chicago, 28 August 1974).

9. For a general background to the nascent theory construction offered in this chapter the reader is invited to consult Raymond Tanter and Richard H. Ullman, eds., "Theory and Policy in International Relations," *World Politics*, 24 (Spring 1972): 1–248 (supp.); Nazli Chouchri and Robert C. North, *Nations in Conflict: National Growth and International Violence* (San Francisco: Freeman, 1975); J. David Singer and Melvin Small, *The Wages of War, 1816–1965: A Statistical Handbook*; R. J. Rummel, "A Field Theory of Social Action with Application to Conflict within Nations," *Yearbook of the Society for General Systems*, 10 (1965): 183–211; J. Rosenau, "Foreign Policy as Adaptive Behavior," *Comparative Politics*, 2(1970): 365–387; Jonathan Wilkenfeld, Virginia Lee Lussier, and Dale Tahtinen, "Conflict Interactions in the Middle East, 1949–1967," in "Research Perspectives on the Arab-Israeli Conflict: A Symposium," ed. J. D. Ben-Dak and Edward E. Azar, *Journal of Conflict Resolution*, 16, no. 2 (June 1972); and Charles F. Doran, *The Politics of Assimilation: Hegemony and Its Aftermath* (Baltimore: Johns Hopkins Press, 1971).

10. Here economic size is perhaps less important than the size of petroleum reserves but the argument can be made on either grounds. Bruce M. Russett, *What Price Vigilance? The Burdens of National Defense* (New Haven: Yale Univerity Press, 1970), pp. 91–126; and Mancur Olson, *The Logic of Collective Action* (Cambridge: Harvard University Press, 1965).

11. Thomas O. Enders, "OPEC and the Industrial Countries: The Next Ten Years," *Foreign Affairs*, 53, no. 4 (1975); M. A. Adelman suggests a more controversial interim shortcut in "Oil Import Quota Auctions," *Challenge*, 18, no. 6 (January–February 1976): 17–33; the U.S. government's own modified program is found in U.S., Energy Research and Development Agency, *A National Plan for Energy Research, Development, and Demonstration: Creating Energy Choices for the Future* (Washington, D.C.: U.S. Energy Research and Development Agency, 1975), vols. 1, 2.

12. Energy is a most central resource because its abundance ensures that even diffuse minerals and other commodities can be aggregated and processed cheaply. Hence the importance of coal after 1990. U.S., Department of the Interior,

Geological Survey, *Coal Resources of the United States* (Washington, D.C.: Government Printing Office, 1974).

13. A neogrowth perspective would recognize that the advanced industrial countries must trade certain constraints on future consumption for a brake on population growth among the developing countries. But continued economic growth of a qualitatively new variety is absolutely critical, providing hope for the world's poor and a reasonable chance for success in tension management.

CHAPTER VII

1. For an informed discussion of the broad energy situation see Mason Wilrich, with Joel Darmstadter, *Energy and World Politics* (New York: Free Press, 1975).

2. Robert W. Campbell, *The Economics of Soviet Oil and Gas* (Baltimore: Johns Hopkins Press, 1968); and William E. Griffith, "Soviet Influence in the Middle East," *Survival*, 18, no. 1 (1976): 2–9.

3. Furor over the recycling of petro-dollars has been rather short-lived. See S. D. Krasner, "The Great Oil Sheikdown," *Foreign Policy*, 13 (Winter 1975–1976): 123–138; and H. Chenery, "Restructuring the World Economy," *Foreign Affairs*, 53, no. 2 (1975): 242–262.

4. David S. Landes, *The Unbound Prometheus: Technological Change and Industrial Development in Western Europe from 1750 to the Present* (Cambridge: At the University Press, 1969), p. 36; John U. Nef, *The Conquest of the Material World: Essays on the Coming of Industrialism* (New York: Meridian, 1967); and Angus Maddison, *Economic Growth in the West* (New York: Twentieth Century Fund, 1964).

5. Landes, op. cit., p. 36.

6. For the official U.S. statement of its long-term strategic priorities consult U.S., Energy Research and Development Agency, *A National Plan for Energy Research, Development, and Demonstration: Creating Energy Choices for the Future* (Washington, D.C.: U.S. Energy Research and Development Agency, 1975), vols. 1, 2.

7. Positive spillovers of high-level research collaboration between the United States and its two major allies, Japan and West Germany, could be important. While these two governments are in some sense the pillars of the American alliance system, they also represent the points of some strain, future volatility, and possible alliance alteration. Stanley Hoffman, "Weighing the Balance of Power," *Foreign Affairs*, 50, no. 4 (1972): 618–643.

8. Richard R. Nelson, Merton J. Peck, and Edward D. Kalachek, *Technology, Economic, Growth, and Public Policy* (Santa Monica and Washington, D.C.: Rand Corporation and Brookings Institution, 1967), pp. 23–43; Jacob Schmookler, *Invention and Economic Growth* (Cambridge: Harvard University Press, 1966); and H. J. Habakkuk, *American and British Technology in the Nineteenth Century* (New York: Cambridge University Press, 1962).

9. For a useful background to these matters consider Mordechar Abir, *Oil, Power, and Politics: Conflict in Arabia, the Red Sea, and the Gulf* (London: Cass, 1974). A game-theoretic treatment is Charles Bird and Martin W. Sampson III, "A Game-Theory Model of OPEC, Oil Consumers, and Oil Companies Emphasizing Coalition Formations," in *Mathematcial Models in International Relations,* ed. John Gillespie and Dinna A. Zinnes (New York: Praeger, 1976), pp. 376–397.

10. Maurice J. Williams, "The Aid Programs of the OPEC Countries," *Foreign Affairs,* 54, no. 2 (1976): 308–324.

CHAPTER VIII

1. Richard Cooper, *The Economics of Interdependence* (New York: McGraw-Hill, 1968); George Liska, *Nations in Alliance: The Limits of Interdependence* (Baltimore: Johns Hopkins Press, 1962); Nazli Chouchri, *Global Energy Interdependence* (Cambridge: MIT, Center for International Studies, 1974); and L. R. Beres and A. Tarr, eds., *Planning Alternative World Futures: Values, Methods, and Models* (New York: Praeger, 1975).

EPILOGUE

1. Published after my own manuscript had been written, John M. Blair's *The Control of Oil* (New York: Pantheon Books, 1976) has created a stir in the public media with its plea on behalf of divestiture. While I cannot at this late stage devote as much space as I would like to Blair's contentions, several points must be stressed. Blair contributes importantly to the discussion of the oil question by bringing the details of industrial price leadership prior to 1973 into the public forum (Chapter 5). His study assumes, however, that the industrial control exerted from the early twentieth century through the first years of the post-World War II period continues today in the aftermath of the 1973 price revoluion, a position he fails to justify (and at one point himself questions, pp. 319–320) for the current period. For him, the industrial leadership, not OPEC, is the senior partner in oil decision matters today. He is led to this conclusion, despite his proper emphasis on the origins of control rather than market considerations, in part by neglecting politics. For instance, the chapter on the Libyan take-over of the companies underestimates the political leverage used against them. Likewise, the author never addresses the international political implications of divestiture. Very dependent for information upon the Senate and Congressional hearings regarding oil company and OPEC operations and not evidently familiar with much of the best scholarly research on the subject, the author fails to reason beyond the confines of past relationships in assessing the new balance of power in oil matters. Everything smacks of industrial conspiracy: for example, the rapid depletion of the Texas oil fields was consciously spurred under cover of the oil import quota, but it was not pointed out that reduced domestic drilling incentives relative to foreign incentives have for years

added very little to proven reserves and that lags of many more years will be required to correct this deficiency. One of the most dangerous conclusions of the book is that no relationship exists (even for the independents) between profitability and new discoveries, a philosophy which is guaranteed to preserve whatever petroleum reserves yet remain inside the U.S. region in their undeveloped condition (contrast Britain's energy policy) and thus to ensure continued foreign oil dependence.

INDEX

Index